Common Law Judging

Are judges supposed to be objective? Citizens, scholars, and legal professionals commonly assume that subjectivity and objectivity are opposites, with the corollary that subjectivity is a vice and objectivity is a virtue. These assumptions underlie passionate debates over adherence to original intent and judicial activism.

In *Common Law Judging*, Douglas Edlin challenges these widely held assumptions by reorienting the entire discussion. Rather than analyze judging in terms of objectivity and truth, he argues that we should instead approach the role of a judge's individual perspective in terms of intersubjectivity and validity. Drawing upon Kantian aesthetic theory as well as case law, legal theory, and constitutional theory, Edlin develops a new conceptual framework for the respective roles of the individual judge and of the judiciary as an institution, as well as the relationship between them, as integral parts of the broader legal and political community. Specifically, Edlin situates a judge's subjective responses within a form of legal reasoning and reflective judgment that must be communicated to different audiences.

Edlin concludes that the individual values and perspectives of judges are indispensable both to their judgments in specific cases and to the independence of the courts. According to the common law tradition, judicial subjectivity is a virtue, not a vice.

Douglas E. Edlin is Associate Professor of Political Science at Dickinson College.

Common Law Judging

Subjectivity, Impartiality, and the Making of Law

Douglas E. Edlin

UNIVERSITY OF MICHIGAN PRESS

Ann Arbor

Published in the United States of America by the
University of Michigan Press
Printed and bound by CPI Group (UK) Ltd, Croydon, CR0 4YY

2019 2018 2017 2016 4 3 2 1

A CIP catalog record for this book is available from the British Library.

Library of Congress Cataloging-in-Publication Data

Names: Edlin, Douglas E., author.
Title: Common law judging: subjectivity, impartiality, and the making of law / Douglas E. Edlin.
Description: Ann Arbor: University of Michigan Press, 2016. | Includes bibliographical references and index.
Identifiers: LCCN 2016006681| ISBN 9780472130023 (hardcover: alk. paper) | ISBN 9780472122158 (e-book)
Subjects: LCSH: Judicial process—English-speaking countries. | Common law.
Classification: LCC K2146 .E35 2016 | DDC 340.5/7—dc23
LC record available at http://lccn.loc.gov/2016006681

To N.B.E.

For M.A.E.

The business of the judge, they told us, was to discover objective truth. His own little individuality, his tiny stock of scattered and uncoordinated philosophies, these, with all his weaknesses and unconscious prejudices, were to be laid aside and forgotten.

—BENJAMIN N. CARDOZO

Contents

Common Law Judging

is made must also be objective (in the same sense). The common law tradition does not equate the law and the process so rigidly. In this book, I hope to disentangle the judicial process and its legal product. More specifically, I will argue here that an important aspect of the common law judicial process is irreducibly and inescapably subjective and that this is not a bad thing. Indeed, the subjective aspect of the process is due as much to the nature of judging as it is to the nature of judges.

Concerns about objectivity in law and subjectivity in judging are familiar. The conventional view holds that judges must enforce the law "as written" or else the rule of law and democratic government are jeopardized.[12] We are told that "a government of laws, and not of men"[13] requires that we be governed by the objective rules of law rather than the subjective preferences of judges. Otherwise, we will be governed by the preferences of a coterie of unelected, unrepresentative, unaccountable, and unconstrained officials, rather than by the laws enacted by our elected representatives. Therefore, the story goes, judicial decisions must be made according to what the law says rather than according to what the judge says.

Concerns about the threat of judicial subjectivity pervade our discussions of judicial discretion, judicial activism, judicial supremacy, and judicial responsibility,[14] and they frame our debates about legal language, legal rules, constitutional meaning, and constitutional interpretation. The perceived tension between the subjective values of judges and the objective qualities of law animates long-standing debates about formalism,[15] realism,[16] behaviorism,[17] attitudinalism,[18] originalism,[19] and textualism.[20] In many instances, these debates exaggerate the definitiveness of rules[21] or the discretion of judges.[22] And, of course, these debates may also lead one to wonder whether the views of, say, an originalist or a behaviorist, derive from that individual's subjective preference for originalism or behaviorism.

My goal here is to reconsider the role that subjectivity plays and is meant to play in common law judging and to challenge certain assumptions that are typically made about objectivity in law. I will argue that, contrary to conventional views, the subjective element in common law judging is a necessary and valuable part of the judicial process. I will also argue that objectivity, in the strong sense that is often assumed for law, is not a plausible goal for judging. Our understanding of common law judging would benefit significantly if we replace the outmoded and inaccurate fixation on objectivity (and truth) with the more conceptually and descriptively accurate notion of intersubjectivity (and validity). Intersubjectivity means that the judge decides as an individual within a larger community, that the judge produces judgments with the understanding that they must contain statements of justificatory reasons for legal conclusions, and that these conclusions depend on their evaluation and validation by the community as legal judgments. The judgments are constituted by both their subjective and intersubjective components. By reorienting the discussion of legal judgment in terms of intersubjective validity rather than objective truth, and by examining the relationship between individual responses and publicly articulated reasons in the form of universalizable propositions of law, I hope to explain the nature and value of common law judicial decision making.

My position should not be misunderstood as an argument against objectivity or for subjectivity. A distinction I will develop further in the next two chapters is that the objective aspects of the laws produced through the judicial process should be understood as separate from the judge's process of judging and communicating her decision.[23] However estimable objective truth or objective judgment may appear in the abstract, common law judges do not decide cases in the abstract.[24] Within the common law tradition, the point is that "the idea of objectively good judgments, as distinct from judgments that are good under certain (perhaps quite broad ranges of) conditions and from the perspectives of (perhaps highly relevant sets of) people, appears fundamentally untenable."[25]

Common Law Judges

The problem with an expectation of objectivity in common law judging is that it is not the common law's expectation. Common law judges must resolve concrete legal disputes about claimed legal injuries presented by the parties whose legal rights are at stake. As a result, by reifying objectivity as an ideal for common law judging and judgment, the authentic process of legal judgment will inevitably appear partial (in both senses of that term). By treating impartiality as synonymous with objectivity, and subjectivity as the opposite of both impartiality and objectivity, we are left with no room for a subjective element in responsible judging. By distinguishing impartiality from objectivity, however, and by recognizing that a judge may be impartial while still bringing her own values to her judgments, we are left with a more expansive and realistic view of the process by which judges formulate legal judgments and how those judgments acquire their salience as authoritative legal sources.

Objectivity is not the goal of the judicial function and subjectivity is not the price of judicial dysfunction. Instead, we should expect impartiality as the goal of common law judging and understand subjectivity as a necessary corollary of genuine judicial independence and the traditional function of common law judges. The process of common law judging combines the individual perspectives of judges with a recognized form of legal argumentation that is expressed to a larger community. A judge's perspective on the law is an essential part of that judge's contribution to the law. The expression of the individual response within the forms of legal judgment ensures that the judgment will be recognized as a source of law and enhances the judge's contribution to the common law system and process.

The search for objectivity in common law judging is an attempt to eliminate the judge from the judgment. This search is not just impractical and unavailing; it is undesirable. By integrating the judge's personal response as a component of the formal legal judgment, the common law process and the law it produces remain dynamic and organic. In addition, by ensuring that the judge does not disconnect himself from his judgments, the common law expects that judges will remain personally accountable and responsible to their institution and to the people their institution serves.

In this book, I argue that common law judging requires four interrelated components: individuality, impartiality, independence, and intersubjectivity. The first three of these components are familiar and are understood in various ways. The fourth is not well understood at all in relation to law and the judicial process. I hope to clarify each of these aspects of common law judging and their various relationships with one another. Throughout this book, I will distinguish each of these elements from objectivity. In doing so, we can arrive at a fuller and more accurate appreciation of common law judicial law making and of the law that judges make. Moreover, by contrasting these four components with objectivity, I hope to eliminate some fundamental misconceptions about the common law, some misguided criticisms of common law judges, and some cynicism about the common law system.

The criticism of common law judges for acting subjectively takes many familiar forms: judges should "not legislate from the bench,"[26] "judges have grounded particular constitutional rulings in their own preferences rather than in law,"[27] "it is illegitimate for judges to impose their own values in place of those of the legislature,"[28] a judge must "overcome her own subjective preferences for a given outcome, so as to make decisions based on the legal merits of the case,"[29] etc. Sometimes these criticisms are well-founded. Sometimes these criticisms fundamentally misconstrue the nature of the common law system and its traditional judicial process. For example, to the extent that "legislating" is taken as synonymous with "law making," the

phers conceptualize objectivity in metaphysical, epistemological, and semantic terms. Metaphysical objectivity focuses on what exists in the world external to us, but it is not necessarily limited to the physical world. This category could include, for example, an external moral reality or a mathematically postulated but not yet observed physical particle. Epistemological objectivity concerns how we acquire knowledge of that external world. Semantic objectivity examines the conditions under which our statements about the external world may be determined to be true or false.[55] Philosophical positions on objectivity can be organized into four categories: (1) subjectivism denies objectivity wholesale and claims that the existence or meaning of the world depends entirely upon our individual beliefs about the world, (2) minimal objectivism is the view that the existence or meaning of the world is determined by our shared understanding of the world, (3) modest objectivism is the view that the existence or meaning of the world is determined not by what we may happen to believe, but rather by what we would believe under ideal epistemic conditions, and (4) strong objectivism is the view that the meaning or existence of the world never depends upon what we may believe about the world.[56]

Although nothing in my argument depends on this point, I might add a fourth type of objectivity, between minimal and modest objectivism. It seems to me that there may be a place for determining the existence and meaning of the world in reference not to an entire community or to ideal conditions, but rather to a particular community under ordinary conditions.[57] We can call this mediated objectivism, according to which the received meaning of, say, law or art is determined through a process of considered judgment by a community that has particular training or expertise in formulating and evaluating judgments of this type. The process of making and evaluating these judgments constructs a broader meaning for a larger political, legal, or social community.

In all senses of objectivism (but not subjectivism), the existence or meaning of the world is determined in some manner beyond or outside one's own perspective or belief. These notions of objectivity may apply best in different circumstances (*i.e.*, judgments of taste are subjective, judgments of fashion are minimally objective, judgments about color are modestly objective, and scientific judgments are strongly objective).[58]

The objectivity often assumed for law is strong objectivism, even though it is the least defensible form of objectivity from a philosophical perspective.[59] Michael Moore is probably the most prominent legal scholar who defends strong objectivity in law on philosophical grounds.[60] Moore's view is that we ordinarily attempt to understand the world around us, the physical and the moral worlds, and that we attempt to use language to describe them as accurately as we can. Natural objects, evaluative concepts, and legal norms have an existence that we encounter and attempt to explain.[61] That is to say, trees, fairness, and malice have a true meaning, and we use our language correctly or incorrectly to correspond to that reality.[62] Moore's view has been extensively criticized.[63]

On the other end of the spectrum, legal realists take a subjectivist view of law.[64] This view seems motivated by the observation that law cannot be understood in strongly objectivist terms. In other words, because the meaning or existence of the law always depends upon judgments about the law's content or applicability, legal realists deny that the law exists as a genuine constraint on judicial behavior.[65] Legal realists seem to ignore or deny the possibility that law may exist and possess meaning in minimally or mediatedly or modestly objective terms.[66] As I will argue in the next two chapters, the law is not best understood in strongly objective terms and, despite subjectivist protestations, the law does function as a meaningful influence on judicial decision making.[67]

Contemporary subjectivist views of law assume a rigid "subjective preference vs. objective law" dichotomy:

> In the traditional legal model, judges use as their guidelines the standards set in constitution, statute, precedent, or court rule. Inputs are carefully screened to avoid the personal and subjective in favor of the neutral and objective.[68]

Subjectivists then observe that law understood in this way does not fully determine judicial rulings, therefore judicial rulings are not controlled by neutral and objective legal rules. But demonstrating that judges do not decide cases according to this model cannot establish that the law is not influencing judicial decision making, because this model has so little to do with the way law actually functions in judicial decision making. To begin with, different sources of law and areas of law should not be regarded as operating monolithically and uniformly in judicial reasoning. We need to categorize different sources of law (such as constitutions, statutes, and precedents) and analyze their different operative nature and force in legal reasoning and judicial decision making.[69] Additionally, as I explain in more detail in the next chapter, in thinking about legal objectivity, we need to distinguish the legal norms produced by the judicial process and the judicial process itself. The strong objectivity of law rejected by legal realists is not a form of objectivity that can possibly capture the function of legal sources or the operation of the judicial process in the common law tradition: "The nature of the common law, however, is that subsequent cases alter prior precedential cases, yielding a new rule. . . . A 'rule' in the common law is not some abstract principle of law, but the interaction of an abstract principle with the facts of the present case. Later cases necessarily refashion the prior rule."[70]

The fundamental problem with equating legal objectivity with strong objectivity, or criticizing law and judging for failing to exhibit strong objectivity, is that it results in an unnecessarily blinkered vision of judicial decisions as determined by either legal rules or judicial attitudes. A finer understanding of legal objectivity would allow that neither laws nor attitudes are ever absent from judicial decision making. The better approach, then, is to consider more carefully and realistically the manner in which the law and judicial values are translated into judicial decisions:

> At some level, every law student, lawyer, and judge understands that a judge's values can influence the choices that a judge makes and that judicial decision making cannot always be explained with reference to legal doctrine alone . . . [J]udicial decisions are influenced by law and personal preferences in complex and varying combinations . . . value preferences influence case outcomes, but the universe of possible outcomes is constrained and channeled by legal text and precedent that judicial independence protects against encroachment.[71]

The judicial process cannot simply be reduced to a "law-based and preference-based decision-making dichotomy"[72] according to which judges act either "as detached and neutral arbiters of rules in contests between combatants"[73] or "judges employ law as a shill to conceal nakedly political decision making of a sort best reserved for Congress or the people."[74] We need to consider more accurately the relationship between judicial values and legal doctrine in the process of judicial decision making, a process that incorporates the judge's response to the facts and law at issue in a case within a formal written opinion that communicates the judge's reasoning and ruling to the parties and to the public.

I hope to engage different readers in different ways with my argument. This book is an argument against subjectivist and strong objectivist understandings of law and judging.[75] In general, when I refer to objectivity in law, I am referring to strong objectivity, because that is the understanding so often assumed in discussions of law and judging. In addition to arguing against subjectivism and strong objectivism, my argument is an effort to move past a pitched battle that has either been won or cannot really be joined. I want to think about subjectivity as it actually operates in the formulation of legal judgment and to suggest a way of thinking about the reception of that judgment as a legal source through an intersubjective process of communication and evaluation.

Subjectivity is not a synonym for bias, arbitrariness, idiosyncrasy, or solipsism.[76] Judges decide for themselves, but they do not decide for themselves alone.[77] Acknowledging an element of subjectivity in judging is not conceding that "anything goes" or that one can no longer evaluate the quality of a judge's decision.[78] On the contrary, the common law tradition requires judges to communicate their judgments to the parties and the public, and it presupposes a broader systemic process of appraising the merit of those judgments. The communication of legal judgments demands justificatory reasons for decision and action. The integrity of the process is predicated on the responses of judges, expressed as legal judgments and communicated in a form that is recognized by the community as fulfilling the individual's and the institution's judicial function.[79]

Subjectivity alone cannot sustain a formal legal judgment. The recognition of a subjective element in judging does not require us either to abandon a conception of meaningful legal norms or to seek a form of judging that eliminates or exaggerates judicial personality in judicial decision making.[80] This reductive, either-or mentality ("either judges enforce legal rules or the rules do not matter"—"either judges are political actors pursuing ideological agendas or they are neutral umpires applying the law") utterly fails to capture the authentic common law judicial process.[81] Instead, we need to see the interaction between an individual judicial response and a formally articulated legal judgment.[82]

The subjective element in judicial decisions remains a source of discomfort and discontent for many scholars and students of the common law system. My hope is to alleviate some of that discomfort by demonstrating that the personal and subjective aspect of judging can be accepted and valued once it is situated within the complementary aspects of common law judging that require the public justification of an intersubjective judgment cast in universalizable terms. As long as we can agree that the existence and meaning of law are not best understood as entirely external to a shared human process of communication and evaluation, and as long as we can agree that law has some existence and meaning external to individual perception

concept and term for thinking about how we answer evaluative questions about legal judgments. In terms of my argument, once a judgment has been reached, the intersubjective reception of that judgment as valid is an evaluation that the judgment was proper.[95]

For purposes of this book, the operative understandings of objectivity and truth involve a reference to a standard or perspective external to the judge, which validates the judgment, because it can be evaluated as distinct from the subjective preferences and values of the judge.[96] In an effort to distill these various conceptions of objectivity in a way that will allow me to discuss them usefully here, I will focus mainly on objectivity in terms of "mind-independence"[97] and "the rule of law and not of men."[98] Mind-independence means that the existence and meaning of legal norms is determined through a process external to the perceptions or beliefs of an individual.[99] The rule of law aspect of objectivity means that the existence and content of legal norms is determined through a process that identifies these norms as legal sources, which play a uniquely important role in legal reasoning.[100] Both conceptions capture the philosophical and legal sense that objectivity delineates a basis for judgment beyond or besides the subjective preferences of the judge.

Impartiality, Intersubjectivity, and the Art of Judging

As I explain in chapter 2, thinking about law in terms of objectivity has produced important scholarship, but it has also resulted in confusion about what objectivity means and how it applies to law and judging. One of the many problems with the use of objectivity in discussions of judging is that the term is sometimes used to refer to a quality in judges and sometimes to refer to a quality in rules. I will distinguish different forms of objectivity and explain how they result in different understandings of law. I will distinguish objectivity from impartiality and situate my argument within the existing discussion of issues of subjectivity and objectivity in law and judging. I also begin in chapter 2 to suggest an alternative to thinking of law and judging as only subjective or objective. My point here is not that the dichotomy is false; it captures something important about our relationship to the world and a judge's relationship to the law. It also, however, sharply restricts and ultimately distorts our best understanding of the judicial process in the common law tradition.

The purpose of chapter 2 is to explain that we should distinguish among the formulation of legal judgments by judges, the legal norms expressed in those judgments, and the evaluation and reception of those judgments by the community. Functional effectiveness is the term used to describe the objectivity associated with the judicial process of reviewing the evidence, arguments, and sources that are distinctive of the common law tradition and arriving at the legal judgments that articulate legal norms. Universalizability or universality is the term used to describe the legal norms of a jurisdiction that are produced through the judicial process and articulated in a legal judgment (or in some other fashion recognized by that jurisdiction as generating an authoritative source of law). Intersubjectivity is the process by which the legal judgments issued by judges are evaluated by a larger constitutive community. My overarching point in this chapter is to argue that however we conceive of objectivity in law, we should distinguish among the objectivity of judges and judging, the objectivity of legal sources and judgments, and the process of evaluating and validating those judgments by the larger legal or political community. The focus on objectivity and the failure to differentiate the objectivity of law, the objectivity of judging, and the evaluation of judgments has led to serious misrepresentations and distortions of the process of adjudication and the operation of legal sources in legal reasoning.

Chapter 3 develops an alternative conception of judging, one that is influenced by Immanuel Kant's aesthetic theory. In this chapter, I explore a number of connections between common law legal judgment and Kantian aesthetic judgment. In brief, Kant described a process of judging art that involved an individual's personal, internal response, which is then communicated and claimed as a shared judgment for all viewers of the work of art. I argue in chapter 3 that this mode of response and reasoning captures more fully the common law process of judicial decision making than the familiar alternatives. Connecting Kantian aesthetic judgment with common law legal judgment avoids the misguided and widespread view that the subjective element of judging somehow compromises the integrity of the process or the decision or, conversely, that principled judging requires that a judge disregard his personal values or perspectives when judging. As with Kantian aesthetic judgments, common law judicial efforts to articulate legal doctrine from the perspective of the individual judge are necessarily evaluative and communicative. Kant's theory helps us to see that a human judgment (of law or art) exists apart from the individual who reached that judgment, but cannot be abstracted entirely from the human beings who make, evaluate, and share those judgments.[101] Similarly, we see why it is difficult to assess judgments of law or art through falsifiable models or measurements.[102]

Why aesthetic theory as a way of examining judicial decision making? Whatever may be the case in the civil law tradition, there is an undeniable element of art in legal judgment in the common law world. But I do not mean this simply in the "lawyering is an art not a science" sense. I mean that the formulation of a legal judgment mirrors the process of aesthetic judgment in that an individual's subjective response and considered conclusion are proffered to a larger community with a claim that that community will share the individual's view, and the community then engages in an intersubjective evaluation through which the received meaning of the judgment is determined. Kantian aesthetic theory describes this relationship between the individual judgment as an independent and interdependent judgment through the reception of that judgment within a broader constitutive community. In the common law tradition, the parallel of aesthetic and legal judgment is a valuable way to understand the contribution of a judge's opinion to the developing understanding of the law within a broader legal and political community. There is an individual and communal sense of justice that correlates well with a sense of beauty, and there is an aesthetic to legal reasoning. When we read an exceptional legal opinion—one that concentrates on the important factual circumstances, that captures correctly the application of the law to these facts, that reaches the proper outcome for the right reasons—we do not just think it is right. We feel it. There is a momentum to these opinions that builds through their structure and reasoning. Powerful legal arguments have an emotional force. Art and law combine human faculties of thought and feeling, reason and passion.[103]

In chapter 4, I provide some examples of judicial decisions in which the relationship between the subjective and intersubjective elements of judicial decision making are evident and in which the individual responses of judges are then translated into legal judgments that form precedents for future judicial decisions. By changing and developing property law, tort law, and criminal law, judges in the United States and the United Kingdom function within their institutions when fashioning doctrine and applying legal standards that then guide and govern behavior, and as I argue in this chapter, we should understand a fundamental aspect of this decision making process to be the judges' individual responses to the cases they are asked to decide.

In chapter 5, I explore the meaning of judicial independence in terms of judicial individuality. More specifically, I consider legislative attempts to interfere with the internal reasoning process of judges as a threat to judicial independence. And I challenge conceptions of judicial independence that focus exclusively or predominantly on institutional independence. By ex-the judicial process. A lack of impartiality in a judge is a violation of due process for a litigant.[21] The individual before the court has the right to an impartial judge whose views about her as an individual will not prejudice his decision and who possesses no personal stake in the outcome of the case.[22] But the individual before the court does not have a right to a judge with no views about the law and with no value system of his own that frames his understanding of the law or the world.[23] With this distinction in mind, the common law tradition requires judges to be impartial, but it cannot and does not expect them to be objective:

> We are born with predispositions; and the process of education, formal and informal, creates attitudes in all men which affect them in judging situations, attitudes which precede reasoning in particular instances. . . . The judge in our society owes a duty to act in accordance with those basic predilections inhering in our legal system (although, of course, he has the right, at times, to urge that some of them be modified or abandoned). The standard of dispassionateness obviously does not require the judge to rid himself of the unconscious influence of such social attitudes. In addition to those acquired social value judgments, every judge, however, unavoidably has many idiosyncratic 'learnings of the mind,' uniquely personal prejudices, which may interfere with his fairness at a trial. . . . The conscientious judge will, as far as possible, make himself aware of his biases of this character, and, by that very self-knowledge, nullify their effect. Much harm is done by the myth that, merely by putting on a black robe and taking the oath of office as a judge, a man ceases to be human and strips himself of all predilections, becomes a passionless thinking machine. The concealment of the human element in the judicial process allows that element to operate in an exaggerated manner; the sunlight of awareness has an antiseptic effect on prejudices. Freely avowing that he is a human being, the judge can and should, through self-scrutiny, prevent the operation of this class of biases.[24]

Once we distinguish impartiality from objectivity, we can see the difference between prejudices and values. We also can begin to appreciate the problem with referring to a judge's values, experiences, and perspectives—as well as his prejudices, biases, and financial interests—as the subjective element of judging, and then contrasting this with the image of the objective, neutral, and dispassionate judge with a blindfold and scales.[25]

Two core institutional standards reinforce this differentiation of impartiality from objectivity and emphasize impartiality, rather than objectivity, in the common law judiciary. First, the sort of improper interest that precludes a judge from deciding a case is a "direct, personal, substantial" interest in the case, "because his interest would certainly bias his judgment."[26] Similarly, the statutes codifying the standards for recusal indicate that a judge should recuse himself only where there is a bias specific to a litigant, or a case, or a financial interest.[27] A judge is not required or expected to recuse himself simply because of general values or perspectives[28] or because of personal characteristics such as race or gender.[29] My argument here is that the differentiation of impartiality from objectivity tracks the basic distinction between the biases or prejudices that should lead to recusal and the values or perspectives that any judge brings to her judgments: "[N]eutrality in the absolute sense cannot be expected. 'Personal bias or prejudice' calls only for practical objectives. For example, prior judicial views will not disqualify. [I]t would be strange if a judge became less qualified the greater his judicial experience. Obviously, too, a judge is not prevented from sitting because he comes into every case with a background of general personal experiences and beliefs. There must be something unique."[30]

The claim that a judge cannot be impartial must be supported by specific factual allegations, and the determination that a judge's impartiality has been compromised is left to that judge himself. The reasons for this are easiest to see when we consider impartiality in relation to judicial independence, which I will discuss further in chapter 5. A judge must determine for himself whether he possesses a bias that might interfere with his ability to decide a case fairly. Otherwise the judicial institution could be manipulated by having the parties rather than the courts determine which judges shall hear which cases.[31]

Thinking about the relationship between judicial impartiality and judicial independence leads to the second institutional basis for distinguishing impartiality from objectivity. In the common law tradition, judges cannot be removed from office for their legal judgments.[32] The basis for this constitutional protection of the judiciary's independence is closely linked with the judiciary's impartiality. Because judges are expected to determine the law's meaning and application on the basis of their own legal judgment, rather than on the basis of personal prejudice or external influence, the judiciary merits the unique institutional protections it enjoys. If judges cannot point to a basis in the law for their legal rulings, they will no longer be able to justify their institution's independent position and role in public life and government.[33] Judges are expected to decide impartially because they are uniquely positioned, constitutionally and institutionally, to decide that way.[34] Their position places significant obligations upon them, individually and as members of a larger community, to explain their judgments by reference to authoritative legal sources and forms of legal reasoning.[35]

In relation to the courts' institutional independence, the distinction between impartiality and objectivity can help us analyze politically charged cases such as *Bush v. Gore*.[36] As Howard Gillman observed, we cannot simply equate or correlate decisions traced to judicial party affiliation with decisions based on improper judicial partisanship.[37] My point is not that the Court decided *Bush v. Gore* correctly, or that the decision was not improperly influenced by partisan behavior on the part of certain justices. My point is that we cannot simply point to the party affiliation of the justices in the majority and conclude on this basis alone that a decision was improperly influenced by partisanship. Put another way, we need to do more than assert that certain justices lacked objectivity because they share an ideological perspective with the litigant who prevailed in the case. As Gillman points out, we must determine, on the basis of specific aspects of the judges' actions or decisions, whether the impartiality of certain justices was compromised by partisanship. Perhaps, in *Bush v. Gore*, there are specific facts toward which we might point.[38] In any event, differentiating impartiality from objectivity allows us to evaluate judicial behavior in a manner that is more precisely linked to the actions of a particular judge in a particular case.[39]

Objectivity

The longstanding view of objectivity as the opposite of subjectivity has led people to assume that since judges should not decide cases in an entirely subjective way, they must decide in an entirely objective way. There is a problem, though, with seeing subjectivity and objectivity solely in oppositional terms. First, subjectivity and objectivity are strictly oppositional only if we assume that the relevant meaning of objectivity is strong objectivity.[40] Second, the meanings of "objective" used to describe law and to describe judges do not overlap perfectly. The existence and meaning of the law may be identified in a meaningfully objective sense, but the process by which the law is identified does not necessarily operate in the same way. What people (officials, citizens, litigants, jurors) believe and do in reference to the law *is* what determines its meaning and existence.[41] In other words, in terms of objectivity, the process of identifying legal norms should be understood differently from the norms themselves, and since the production and identification of

than a minimally objective consensus of opinion about meaning; the recognition of a dynamic process of evaluating judgments in a community contemplates a place for judgments that deviate from a preexisting consensus and yet may still be validated as legitimate or even correct judgments.[49] Intersubjectivity in legal and aesthetic judgment produces meaning through reception, evaluation, and translation. To begin addressing intersubjective judgment in legal terms, in the next section I consider some of these issues in relation to the trial process as the traditional institutional starting point for the production of legal judgments.

Trials and Truths

The goal of the trial process is sometimes understood as translating into and through legal evidence the historical events that are at issue in a given case. Even here, people frequently confuse more abstract conceptions of objectivity and truth with the determination of factual and legal issues at trial. The physical and testimonial evidence that is presented at trial to establish the relevant facts of the case can be thought of in terms of mind-independence or objective truth, but that will quickly become misleading. For example, the physical evidence (a gun or a pair of eyeglasses) exists in the world apart from what we may think about it. The testimonial evidence exists as an independent record of the perceptions, recollections, and opinions of the people who testify. But what the physical and testimonial evidence *means*, how that evidence is deemed to be relevant and probative of the legal issues, depends upon the conclusions of the judge or juror whose role is to determine the legal truth of what happened and how the facts established in court relate to the law.

The legal concepts that structure and govern the trial process are not directed solely toward a simple investigation or reconstruction of historical events. The historical facts are, of course, a crucial part of the process, but they do not make up the values, virtues, and shortcomings of the adversary trial process. At trial, the evidence must be presented in a manner that ideally ensures the fairness of the process and the rights of the litigants, with particular regard for the criminal defendant.[50] This is one of the many reasons that in our discussions of the legal world we would be better off thinking in terms of intersubjective validity rather than objective truth.[51] Our discussions will benefit because thinking this way can help us to identify mistakes in the identification or interpretation of the law and in the determination of the facts and to distinguish such errors from failings of the trial

upon authoritative legal sources according to which legal arguments are articulated and evaluated by a community of judges, lawyers, and others.[73] Among other things, the effort to keep legal reasoning autonomous from other forms of reasoning will help to ensure that adjudicative outcomes are determined by legal sources and not by extra-legal values that might otherwise be smuggled by judges into their legal decisions. According to this conception of legal positivism, statements about the law may be determined to be true or false solely with regard to the content of legal sources and their anticipated application in legal reasoning.

My purpose in this section is not to defend legal positivism; it is to defend my argument by anticipating and preempting certain criticisms that are commonly made against positivism and might also be made against my position. In thinking about these claims it is useful to differentiate, as Frederick Schauer does, among different meanings or versions of legal positivism. Schauer suggests three: conceptual positivism, decisional positivism, and normative positivism.[74] Conceptual positivism is the theoretical claim that "morality is not a necessary condition of legality."[75] This describes, in effect, positivism's commitment to the separability thesis. Decisional positivism "is a view about the role of posited law in legal decision-making."[76] This represents positivism's commitment to the sources thesis. Normative positivism is a view of conceptual positivism as itself a socially constructed thesis about the meaning of law. In other words, normative positivism sees the separation of law from morality as presupposing a conception of law that is, by definition or conceptual extension, necessarily distinct from morality. This view of positivism is normative in the sense that a positivist conception of law should be chosen as *the* conception of law "because of the good that such an understanding will produce."[77] The good that may be engendered by a positivist conception of law might include, for example, fostering an individual and societal perspective of moral distance from or evaluation of the law.[78]

Joshua Cohen's discussion of legal positivism reflects a common understanding of the purpose of judging as getting to the truth of how the law applies in a given case and, more simply, what the law is (as opposed to what the law ought to be): "The notion of truth is also fundamental in our understanding of reasoning. Thus, truth is tied to judging, in that judging whether p is closely connected to judging whether p is true. . . . Truth is connected as well to norms of thought and interaction that call for accuracy in representation, sincerity in expression, consistency, 'getting it right,' and being attentive to how things are and not simply how we wish them to be."[79] Cohen defends the concept of truth against various forms of the claim that truth cannot be invoked in public discourse about democratic politics (because of the challenges of cultural diversity, moral relativism, ideological pluralism, etc.). He frames his analysis of truth as a response to John Rawls' argument that political judgments should not "use (or deny) the concept of truth. . . . Rather, within itself, the political conception does without the concept of truth."[80]

Cohen argues that "a political conception of truth is . . . a genuine conception of truth."[81] By truth, Cohen sometimes indicates that he understands truth in relation to "our practices of making and defending assertions, in our reasoning, and in ordinary understandings about the content and the correctness of thoughts."[82] So Cohen does not assume a strongly objectivist notion of political truth. Instead, Cohen argues that "political justification . . . should proceed on a terrain of argument that can be shared."[83] The problems with Cohen's view arise when he shifts his discussion from political to legal conceptions of truth. As I explain in the next section, Cohen's defense of truth in relation to legal judgment will inevitably lead us back to the confusions created by the assumed relationship between truth and objectivity.[84]

Cohen intends his argument about truth to extend into the field of law and legal judgments. For example, in his discussion of Thomas Hobbes and legal positivism, Cohen writes:

> Hobbes's thesis is about legal validity, not about justice. The idea is that legal validity is fixed entirely by an act of authority, and not at all by moral rectitude. . . . That position is legal-positivism, which is consistent with the view that there are natural standards of rectitude to be used in evaluating laws. But Hobbes was arguably (only arguably) led to his legal positivism from positivism about justice itself: *auctoritas non veritas facit justitiam*. As Hobbes says, there are no unjust laws, because, antecedent to the sovereign's law-making activity, there is no just or unjust distinction for laws to be answerable to. So when Hobbes says that truth does not make law, he means that legal validity does not depend on truths about rightness. But that is in part because there are no normative truths available prior to authority that might enter into determinations of legal validity. If that is indeed the rationale for legal positivism, then it follows as well that the truth—that is, truths about what is just and unjust, right and wrong—cannot figure in *assessing* valid laws as just or unjust, because the justice-making facts, too, are exercises of sovereign legislative authority.[85]

There are several points in this excerpt that are important for my argument. First, Cohen correctly indicates that legal positivism is typically characterized by the separability thesis, a general claim that legal validity is not preconditioned upon the law's satisfying a standard of moral rectitude. But when Cohen goes further and attributes to legal positivism the view that "there are no unjust laws because, antecedent to the sovereign's law-making activity, there is no just or unjust distinction for laws to be answerable to," his statement may be true of Hobbes,[86] but it is not true of all legal positivists. In fact, Cohen has made two mistakes here. He has failed to recognize that legal positivism is not inconsistent with moral realism and he has glossed over the distinction between inclusive positivism and exclusive positivism. I will address each of these mistakes in turn.

Commentators frequently misconstrue the separability thesis as a claim not just that law may be identified without recourse to morality but also as a claim that there is no morality through which law may be identified. Properly understood, however, legal positivism does not hold a view on the metaethical question of whether moral truths or facts exist.[87] Put differently, a legal positivist can also be a moral realist.[88] In addition, legal positivists disagree with one another about whether moral claims can enter into determinations of legal validity. Exclusive legal positivists argue that the identification of a law as valid can never depend on its moral worth, because this would violate the separability thesis.[89] Inclusive legal positivists believe that the identification of a law as valid can depend, within a given jurisdiction, upon its compliance with a normative moral criterion.[90]

Legal positivists argue that their theory helps to keep the identification of the law distinct from the moral evaluation of the law,[91] and this is the first point that Cohen missed in the last sentence of his quotation. By arguing that legal positivism does not allow for moral assessment of the law, Cohen assumes either that legal positivism is committed to moral relativism or noncognitivism or that disagreements about moral truth preclude moral evaluation of the law. Whichever Cohen meant as a criticism of positivism, the criticism is unfounded.

The excerpt from Cohen also touches on his misperception of the sources thesis. The differentiation and identification of authoritative legal sources produces a "limited domain" of concepts and norms according to which lawyers and judges formulate and evaluate legal arguments. In H. L. A. Hart's terms, a rule of recognition[92] allows for the establishment of a legal system and a process of legal reasoning: "in the simple operation of identifying a given rule as possessing the required feature of being an item on an authoritative list of rules we have the germ of the idea of legal validity."[93] The use of the term "validity" here is neither accidental nor coincidental. In the identification of certain sources as legal sources, we can see that certain arguments validly refer to the sources recognized by the community as legally authoritative and certain arguments do not.[94] The rule of recognition functions as a "social rule" insofar as legal rules are validated through their acceptance by a legal community.[95] In the next chapter, I will develop an account of the validation of legal judgments through the common law process of their formulation and communication in a larger community.

The role of the rule of recognition in identifying legal sources for purposes of legal reasoning is perhaps its most crucial function. In fact, Hart emphasized this point in a passage that clarifies the value of thinking of law and legal reasoning in terms of validity rather than truth:

> [Some argue] that the rule is meant to determine completely the legal result in particular cases, so that any legal issue arising in any case could simply be solved by mere appeal to the criteria or tests provided by the rule. But this is a misconception: the function of the rule is to determine only the general conditions which correct legal decisions must satisfy in modern systems of law. The rule does this most often by supplying criteria of validity.[96]

For Hart, the value of legal sources for legal reasoning is not to predetermine the outcome of a legal dispute, but to prescribe the distinctive sources and processes by which the outcome will be determined. Hart emphasized this role of legal sources for legal reasoning specifically in relation to the justification of judicial decisions, for the judges who write them and for the community to whom and for whom they are written.[97]

Here we see the problem with conceiving of judging as a search for legal truth contained within existing sources of law: it is not an accurate depiction of legal positivism or of common law judging. It also is not a meaningful criticism of my argument to indicate that I do not assign this role to legal sources in legal reasoning. Legal sources are crucial to legal reasoning, but not because they contain statements of legal truth that judges must locate and articulate in their judgments. We recognize a legal outcome as valid when the sources and process are employed properly in a legal judgment. As Hart explained, we should think of a legal judgment not as finding the truth dictated by the sources, but rather as the result of a process validated by reference to the sources. In fact, this understanding of legal positivism helps us to see why Hart himself did not believe legal standards are best conceived in terms of their objectivity and why he believed that positivism did not need to conceive of the objectivity of moral standards at all.[98] In his discussion of truth in relation to law as well as politics, Cohen misconstrues positivism and the role of authoritative sources in legal reasoning.

Inclusive positivists and exclusive positivists discuss the relationship between law and morality in the rule of recognition in terms of validity rather than truth, as a means of differentiating legal validity from moral truth.[99] One problem with failing to recognize the difference between legal validity and moral truth is that it might lead to a view that there is no differentiation of morality and law in the common law tradition.[100] The separability thesis means, however, that whatever we may believe about the existence of morality, those beliefs have nothing to do with determining the existence of law. And according to the sources thesis, wherever we may believe we find authoritative sources of morality, we all can agree about where we find the authoritative sources of law.

In characterizing positivism (in the person of Hobbes) by its rejection of moral truth, Cohen does not seem to engage the theory on its own terms. In addition, even if we take Cohen's direct reference to Hobbes to indicate that he meant to direct his criticisms solely at exclusive positivism, they are still inapposite. Exclusive positivists generally do not argue that judges do not or cannot engage in moral reasoning when making legal decisions.[101] Furthermore, positivists generally agree that morality will usually influence the evaluation and development of the law.[102] Cohen believes, along with many others, that the combination of conceptual positivism and decisional positivism leaves positivists with no place for morality in the process of legal reasoning by reference to legal sources. Similarly, because I accept that legal sources possess a unique importance in legal reasoning, one might assume that I must be a decisional positivist and a conceptual positivist, and accordingly that I cannot argue that there is a place for a judge's values (moral or otherwise) in the judicial process. As I have explained, Cohen misunderstands positivism on this point. Moreover, positivists are not alone in recognizing that legal sources may be identified without reference to their moral worth and in acknowledging the centrality of legal sources for legal reasoning.[103] Relatedly, while it is open to question whether conceptual positivism entails decisional positivism,[104] nothing about decisional positivism necessitates any commitment to conceptual positivism. My argument explains the place for a judge's values and perspectives within the communication of a legal judgment to a legal community. The process of legal judgment by reference to legal sources does not preclude consideration of judicial values in the judicial process. The process of legal reasoning in accordance with legal sources allows us to distinguish the judge's values from the judgment's value. As I discuss in the next chapter, the communication, evaluation and validation of a judge's reasoning in his legal judgment requires the use of conceptual, rhetorical, and doctrinal sources and modes that distinguish the judgment as distinctively legal. For positivists and nonpositivists, the evaluation and reception of a judgment is often framed in terms of validity rather than truth, because its significance as a legal judgment depends upon its reference to authoritative sources. The sources do not and cannot, however, fully determine the judgment's meaning.

Shifting our thinking away from truth and toward validity in our understanding of legal judgments allows us to recognize that a judgment is legally valid even though we may continue to disagree about its moral value. Indeed, one value of legal judgments as distinctive and authoritative legal sources, which thereby constitute part of the limited domain of law, is that they resolve social conflicts while allowing the underlying moral disagreements to continue.[105]

Judgment and Justification

Considering objectivity in law in terms of truth is not the only way to claim objectivity as a value of law. The "uniform applicability" aspect of objectivity as applied to law requires that legal norms should be created in a "universalizable" form.[106] But many arguments for objectivity in law do not differentiate between universality and functional effectiveness, on the apparent assumption that universality entails a rule that will yield the same result whenever it is applied, by whomever it is applied.[107] The challenge here, however, lies in "determining the extent to which ideology or intellectual perspective governs the selection of universals."[108] In other words, by assuming that the objectivity of a legal rule is defined by its differentiation from the judge who applies it, universality and functional effectiveness are elided in a way that leads people to conclude that a rule that can be applied consistently but is not applied by a judge in a particular case results from a cognitive error or ideological prejudice of the judge who failed to apply the rule. But, in fact, the functional effectiveness of the judicial process in a common law system sometimes depends upon a judge's ability to determine that a rule should *not* be applied in a particular case, or that a rule should be changed.[109] Legal rules in a common law system may be understood as "de-

ences and perspectives in their work on the bench.[118] These individual responses and perspectives are discussed in different terms, such as emotion or empathy, and they also may embrace broader experiential components that inform a judge's decision making. These elements of a judge's decision, when properly understood, do not supplant or controvert the decision's legal merit or substance. Instead, they help to constitute the meaning of the law through its application to the actions of people governed by it. The translation of these responses in the production of legal norms through the judicial process is the common law method of establishing the content of the law as a practical influence on people's lives in a community (also known as a jurisdiction) and concomitantly as a social and institutional expression of the values the members of that community understand the law to embody. The judge articulates the reasons for her judgment in a manner that will be recognized as legitimate by the parties, the profession, and the public. The public justification of her decision in the formulation of her judgment, and the evaluation of her judgment by a larger community, is the "intersubjective" aspect of decision making that I will discuss further in the next chapter.[119]

The most prominent and controversial examples of the perceived influence of individual values and perspectives on legal judgments tend to involve Supreme Court decisions. This is not because the values of other judges on other courts do not play an equally important role in their decision making, and I will discuss some decisions of these courts in chapter 4. It is instead because the nature of the issues confronted by the Supreme Court, the role and position of that Court in the judicial and political system, and the public attention paid to the Court heighten public awareness and scrutiny of its decisions and of the justices who make them. A judge deciding a constitutional case must, perhaps more than most, consider her personal response to the case and the impact of the constitutional concept at issue in relation to the litigants before her and, by extension, all future litigants who would be governed by the Court's conception of that constitutional provision. That is to say, the judge must consider what the concepts of privacy or due process or equality mean for an individual who claims that a law violates a constitutional provision. That consideration cannot be accomplished without the personal response of the judge, because the constitutional provision cannot and should not be abstracted from the meaning of these concepts for those who are governed by their meanings.[120]

A good example of an actual judge whose particular judgments illustrate this point is Ruth Bader Ginsburg. While this is not the place for an extended excursus into judicial biography, Justice Ginsburg's experiences can help us understand her public statements and legal judgments. Ruth Bader Ginsburg began her legal education in 1956 at Harvard Law School as one of nine women in a class of 552.[121] They were welcomed by Dean Erwin Griswold by being asked "what [they] were doing in law school taking a place that could be held by a man."[122] Her academic performance earned her a place on the Harvard Law Review. After her husband (who was a year ahead of her at Harvard) took a job with a firm in Manhattan, Ginsburg requested that Harvard allow her to complete her degree at Columbia Law School so that she, her husband, and their young daughter could remain together. Harvard refused.[123] So Ginsburg transferred to Columbia, served on the Columbia Law Review, and graduated in 1959 as the covaledictorian of her class.[124] But she received no job offers. Justice Felix Frankfurter declined to hire her as a clerk due to her gender,[125] Judge Learned Hand told her he did not hire women as clerks because of his use of "salty language,"[126] and her professor at Columbia, Gerald Gunther, had to prevail upon (and provide guarantees to[127]) Judge Edmund Palmieri for him to hire her as his clerk. As it turned out, Ginsburg performed so well that Judge Palmieri hired another woman to succeed her.[128]

In 1963, Ginsburg joined the Rutgers Law School faculty in Newark. While at Rutgers, Ginsburg helped to found the Women's Rights Law Reporter and began working with the American Civil Liberties Union.[129] Ginsburg cofounded the ACLU's Women's Rights Project, coauthored the first casebook on gender discrimination,[130] accepted a position as the first tenured woman on the Columbia Law faculty, and taught the first course at Columbia on Women and the Law.[131] Through her work with the ACLU, Ginsburg was involved in nine cases before the Supreme Court that established gender discrimination as a constitutional violation; Ginsburg argued six of these cases and prevailed in five.[132] Ginsburg argued that gender shared with race both social characteristics[133] and a related history of legally sanctioned subordination and discrimination,[134] and she patterned her approach in these cases after the NAACP strategy in establishing racial segregation as a constitutional violation.[135]

As a result of these experiences, commentators frequently discuss Ginsburg's opinion in *United States v. Virginia* (*VMI*)[136] as the culmination and realization of her efforts as an advocate for gender equality before the Court through her authored judgment as a member of the Court.[137] Indeed, Ginsburg said so herself.[138] While her decision in *VMI* supports the point I am making, I want to focus instead on a few dissenting opinions that reveal the influence of perhaps less-evident personal experiences on the formulation and expression of Justice Ginsburg's legal judgments.

When Ginsburg was asked at her Supreme Court confirmation hearings before the Senate Judiciary Committee if her experiences had made her particularly sensitive to issues of discrimination, this was her response:

> I am alert to discrimination. I grew up during World War II in a Jewish family. I have memories as a child, even before the war, of being in a car with my parents and passing a place in Senator Specter's State [Pennsylvania], a resort with a sign out in front that read: "No dogs or Jews allowed." Signs of that kind existed in this country during my childhood. One couldn't help but be sensitive to discrimination, living as a Jew in America at the time of World War II.[139]

Ginsburg also expressly linked the realization of what it meant to live as a Jew in Europe during World War II with the end of racial segregation by law in the United States. As she put it at her confirmation hearing, "One of the influences on *Brown*, I think, was a war we had just come through, in which people were exterminated on the basis of what other people called their race. And I don't think that apartheid in the United States could long outlive the Holocaust."[140] And in an exchange with Senator Carol Moseley Braun, Ginsburg was asked about the efforts to disenfranchise blacks that led to the Voting Rights Act of 1965 (the VRA)[141] and the *Shaw v. Reno*[142] litigation. In response, Ginsburg recounted her first personal exposure to socially entrenched racial discrimination:

> I remember going with my husband to an Army camp when he was in the military service. We passed a sign that said—I thought it said, "Jack White's Cafe." But it didn't. It said, "Jack's White Cafe[.]" I had never seen such a sign. I was fully adult, indeed pregnant at the time, so it was not so long ago that such things existed in the United States. I am sensitive to that history. When I spoke about *Brown v. Board of Education*, earlier today, I mentioned specifically the deprivation of the very basic right to cast one's ballot that existed for so long in the United States for black people.[143]

This brief discussion of Justice Ginsburg's background and comments can help us perceive, in some of her notable opinions as a Supreme Court justice, the influence of her experiences as a Jewish woman who lived through legalized racial discrimination and World War II. For example, in *Shelby County v. Holder*,[144] the Court ruled that § 4(b) of the VRA was unconstitutional because it relied upon outdated factual findings in support of its requirement that certain states and counties have changes to their voting regulations "precleared" by the federal government (the US Department of Justice or a three-judge court).[145] The basic premise of the majority in *Shelby County* was that "things have changed dramatically"[146] since the VRA was first enacted.

In her dissent in *Shelby County*, which was joined by Justices Breyer, Sotomayor, and Kagan, Justice Ginsburg comprehensively reviewed the history of voting rights discrimination and deprivation in the United States and the attendant "failure to fulfill the promise of the Fourteenth and Fifteenth Amendments."[147] She reviewed the passage of the VRA, the effectiveness of the VRA's preclearance provision, unrelenting efforts to discriminate against minority voters, repeated congressional reauthorization of the VRA in 1970, 1975, 1982, and 2006, the extensiveness of the hearings conducted by Congress prior to the 2006 reauthorization, and specific attempts to disenfranchise black and Latino voters leading up to the 2006 reauthorization.[148]

Ginsburg's dissent in *Shelby County* was motivated by her view that our nation has not changed so much since the passage of the VRA to allow the Court to disregard the basis for Congress's reauthorization of the statute. In reviewing the legislative record developed by Congress in reauthorizing the coverage formula under § 4(b), Ginsburg observed that "the covered jurisdictions have a unique history of problems with racial discrimination in voting. Consideration of this long history, *still in living memory*, was altogether appropriate."[149] One person whose memory Ginsburg refers to here is herself. As she recounted before the Judiciary Committee, she lived through the period that culminated in Congress passing the VRA, and as she said, "it was not so long ago that such things existed in the United States." We cannot separate Ginsburg's view of the constitutional basis for congressional reauthorization of the VRA from her personal experience as a witness to racial prejudice or from her sensitivity to the history of "deprivation of the very basic right to cast one's ballot that existed for so long in the United States for black people."

In an earlier case involving a challenge to a redistricting plan under the VRA, *Miller v. Johnson*,[150] Ginsburg dissented and drew upon another aspect of her personal experience in formulating her judgment. *Miller* involved the creation of a "majority-minority" voting district in Georgia. The majority upheld the invalidation of the proposed voting district and concluded that a district cannot be constructed on the basis "of purported communities of interest" when the goal was simply "maximizing the District's black population."[151] The Court ruled that the proposed district failed strict scrutiny even though it would have complied with the Justice Department's interpretation of preclearance under the VRA as maximizing majority-minority districts in Georgia.[152] According to the majority in *Miller*, maximizing black voting districts amounted to an assumption that race alone creates a shared voting interest apart from otherwise divergent "political, social, and economic interests within the [proposed] District's black population."[153]

In contrast with the majority, Justice Ginsburg was untroubled by the notion that voters might share interests largely on the basis of their race or ethnicity. That view was almost certainly informed by her experience of being born and raised in Brooklyn's Flatbush area[154] and, as she said, growing up in a Jewish family during World War II. She began her dissent by emphasizing, as she would later in *Shelby County*, that "for most of our Nation's history, the franchise has not been enjoyed equally by black citizens and white voters."[155] Consequently, after considering carefully the other factors that contributed to the formulation of the proposed district in *Miller*, Ginsburg addressed the majority's main contention that the overriding factor was race. In Ginsburg's view, this was politically justifiable and constitutionally defensible because, as she put it in her dissent (and as many of her former neighbors in Flatbush could have attested), "ethnicity itself can tie people together."[156] Moreover, as Ginsburg went on to explain, creating districts in recognition of ethnic or racial ties was nothing new and was a simple recognition of a political reality: "To accommodate the reality of ethnic bonds, legislatures have long drawn voting districts along ethnic lines."[157] To fail to treat race in the same manner as ethnicity would, in Ginsburg's view, amount to denying to black voters exactly the protection that the VRA was enacted to ensure.[158] As with *Shelby County*, Ginsburg's discussion in *Miller* cannot be divorced from her personal experiences of minority communities in the United States and the shared political affinities among minority voters and that the VRA was meant to ensure the full participation of minority voters in the political process.

Burwell v. Hobby Lobby Stores, Inc.[159] offers another example of the traceable influence of Ginsburg's experiences and perspectives on her judicial decisions. In *Hobby Lobby*, the majority ruled that the Religious Freedom Restoration Act of 1993 (RFRA)[160] precludes the government from requiring a closely held for-profit corporation to provide funding for contraceptives to its employees, in violation of the religious beliefs of the corporation's owners,[161] through a group health plan or insurance coverage under the Affordable Care Act.[162]

Justice Ginsburg dissented. Although she challenges several aspects of the majority's reasoning, I will focus on two. First, in reading her explanations of her disagreements with the majority opinion and with Justice Kennedy's concurring opinion, Ginsburg's experiences as a religious minority seem particularly pertinent. Kennedy and the majority chose to focus on the employers' exercise of "their religious beliefs within the context of their own closely held, for-profit corporations."[163] In contrast, Ginsburg believed the focus should be on the provision of health care to "employees who do not subscribe to their employers' religious beliefs."[164] The correct inquiry under RFRA, Ginsburg explained, is whether "the contraceptive coverage requirement 'substantially burden[s] [their] exercise of religion.'"[165]

According to Ginsburg, this inquiry was almost entirely avoided or ignored by the Court.[166] Here Ginsburg links her consideration of the religious beliefs of employees who do not share the views of Hobby Lobby's owners with her consideration of the health care that is denied to those employees as a result of the Court's ruling. Ginsburg noted that this inquiry is proper under the Free Exercise Clause of the First Amendment, because "[a]ccommodations to religious beliefs or observances [of Hobby Lobby's owners] . . . must not significantly impinge on the interests of third parties."[167] More specifically, Ginsburg emphasizes that the effect of the Court's ruling is to deny women who work for Hobby Lobby, but do not share the religious beliefs of Hobby Lobby's owners, access to contraceptives under their health care plan.[168] Consistent with her personal experiences and professional efforts, Ginsburg focuses on the rights and interests of women:

> Any decision to use contraceptives made by a woman covered under Hobby Lobby's or Conestoga's plan will not be propelled by the Government, it will be the woman's autonomous choice, informed by the physician she consults. Even if one were to conclude that Hobby Lobby and Conestoga meet the substantial burden requirement, the Government has shown that the contraceptive coverage for which the ACA provides furthers compelling interests in public health and women's well being. Those interests are concrete, specific, and demonstrated by a wealth of empirical evidence. To recapitulate, the mandated contraception coverage enables women to avoid the health problems unintended pregnancies may visit on them and their children. The coverage helps safeguard the health of women for whom pregnancy may be hazardous, even life

> threatening. And the mandate secures benefits wholly unrelated to pregnancy, preventing certain cancers, menstrual disorders, and pelvic pain.[169]

Ginsburg's experiences as a law student and as a lawyer involved dealing with prejudices based on her gender. Along with the others I have mentioned, Ginsburg has noted the specific challenges she faced not just as a Jewish woman, but especially as a mother.[170]

Ginsburg did not dissent alone in *Hobby Lobby*, *Shelby County*, or *Miller*. The other two women on the Court, Justices Sotomayor and Kagan, joined her *Hobby Lobby* dissent along with Justice Breyer. The *Hobby Lobby* majority, therefore, consisted only of men. This point was not lost on Ginsburg. In an interview about the decision, Ginsburg indicated that the male majority on "the Court has a blind spot today."[171] But she also remains hopeful that "justices continue to think and can change. . . . They have wives; they have daughters. By the way, I think daughters can change the perceptions of their fathers."[172] So we do not have to wonder whether Justice Ginsburg believes that a judge's experiences and perspectives influence her decisions. She has told us, in her judgments and in her statements, that she does. And this is as true for the Court's majority opinion in *Hobby Lobby* as it is for Ginsburg's dissenting opinion.

This analysis of the influence of a judge's personal experiences and values on her understanding of the law and her judgments in particular cases could be produced for any judge. My point here is not that there is any simple or universal experience of gender, race, religion, or ethnicity. My point is that a person's experiences as a Jewish woman, or a Latina, or a white woman raised on an Arizona ranch,[173] or a black man raised in poverty in Georgia during the 1950s and 60s,[174] do influence the perspectives of those individuals, and those perspectives, in turn, influence the understanding each of those judges has of the law. We can locate some of these similarities and differences in their responses and judgments. We find that Justice O'Connor wrote the principal precedent on which Justice Ginsburg relied in her *VMI* judgment.[175] But we also find that Justices O'Connor and Ginsburg disagreed about whether Congress possessed the power to provide a "a federal civil remedy for the victims of gender-motivated violence"[176] under the Commerce Clause by regulating "violent criminal conduct based solely on that conduct's aggregate effect on interstate commerce."[177] And one of the cases in which Justice Thomas chose to speak during oral argument, *Virginia v. Black*,[178] involved the burning of a cross at a Ku Klux Klan rally. During his questioning of Deputy Solicitor General Michael Dreeben at oral argument, Justice Thomas said:

> Mr. Dreeben, aren't you understating the—the effects of—of the burning cross? . . . [I]t's my understanding that we had almost 100 years of lynching and activity in the South by the Knights of Camellia and—and the Ku Klux Klan, and this was a reign of terror and the cross was a symbol of that reign of terror. . . . [M]y fear is, Mr. Dreeben, that you're actually understating the symbolism on—of and the effect of the cross, the burning cross. . . . [I]t was intended to have a virulent effect. And I—I think that what you're attempting to do is to fit this into our jurisprudence rather than stating more clearly what the cross was intended to accomplish and, indeed, that it is unlike any symbol in our society. . . . [T]here was no other purpose to the cross. There was no communication of a particular message. It was intended to cause fear . . . and to terrorize a population.[179]

Thomas's comments at oral argument altered the atmosphere in the courtroom,[180] and their influence can be found in the language and reasoning of the majority opinion.[181] Of course, we cannot know what impelled Justice Thomas to speak, but given the substance of his comments and of his dissenting opinion in this case,[182] it is difficult to deny either that his experiences in the racially segregated South were an important factor or that his position as the only black justice on the Court enhanced the influence of his comments upon his colleagues.[183]

Just as we should not assume that all women share the same perspective based on their gender experience or that all black people share the same perspective based on their racial experience, we also should acknowledge that some experiences are shared.[184] Shared or not, however, we should not pretend that judges will or should suspend their personal experiences and perspectives so that they can judge from an imagined place of abstract neutrality or objectivity.[185] The influence of these personal values on a judge's response to a case cannot be excised from her broader understanding of the purpose and meaning of the law that she interprets and applies in her judgments.[186] To be sure, this influence will be more evident in certain cases or for certain judges. But leaving aside certain instances of misconduct or failures of impartiality, the element of subjectivity in judicial decision making does not detract from the distinctive nature of the opinions as legal judgments or of the judgments as contributions to a broader understanding of the law.

In all these cases, a judge must render a legal judgment that incorporates an individual response within formal and institutional constraints, which allow the law to develop in a manner that the legal community can recognize and validate as a legal judgment. The judge and the community can justify a decision as impartial not because the judge's values played no role in her judgment, but because her judgment is consistent in principle, form, and content with existing modes of legal reasoning that are distinctive of the judiciary as an independent institution.[187] The response of a judge must be contained in and constrained by the formal elements of legal reasoning,[188] and these elements ensure that a judge's decision will be recognized as a legal judgment by the legal community and by the public.[189]

The combination of subjective responses within recognized forms of reasoning and decision making allows a community to evaluate and incorporate that judgment as an authoritative source of law or as a source of potential development of the law. As I will explain further in the next chapter, the bases for a judge's majority or dissenting opinion must be articulated in a manner that allows the judge to claim the assent of other judges who will review that decision in the future.[190] These forms of reasoning, particularly when judges disagree with one another, should properly be conceived in terms of validity or persuasiveness, rather than objectivity or truth, because the full meaning and value of a judgment cannot be determined when the judgment is written.[191]

In an important sense, every judgment implicates a judge's values, and the value of any judgment is determined by its ability to persuade other judges of its correctness as a legal result.[192] There is good reason to believe that judgments are more likely to endure in their persuasive influence if they engage the judge's own values and articulate that judge's view of the impact of the law for those governed by it. This is a further element of the common law process in constitutional adjudication: a lower level of abstraction increases the judge's focus on those individuals who are most directly affected by the law. The more a judge is sensitive to "the lived lives of individuals" in articulating her judgment, the more likely that judgment will continue to exert doctrinal influence in the future.[193] And the more distant the ruling is from its concrete applications, the less likely future lawyers and judges will find it persuasive.[194]

In other words, every legal judgment is a value judgment.[195] Read carefully, Ginsburg's dissents in *Shelby County*, *Miller*, and *Hobby Lobby* can help us see that the purpose and content and application of the Voting Rights Act or the Religious Freedom Restoration Act or the Fifteenth Amendment or the First Amendment—the *meaning* of these laws—cannot be understood in isolation from individual responses and underlying values of the judge who is interpreting them.[196] In writing her dissenting opinions, Justice Ginsburg articulates not only her view of the mistakes in the majority's reasoning and conclusion, she also expresses her implicit hope that the majority's "justices continue to think and can change."[197] In this respect, the substantive development of the law depends on the subjective responses of judges.[198] According to values intrinsic to the common law, a legal judgment claims the assent of other judges who may consider the matter in the future as a universalizable norm,[199] and it is also defeasible and subject to reevaluation and revision.[200]

The Judge in the Judgment

We need to move beyond the familiar civic phobia that judges will decide cases on the basis of their own values rather than the law. We need to recognize that when judges decide on the basis of the law they *are* deciding on the basis of their own values. Every time. The familiar concern either fundamentally misconceives the common law tradition or misconstrues the personal and public dynamics evident in all judicial decision making. As MacCormick reminds us, this concern also overlooks the overarching point that every aspect of the judicial decision-making process, including the judicial decision itself, occurs within a system of law:

> Legal decisions presuppose legal disputes. That is, they presuppose cases in which one party makes some kind of a claim about or from another person. . . . Particular rulings will have to take their place under constraints of consistency, coherence, and a reasonable evaluation of consequences in an existing even if incomplete corpus of law. So the parties and the judges have only quite restricted freedom of manoeuvre as they try to work through to a reasonably justifiable conclusion *justified as a conclusion of law* in the case seen as a *legal case*. The concept of universalizability, which I propound as essential to that of justification in law . . . is a concept limited by the requirements of legality and the Rule of Law. Judges have to universalize rulings as best they can within the context of an existing and established legal order.[201]

It is useful here to connect MacCormick's work with Brian Tamanaha's. In his response to characterizations of law as a political and ideological instrument and of judges as political actors pursuing ideological motivations by legal means, Tamanaha argues for a return to or a reconstruction of a non-instrumental view of law and judging. Tamanaha is motivated in part by his concern that these characterizations exaggerate the subjective aspects of judging and thereby deny the objective qualities of law.[202]

Tamanaha seeks to rescue the concept of objectivity from its modern critics and to reclaim a more meaningful account of objectivity, which better accounts for its genuine meaning and force in the common law tradition.[203] In pursuing this argument, Tamanaha emphasizes, as MacCormick does, the preexisting formal, doctrinal, and institutional parameters within which a judge's response must be incorporated in a legal judgment:

> Judges indeed approach the law from the standpoint of their personal views. More immediately, however, they see the law from within the lens of the legal tradition into which they have been indoctrinated, and from within the conventions of legal practice and judging in which they participate. The totality of the legal tradition—the legal language, the corpus of legal rules, concepts, principles, and ideas, legal processes and practices, hierarchical legal institutions, the craft of lawyering—has the effect of stabilizing legal meaning and providing restraints on the influence of the subjective views. Law is a socially produced and shared activity that participants are not free to do in any way they desire. . . . This account incorporates . . . the influence of background views on how people see the world, merely adding the reminder that the legal tradition itself is such a body of background views, which becomes an integrated aspect of the judge's own perspective.[204]

Tamanaha's observations connect well to MacCormick's discussion and help us see that a judge's subjective response is not exogenous to the legal tradition within which the judge functions. The judge's perspective and subjective response are themselves always formed and expressed within the background of a shared legal tradition and legal community.

We need judges with broad and varied experiences on our courts. The more breadth in personal experience and perspective that judges can bring to the law, the more that the law will reflect, over time, the plural community that it governs and through which judicial decisions acquire their full meaning as sources of law.[205] The inherently public, justificatory aspect of common law judicial decision making both predetermines the form a legal judgment must take and creates the community or communities that will evaluate and validate the judgment's legal status.[206] By referring to the forms of legal argument and the sources of legal authority, the judge both acknowledges his membership in the legal community and offers his judgment as a contribution to that community. The judge decides as an individual whose judgment must be formulated and expressed within the common law tradition of legal process, legal argument, and legal sources. The judgment cannot depend entirely on the judge's values or experiences, but it also cannot be entirely disconnected from them. A judge's failure to articulate his judgment in accordance with the forms of argument and legal sources of the common law tradition will undermine or extinguish his judgment's legal validity and status as a legal source.

The long-standing tendency to conceptualize law and judging in dichotomous subjective-objective terms has led to some overheated, but undercooked, depictions of judging:

> Judges are said not to have discretion; they do not decide their cases; rather it is the law or the Constitution speaking through them that determines the outcome. Judges, in short, are the mouthpieces of the law. To deny the falsity of the foregoing, we adopt an ostrich posture . . . We do so because we have given judges the authority to play God with regard to the life, liberty, and property of those who appear before them. . . . Such autotheistic power ought not to be vested in mere mortals. . . . Over the last century, dominant legal models include mechanical jurisprudence, which posited that legal questions had a single correct answer that judges were to discover. The most apparent legacy of this model is the assertion that judges in deciding their cases 'find' the law, as though it were a bedbug in a mattress. . . . Currently, the vogue is 'post-positivism,' for whose adherents the only required influence of the law is a subjective influence that resides within the judge's own mind.[207]

It seems from this quotation that even the dichotomy of "objective law vs. subjective preferences" can be inverted so that the law itself need only be a subjective influence on what judges tell themselves they are doing. This tendency has led us to a situation in which scholars argue over the best conception of judging in terms of the "legal model" (according to which a "judge aims to interpret the law accurately, without concern for the desirability of the policies that result"[208]), the "attitudinal model" (according to which "judges act directly on their policy preferences without calculating the consequences of their choices"[209]), or the "strategic model" (according to which "judges choose among alternative courses of action, [and] they think ahead to the prospective consequences and choose the course that does most to advance their goals in the long term"[210]). These scholars usually assume that a judge's perspectives and values will remain static throughout his time on the bench.[211]

We need a conception of judging that allows for the influence of value judgments on legal judgments and that considers the influence of legal rules on judicial discretion, one that apprehends the dynamics of individual responses to facts and law within a process that constructs the meaning of the standards according to which those facts and rules are understood. We also need to accept the possibility that this process of judging may not be reducible to a single model of judicial behavior. I discuss this alternative conception of judging in more detail in the next chapter.

3 Subjectivity and Intersubjectivity

> Not till Kant's *Critique of Judgment* did this faculty [of judgment] become a major topic of a major thinker.[1]
> —Hannah Arendt

This chapter considers some connections between Kant's theory of aesthetic judgment and the common law tradition of legal judgment. Specifically, I examine Kant's theory of synthetic a priori judgments in the realm of aesthetics and indicate their significance when applied to common law adjudication.[2] This chapter is not meant to demonstrate, or even to suggest, that Kant's work translates fully as a framework for or a commentary on the common law. This is why, among other reasons, I do not in this chapter discuss Kant's writings on law, government, or justice. Where common law judicial decision making is concerned, these aspects of Kant's work are less germane for my purposes than his discussion of aesthetic judgment. In addition, for similar reasons, I limit myself solely to Kant's analysis of aesthetic judgment, without considering his comments on the sublime or on teleological judgment.[3] I argue that there are enlightening parallels between Kant's and the common law's approaches to the formulation and communication of reflective judgments. I hope to explain the fundamentals of Kant's aesthetic theory in a way that is faithful to its subtlety and salience while ensuring that this discussion will be both accessible to readers who may not have any formal background in analytic philosophy and engaging for readers who do.

It might seem unlikely that a book published toward the end of the eighteenth century by a Prussian philosopher who never traveled more than one hundred miles from the city of his birth would have much to offer in explaining a legal tradition that began in England centuries before he was born.[4] Nonetheless, I am not the first person to think that revealing correlations exist between Kant's theory of the process of aesthetic judgment and the common law process of judicial decision making:

> If Kant had been an Englishman he might have noticed that the same sort of reflective judgment [operative in aesthetics] seems to work in the common-law tradition . . . a sense of justice develops through case precedents much as a taste for beauty develops through the appreciation of exemplary models of artistic excellence.[5]

This observation aside, however, very little has been written relating Kantian aesthetic judgment directly to common law legal judgment.[6] The value of pursuing the connections between Kant and the common law is in thinking more carefully about the parallels in the faculty of taste and the sense of justice. As I will argue here, the faculty of taste[7] combines feeling and imagination with reason and reflection to arrive at an aesthetic judgment that is communicated to and evaluated by a larger community. Similarly, a sense of justice combines an immediate and individual response with doctrinal sources and processes of reasoning to produce a legal judgment that is communicated to and validated by a larger community. Moreover, both types of judgment cannot depend entirely on nor be divorced entirely from a subjective response, and neither type of judgment is directed toward objective truth. Both the individual and interpersonal aspects of aesthetic and legal judgment must be recognized as vital to the validity of both types of judgment. It is a mistake to deny or denigrate the subjective aspects of this process. It is also a mistake to assume that the interpersonal validity of a judgment depends on an impersonal stance or distance of the judge.[8] Considering the correspondence between aesthetic and legal judgments helps us to understand more sensitively and more accurately the dynamics of the decision-making process and the nature of the judgments reached.[9]

This chapter is an extended study of Kantian aesthetic theory as it applies to the dynamics of judicial reasoning and legal judgment in the common law tradition. I will describe these aspects of Kant's theory and then explain how they might be employed in relation to the common law and judicial decision making. The chapter is divided into subsections—judgment, communication, community, and disinterestedness—that correspond to elements of Kantian aesthetic theory applied to specific aspects of the common law.[10] Like Kantian aesthetic judgments, common law judgments cannot be reduced to moral intuitions or abstract deductions.[11] Instead, as the comparison to Kantian aesthetic theory helps us to see, common law judgments combine a personal response with preexisting parameters of legal sources and processes that establish the framework of possible substantive outcomes and their formal expression.

Judgment

To look for connections between Kant's writings and the common law, the third *Critique* seems a sensible place to start. After all, it was in this work that Kant sought to explain "the power or faculty of judging,"[12] an apt description of this book's motivating concern, as well.

For purposes of Kant's theory and this book's overarching theme, the most important single facet of synthetic a priori aesthetic judgment is the idea "that the aesthetic quality ascribed to the object is purely and inescapably subjective; yet, despite all this, he [Kant] teaches that the aesthetic judgment of taste 'lays claim . . . to be valid for everyone.'"[13] The central idea here is that according to Kant, one's reaction to a work of art combines pleasure and judgment in a process that is creative and reflective. Crucially, though, one should not assume that the feeling of pleasure at the apprehension of the object occurs first, and then, if the object truly deserves to be adjudged beautiful, one formulates a considered opinion that the object is in fact beautiful.[14] In Kant's view, the pleasure at the apprehension of a beautiful object follows the formulation of the judgment.[15] This serves to ensure that the considered judgment of beauty is not merely a statement of personal preference. I will return to this point later in the discussion of disinterestedness.

So while the pleasure at apprehending a beautiful object cannot be purely personal, the formulation of a judgment that the object is beautiful is, in part, necessarily subjective. One has that feeling for oneself and by oneself. The reflective, considered judgment is also intersubjective. One does not simply say that the object is beautiful "to me" as an individual; instead, one makes a judgment that all other individuals who evaluate the object aesthetically would reach the same conclusion.[16] This conjoined personal and interpersonal evaluation of the object is the crux of Kant's theory of synthetic a priori judgment. A Kantian aesthetic judgment begins with a purely subjective response, but it cannot end there. The subjective response must be coupled with a considered judgment that the claim of beauty may reasonably be imputed to all other judges of the object.[17]

Subjectivity

To understand Kant's aesthetic theory more completely, we need to define subjectivity, intersubjectivity, and synthetic a priori judgment, for purposes of Kant's theory and its application to the common law. In Kantian aesthetics, the subjective element in aesthetic judgment requires singularity and autonomy.[18] Singularity means that aesthetic judgment begins with an individual's felt response to an artistic object.[19] At the same time, though, individual responses are not judgments and the ability to feel is not identical to the capacity to judge.[20] If our aesthetic judgments were nothing more than our internal feelings (which might or might not be articulable), then they could not accurately be described as judgments. Rather, our individual responses must also be reflected upon in the articulation of a judgment that may be communicated to others and with which we may claim that others should agree.

The function of singularity in Kantian aesthetic theory is found in two features central to the common law judicial process. First, common law judges are ultimately expected to arrive at their decisions by themselves, as individuals. Probably the most evident demonstration of this expectation in the common law tradition is the production of signed opinions.[21] The judge may author the opinion himself or he may join an opinion written by another member of the panel, but in the common law tradition judges sign their names to the opinion they endorse.[22] This individualized expression of each judge's opinion serves to reinforce systemic commitments to transparency and accountability and to the notion that attempting to do "justice in the individual case"[23] demands that judges make that effort as individuals. In addition, the tradition of producing and publishing dissenting opinions is perhaps the most telling indication of the common law's expectation that judges reach and render their judgments for themselves, even when they speak for themselves alone.[24]

Second, and related to the previous point, the autonomy of subjective judgment in Kantian aesthetics means that each individual reacts and decides for herself, as a self-legislating agent, in adjudging an artistic object. No one else decides for her and no one else can tell her how she should feel about or react to a work of art. Analogized to the common law, each judge's subjective autonomy is expressed in the structural and constitutional mandate of judicial independence. I return to this point at length in chapter 5, but for now the point is that, individually and institutionally, the common law preserves for judges the freedom[25] to reach legal determinations by their own lights and in the absence of external pressures or precommitments. In this regard, judicial independence is described as decisional and institutional.[26] In accordance with decisional independence, judges are empowered and expected to reach their own decisions, and the capacity to decide freely for themselves what the law means is the distinguishing and definitive characteristic of their institution and the signature value of that institution for the larger governmental system in which it operates. Like Kantian aesthetic theory, the common law does not attempt to deny that an integral part of judging involves a personal response.[27] And like Kantian aesthetic theory, individuated responses are recognized as an essential and desirable component of the process of formulating and expressing a considered judgment about the law.[28]

Most discussions of judicial independence in the Anglo-American legal tradition tend to focus principally on institutional independence. Institutional independence protects judges from being penalized by others for the legal judgments they reach, and it protects the judicial process of reasoning and decision making from being interfered with by other branches.[29] As I will explain later, an interesting and troubling element of certain legislative attempts to constrain judicial reasoning and to cabin decisional resources is that they seek to limit the courts' institutional independence by limiting the judges' decisional independence.[30]

The importance of judicial independence not just externally (i.e., in relation to other branches of government) but internally (i.e., in relation to the judges who constitute the judicial institution) is less widely considered. Employing Kant's aesthetic theory in this regard helps us see that the independence of the judiciary depends upon the independence of individual judges and the preservation of their individuality within their institutional role.[31]

The importance of the individual judge's perspective within his institutional role as a judge helps to differentiate the judiciary from the legislature. Jeremy Waldron argues that "Kant does not have a robust, participatory image of politics; the supersession of individual judgments of right by the centralized deliverances of a civil legislator, in his scheme of things, might involve a decline in genuine 'omnilateralism.' He does not claim for positive law that it actually takes account of everyone's circumstances or everyone's point of view. The virtue of positive law resides in its univocality, its power, its being put forward in the name of the whole community."[32] There are several problems with Waldron's reading of Kant here, but I will focus on only one. A central value of looking to the *Critique of Judgment* for Kant's account of judging, and for relating his account to the common law, is that it helps us see more fully the differences between judges and legislators in individual responsibility and institutional function. Leaving aside Waldron's assertion about Kant's not having a participatory image of politics (which Arendt's reading of the third *Critique* leaves seriously in doubt), his claim that a centralized legislature's legal pronouncements demonstrate (in Kant's view) the "virtue of positive law" due to its univocal pronouncement on behalf of the community can be, at best, only partially accurate. Judicial decisions and legislative provisions differ in any number of ways, including the observation that judges must justify their judgments with respect to legal sources and processes, while legislators need not do so. Moreover, and more directly responsive to Waldron's point, the virtue of legislated positive law may be its univocality and practical resolution of contentious political and moral questions, but the virtue of positive law made via an adjudicative process is precisely that it requires judges to consider arguments from multiple points of view, including their own, before communicating their understanding of the law's meaning to the community. Individual judgments are not superseded by generalized deliverances to realize their value as legal pronouncements; individual judgments *are* the individual judge's and the judicial institution's contribution to the community's positive law.[33]

The ability to decide as an individual is, in fact, a central component of the authentic meaning of judicial independence in the common law tradition.[34] Kant helps us to see that judges cannot make decisions independently unless they make their decisions individually. But making decisions individually does not thereby afford judges of art or law license to make their decisions idiosyncratically.[35] A judge's subjective response is a necessary component of his judgment, but a judge can produce a judgment qua judgment only insofar as it is communicated to a larger community in which that judge functions. That communication requires the judge to articulate his judgment in accordance with the forms, sources, arguments, and processes of the relevant community.[36]

Intersubjectivity

Turning from subjectivity to intersubjectivity, Kant's interest is to demonstrate that an aesthetic judgment differs from an aesthetic response to the extent that the judgment expresses "the transition from a statement of private liking to one claiming universal validity."[37] The transition from a purely subjective aesthetic response to an intersubjective aesthetic judgment is captured by the linguistic and conceptual transition from saying that an artistic object "*seems* beautiful to me" to the claim that the object "*is* beautiful."[38] The shift from response to judgment, then, is captured by the shift in language and meaning from statements by and for me to statements by me and for everyone who has the capacity to judge.[39] It is the shift from a statement about me ("this object is beautiful to me") to a statement about the object ("this is a beautiful object"). However, and this is where the confusion sometimes arises, such a statement about the object itself is presumed valid for "the whole sphere of judging subjects."[40]

Kant does not claim that the transition from subjective response to intersubjective judgment somehow transmogrifies the object itself. Aesthetic judgments do not alter the object or recognize a latent quality of the object. Rather, the judgment is a claim made by an individual and imputed to all other individuals with the capacity to judge. Kant describes this distinction as the difference between judgments of "objective universal validity" (objectivity) and judgments of "subjective universal validity" (intersubjectivity).[41] The former type of judgment "is valid for everything which is contained under a given concept" while the latter type of judgment "does not rest on any concept . . . because judgements of that kind have no bearing upon the Object."[42] In other words, aesthetic judgments help us to appreciate further the distinction between objectivity and intersubjectivity, which was discussed in the previous chapter. On this account, and oversimplifying for the sake of clarity and emphasis, an objective judgment makes a claim about an object (which need not be a physical object) while an intersubjective judgment makes a claim about other subjects (as potential judges of an object).[43]

The distinction between objectivity and intersubjectivity is helpful in thinking about the province of aesthetic and legal judgment because, like aesthetic judgments, legal judgments are not evaluated for truth in relation to an externally existing natural reality. Laws are not natural kind objects. But legal judgments, like aesthetic judgments, are evaluated as valid and persuasive according to a shared human capacity to make considered assessments in accordance with recognized forms of articulation and standards of reason.[44] Judgments about law or art are not best evaluated in terms of their objectivity. As Stephen Perry and others have explained, thinking about law in terms of objectivity amounts to a characterization of law that is inaccurate and seriously misleading:

> The claim would be that law is equivalent to a natural kind, such as water or gold, and all instantiations of that kind exhibit certain characteristics; that is, they necessarily have those characteristics. . . . [B]ut that is not an

easy view to defend. It requires us to assume that law has an essence, presumably determined by some natural function that must be served by all true legal systems. Yet the idea of a natural essence, which is problematic at the best of times, seems especially ill-suited as a characterization of a humanly-created institution—more accurately, a highly diverse set of independently-created institutions—such as law.[45]

In terms of strong objectivity,[46] the opposite of truth is falsity. In terms of intersubjectivity, however, the opposite of validity is arbitrariness.[47] In terms of "intersubjective validity,"[48] a legal or aesthetic judgment may be "valid but erroneous"[49] but a judgment cannot be both valid and arbitrary, even if the result is perceived to be otherwise "correct."[50]

In distinguishing between objectivity and intersubjectivity, Kantian aesthetic theory again offers a useful means of approaching the theory and practice of common law judging. For Kant's theory and for my argument, intersubjectivity and intersubjective validity must be differentiated from objectivity and objective truth.[51] The important point here is that the contrast between intersubjectivity and objectivity ultimately relates to the distinction between the objects themselves and the individuals who evaluate them:

> A logically universal judgment connects a predicate-concept to a subject-concept in such a way that the former is valid of any object falling in the extension of the latter; the extension of a subjectively universal judgment, by contrast, is not a class of objects, but the class of possible human judges. 'Aesthetic universality' thus does not connect a predicate with the concept of an object, 'considered in its whole logical sphere,' but rather 'extends [the predicate of beauty] over the whole sphere of the *judging* [subjects].'[52]

In other words, Kant's theory of aesthetic judgment is not meant to demonstrate that beauty is a quality that inheres in objects themselves, independently of our judgments of them.[53] According to Kant, the quality of beauty as it relates to an artistic object is the product of an individual assessment of that object that is then extrapolated and attributed to all future appraisers of that object. Of course, Kant did not mean to deny that people may disagree about aesthetic judgments, but the judgment that an object is beautiful is made by me and claimed for you. If it turns out that you disagree with my judgment, it means one of us is mistaken in our judgment, but not about any quality intrinsic to the object itself about which one of us is right and the other is wrong.[54] Put differently, beauty is no more a quality of a painting than pain is a quality of a knife; beauty is the feeling that the painting engenders in us and the judgment that we make about that work of art. We communicate our judgment to other subjects with the demand that they share our response and our judgment about the painting.

There is a further point here with respect to the connection between artistic and legal judgment. Kant frequently writes as though judgments of taste assess the quality of beauty.[55] Similarly, we often assume judgments of law concern the quality of justice. But it is important to remember that not all artists attempt to convey beauty through their art. A work of art may succeed as a work of art precisely insofar as it forces us to confront something we do not wish to see: something aversive or unpleasant or, in a word, ugly. So a judgment that an artistic object succeeds as a work of art may not always be an assessment of beauty.[56] Likewise, common law judges may for many reasons be unable to achieve the most just result in their judgments, and that outcome will not necessarily be a legitimate basis for criticizing those judgments. Indeed, in certain circumstances, a judicial decision may succeed as a legal judgment because it forces us to confront the law's injustice.[57] So the evaluation of a legal judgment may not always be an assessment of its substantive justice. Nevertheless, it is fair to say, as Kant does, that in general the goal of art is the expression of beauty. And it is fair to say, as the common law does, that in general the goal of law is the pursuit of justice.[58] More simply put, judgments of taste are directed toward beauty, and judgments of law are directed toward justice.[59] This directive and interactive quality of aesthetic and legal judgments is an added felicity of thinking of judgments of art and law in terms of their intersubjective validity as judgments (whose meaning and force are not fixed by the individual judge), rather than in terms of their objective truth or correctness as conclusions.

For Kant, intersubjective validity is "the rational expectation of agreement among different subjects."[60] For the common law, a judge does not search in his decisions for an abstract notion of justice or truth that exists naturally or objectively, but he does make his best effort to express his best judgment of what the law requires in the context of a given case. Moreover, as I discuss more fully in the next two sections, the judge offers his judgment for the consideration of future judges and claims that future judges should and will agree with his determination of what the law requires in cases of this kind.[61] In doing so, a judge is obliged to communicate his reasons for arriving at his judgment to other subjects as potential judges of that case or similar cases in the future. The process of judging in Kantian aesthetics and in the common law tradition requires judges to provide the reasons for their decisions to aid others in their consideration of that judgment and in justifying the outcome through a claim to the assent of other future judges.[62] We demand the assent of others to a judgment we proffer as correct, not because our judgment must necessarily be true; we demand the assent of others because they share our capacity to feel, think, and judge. If our judgment is correct, we believe that others will and should arrive at the same judgment we did. Like legal judgments, however, the defense of an aesthetic judgment "cannot be the presentation of a fact to verify a truth claim, nor like a correct logical argument whose denial is merely self-contradictory. . . . [B]y their very nature, judgements of taste are bound to be persuasive."[63]

The discursive and heuristic process of common law judging is similar to the Kantian process of aesthetic judging in that they share an integration of individual response contained within a reasoned and communicated judgment, together with an expectation that others will agree with the judgment when they consider the matter for themselves. In addition, the goal for the common law and for Kantian aesthetics is not judgments that are true but rather judgments that are shared. In distinguishing intersubjectivity from objectivity, Kant stressed the role of the self and the community in the formulation and instantiation of a judgment. Correspondingly, the common law process of adjudication does not seek something like objective truth but rather a public justification achieved over time through sustained efforts by judges to communicate their best understanding of what the law means.[64]

Similar mistakes are made about both Kantian aesthetic theory and the common law in this regard. People sometimes mistake the goal of Kantian aesthetic theory as "possible true judgements."[65] Making truth the goal of aesthetic judgment undermines the Kantian analytic project. Truth demands a means of assessment to which aesthetic judgment is not suited. And if truth is conceived as the goal of aesthetics, the realized result of actual aesthetic judgments will seem partial and inadequate. Likewise, as I discussed in the previous chapter, people often view the goal of law as objectivity. If a purely neutral, objective rule or a singular legal result is perceived as the goal of law, the realization of its unattainability may lead to cynicism about the law and its judges.[66] Kant's view of aesthetic judgment helps us to see something important about the common law tradition of legal judgment: both types of judgment seek a kind of validity that depends not on empirical correlation with external reality but instead on the intersubjective nature of considered judgments, which depend in turn on communication and evaluation. The legitimate claim to the agreement of the community determines the validity of the individual judgment.

By seeking intersubjective validity rather than objective truth, aesthetic and legal judgments combine individual subjective responses with reasoned deliberative assessments that are ultimately tested by their persuasiveness in capturing a shared communal response.[67] Once the goal of truth or objectivity is set aside, the value of validity and intersubjectivity becomes more apparent. Errors and disagreements no longer appear to challenge the usefulness of the enterprise; instead, they are recognized as a necessary, inevitable, and worthwhile part of the process.[68] Indeed, the communication of the judgment to the community and the reception or rejection of the judgment by the community are necessary for Kant and for the common law in determining its ongoing validity.[69]

Synthetic A Priori Judgment

Now that we have considered the interplay between subjectivity and intersubjectivity in Kantian aesthetics, we are ready to approach his theory of synthetic a priori judgment. Here is a presentation of the point in full:

> On Kant's view, the justification of a judgment of taste . . . requires a deduction of a synthetic *a priori* judgment because in calling an object beautiful, we each express our own pleasure in it, yet go beyond the evidence furnished by that feeling to impute it to the rest of mankind, as the potential audience for that object. We presume that our feelings . . . can be the subject of publicly valid discourse, and that . . . [we are] entitled to respond to a beautiful object with a 'universal voice . . . and lay claim to the agreement of everyone.' But the universal validity of our response to a beautiful object can neither be deduced from any concept of the object nor grounded on any information about the actual feelings of others, Kant believes, and so it can be based only on an *a priori* assumption of similarity between our own responses and those of others.[70]

Guyer describes several details of Kant's aesthetic theory that can usefully be applied to the common law. In addition to those I have already discussed, I want now to highlight the expectation that there is a "similarity between our own responses and those of others." I will return to the importance of "publicly valid discourse" in the discussion of "community" a bit later.[71]

Where similarity of our response with those of others is concerned, there is a notable congruence between Kant's notion of an a priori assumption and the framework of legal reasoning that structures and informs any common law judge's judgment about the law.[72] When a judge reaches a decision, and particularly when she writes that decision into a legal judgment, the form and nature of the judgment are, in an important sense, established prior to her writing of it in a specific case.[73] The common law makes an assumption that the judge's response in the form of a judgment will be recognizably similar to the responses of other judges. More specifically, when a judge articulates the reasons for her decision in a written judgment, she also proffers that judgment as her best evaluation of what the law means and how it applies to the case she has decided.[74] Moreover, the common law doctrine of precedent means that other judges are always obligated to consider her prior judgment and are frequently obligated to follow it.[75]

Just as in Kantian aesthetic theory, the common law judge's decision possesses a subjective and an intersubjective quality. The judge decides for herself and yet she also decides for future judges, in the sense that she claims her judgment is correct and expects other judges will follow it in the future without depriving them of their own capacity and opportunity for independent assessment. In addition, in the same way that Kantian aesthetic judgments are not claimed to be objectively true but instead are claimed to be intersubjectively valid, common law legal judgments are not claimed to describe a natural reality or a logical necessity. They are claimed as a judge's authoritative statement of the law's meaning and normative force.[76] It is more accurate here to characterize the judgment as the judge's best effort to articulate the content of the law, particularly because in the common law tradition the judgment is itself a source of law that ultimately depends for its continuing validity on its ability to persuade future judges to incorporate it into their judgments.[77] Here we see the importance of communication in aesthetic judgment for Kant and in legal judgment for the common law.

Communication

For Kant and the common law, a judgment is not a judgment until it is communicated. The act of reaching a decision is importantly subjective, and the act of rendering a judgment is inherently communicative. An entirely subjective feeling cannot be a judgment.[78] To begin with a practical point, a judgment cannot be claimed as universal or intersubjective until it has been communicated to other judging subjects or unless it is at least communicable in this fashion.[79] In fact, the judgment's communicability is necessary for its normativity, because the claim to intersubjective validity turns on the assertion that other subjects *should* agree with one's judgment, but not necessarily that they will.[80] The claim being communicated is that the subject's judgment should be shared by others.[81]

The transformative step from subjective responses to intersubjective judgments of taste lies in the social process of communicating the subjective aesthetic experience to others. The societal components of aesthetic judgment possess an analogous provenance in the common law tradition,[82] where judicial decisions are announced and often published in written opinions for the parties, the profession, and the public.

It is usually insufficient for common law judges simply to make a decision. They must justify their decisions. Justification is itself an important correlative between Kantian aesthetic judgment and common law legal judgment. The requirement of public articulation as a judicial obligation serves to justify results in particular cases and to provide a basis for later decision making.[83] Purely internal and individual experiences of aesthetic pleasure are distinguished normatively from reflective judgments of taste because of the imputation of universal agreement or acceptance through a communicative process. Similarly, idiosyncratic and unregulated judicial responses are distinguished normatively from considered decisions rooted in legal doctrine and argumentation—from *judgments*—by the provision of a judge's written decision as a statement of the deciding judge's understanding of the law and expectation that others will choose to follow that judgment in the future.

The normative force of this expectation is easy to misconstrue. A deciding judge may not necessarily believe—for instance, if she is writing a dissenting opinion—that other judges will in fact decide as she does. She must, however, believe that they *ought* to decide as she has, because she believes in good faith that her judgment is correct.[84] In fact, the *ought* in the previous sentence can be understood in two ways. First, a judge may say that other judges ought to decide as she has because hers is the best conception of what the law requires. Other judges ought to decide similarly because her judgment is legally correct. Second, assuming the correctness of her judgment, a judge might also say that other judges ought to decide as she has because they are judges. As judges, they have a moral and legal obligation to decide in a certain way and in accordance with a particular tradition.[85] Other judges ought to decide similarly because they have a duty to say what the law is, to the best of their ability and according to their best understanding.[86]

Both of these connotations of the normativity of judgment—the correctness of the judgment and the nature of the judicial role—apply to and connect the aesthetic and the common law conceptions of judging. Both connotations turn on the dynamics of communication:

> Kant's association of universal validity, publicity, and a reciprocity by which a person's contribution to the whole is the basis for defining his role and position in it, may be understood as a matter of having a certain viewpoint. Publicity, universal validity, and the proposed reciprocity require subjects to make judgements from a viewpoint which encompasses those of other subjects. . . . [I]n this context 'publicity' may be seen as the exemplification of the a priori moral demand in our actual political, legal, cultural, and aesthetic lives. The 'public' then denotes a relation between imperfectly rational subjects, who are capable of entering into discussion, of making decisions, and of having feelings. . . . In legal, civil, and international relations, 'all actions affecting the rights of other human beings are wrong if their maxim is not consistent with being made public'. The 'form of publicity' is what remains if we 'abstract from all the material of public law. . . .' Similarly, by comparing judgements of taste with a public sense Kant brings our subjective lives into the domain of duty and right. . . . [B]y showing the universal validity of aesthetic judgements and their comparison with a public sense Kant shows them capable of value.[87]

Several aspects of this quotation relate to my argument. The first sentence refers to universal validity, publicity, and reciprocity. I discussed universal validity previously and I will discuss publicity in the next section. For now, I want to concentrate on the reciprocity between a judge's own viewpoint as a contribution to the whole and as a basis for defining his role. In relation to the subjective and the intersubjective, the judge's own viewpoint is essential. And that viewpoint informs both the judge's subjective response to the artistic object or the legal dispute as well as the judge's considered judgment about that object or that dispute. In other words, the judge is always aware that she is engaged in the process of judging.[88] This means, first, that the subjective response is that of a member of a community of judges (as I discuss further in the next section). Her membership in this community helps to establish the viewpoint from which she initially approaches the object or dispute and through which her subjective response takes shape. Second, she is expected (as she is also aware) to articulate her judgment in a form that will be recognized as a judgment by other subjects.

Kant helps us to see that judges cannot and should not attempt to suspend their humanity when judging. To judge as a human being, the judgment must incorporate a subjective response within a considered judgment that is communicated to others. Whatever may generally be the case with man, no judge is an island.[89] A judgment depends, in its subjective and intersubjective aspects, on the mutuality of these components in the process of judging. As Kant explains in the third *Critique*, judging combines imagination and understanding,[90] feeling and reason,[91] creativity and reflection,[92] within a process that both defines a community of judging subjects and depends upon that community's evaluation for the validation of the judgments reached by its members. The process of constituting a community through the shared experience of communication requires us as judging subjects to recognize our role in a reciprocal process of creating and evaluating judgments, sometimes speaking and sometimes listening, and this is the process that ultimately results in the apprehended meaning of a judgment.[93] Both dynamics of the communication—the articulation and the evaluation, the speaking and the hearing—are always operative, all the time.

Community

For Kant and the common law, communication requires a community.[94] In this critical aspect, a judgment is intersubjective, and its intersubjectivity is necessary to its expression as a judgment rather than just as a subjective response, because the response must be communicated in and to a community in a form that allows for and isintended to engender agreement and assent.[95] The judgment is not completely realized until it is communicated, because the judgment depends, in an important sense, upon its evaluation and reception as a valid judgment by the community.

The community's evaluation of a judgment involves more than simple consensus, however, no matter how strong the consensus may be or how long it has lasted. The fact that a legal judgment has long been regarded as correct is, of course, an important element of its authority as a source of law. But the common law processes of articulation and evaluation of legal judgments also require their constant re-evaluation in light of evolving social and institutional factors to which the law must adapt. Established precedents are sometimes overruled and dissenting judgments sometimes become accepted as settled doctrine.[96] No matter how broadly or narrowly we construe the community to which a judgment is communicated, the intrinsic merit of a judgment must be continually be considered and reconsidered by the community through the intersubjective dynamic of articulation, evaluation, and validation.[97] Judgments continue to speak, and communities continue to evaluate them, long after they are written.

The role of the community in the formulation and reception of legal and artistic judgments touches on requirements of form,[98] reason-giving,[99] justification,[100] persuasion,[101] and the inherently public nature of communication and intersubjectivity. In this section, I focus principally on the theme of public discourse, with the understanding that the closely related concepts of form, reason giving, justification, and persuasion, which I have already addressed, are implicitly operative throughout this discussion.

Kant and the common law require that a judge communicate her considered decision as a member of a larger community,[102] and each of these aspects of the judgment is important: the communicator, the communication, and the community. The subjective and the intersubjective, the process and the product,[103] contribute to the validity and authority of the judgment. In moving from subjective experience to intersubjective judgment, the judgment is communicated not merely as an individual belief but as the correct decision, not just in this case but in all similar cases, not just for this judge but for all judges who reflect on the matter.[104] In its expansive reach, we see the normative force of the intersubjective judgment and can appreciate the necessity of intersubjectivity for the judgment to be a synthetic a priori judgment.

If a judgment of taste is correct, any judge who reviews that work of art should come to the same decision.[105] In this way, a judgment is public in the sense that it is offered as a justification for a conclusion and as a basis for the judgments of others in the future. Like the common law, Kant uses the word "judgment" at times to refer to both the process and the product of judging, but this in no way diminishes the salience of the distinction. Differentiating the process of judgment from the production of a judgment helps us to appreciate the distinction between the process of judging at common law and the law that is made as its product. In law and art, the judge communicates his judgment "as a member of a community"[106] and as a contribution to that community:

> If Kant can characterize . . . aesthetic activity as engagement in a dialogue with other subjects, . . . [this] represents a shift in emphasis from a concern with consciousness to one with community. . . . The judgement that an object is beautiful, in which a subject seeks to appreciate an object, involves an individual's relation to others in a community and a dialogue aimed at interpreting and understanding the work.[107]

With respect to the common law, the community that is the principal audience of a judicial decision as a legal judgment is the legal community. Narrowly speaking, this might mean attorneys only and broadly speaking this might include all those professionally engaged in researching, analyzing, and/or practicing law. Judicial decisions are, however, also directed toward a larger political community, which might mean the citizens of a polity, and broadly speaking this might include all those subject to the law of a jurisdiction.[108]

Earlier, in considering Kantian aesthetic judgment as a form of synthetic a priori judgment, I touched on Kant's understanding of aesthetic judgment as a form of publicly valid discourse.[109] Here we return to the concept of publicity to discuss it more completely, particularly as it relates to the function of community in Kantian aesthetics and common law judging.[110] In Kant's conception, the public nature of judgment is immanent in its intersubjectivity. A judgment of taste is a form of participation in a public dialogue with and within the community of judging subjects.[111]

In an important sense, Kant's view of the intersubjective validity of aesthetic judgment is a form of public participation in a process of persuasion through shared experience:

> At most we may change other subjects to our point of view by . . . what may be called 'aesthetic argument by comparison and example'. It is successful when another subject is enabled to gain the experience of beauty for himself. . . . Persuasion respects the autonomy of an individual and treats his capacity for reason and appreciation as an end. Thus, our experience of fine art is not only public and persuasive but is also intersubjective and promotes our humanity through unity with other subjects.[112]

The reflexive process of aesthetic judgment means that these judgments depend for their existence on their audience. In an immediate and direct way, the intersubjectivity of the judgment depends on the imputed assent of the whole sphere of judging subjects. In a less apparent way, the sphere of judging subjects can begin to see itself as a community of judging subjects, in which all potential judges' future opinions are valued because they are necessary to sustain the community and to establish the validity of each prior judge's determinations. Individual judges depend upon and constitute their community.[113]

Aesthetic judgment as a form of publicly valid discourse tracks the process of common law judicial decision making. Ultimately, the validity of a judicial decision depends on its persuasiveness to other judges.[114] The decisions of each judge are valued as that individual's most central contribution to the institutional community, and each judge's decisions ultimately depend upon the community's assessment for their continuing validity. In both of these senses of community construction of valid judgments, the communication of the judgment and the community to which it is communicated are indispensable to the role of the judge and to the product of his deliberations.

Intersubjectivity and community relate to the judging of art and law in another way, too. The community ultimately determines whether a particular judgment satisfies the "criteria for the evaluation of aesthetic response."[115] The criteria imposed by the requirement of intersubjective validity include "a justified demand of assent from others . . . [which requires] an argument sufficient to justify the imputation of specific feelings to others on specific occasions, and this is a very strong constraint."[116] As Paul Guyer points out, judges may not simply demand assent to their judgments. Judges must make a "justified demand of assent," which requires the judge to proffer "an argument sufficient to justify" the claim of assent. On this account, an aesthetic judgment demands of judges the "inclusion of justificatory criteria"[117] even when that judgment incorporates, to some degree, a subjective response.

The criteria that allow the community to evaluate whether an argument is sufficient to justify a judge's claim to the assent of other judges connect aesthetic judgment to legal judgment in the context of a process of public discourse. I have in mind here the role that legal sources and argumentation play in judicial reasoning. Recognized sources of law and processes of legal argument presuppose and impose criteria on a common law judge's evaluation of existing law and on the formulation and articulation of her judgment.[118] In turn, these justificatory criteria provide the basis for the community's assessment of the proffered judgment in relation to the judge's implicit demand that the community endorse the judgment as correct.[119] The formulation and reception of a judgment reflect the reciprocal dynamic of an individual judge's contribution to a community's evolving understanding of the law and the community's contribution to or construction of the meaning of the judgment. Even though the common law expects its judges to respond as individuals to the cases they decide, and even though those responses are a necessary and integral part of the judicial decision-making process, they can be translated into legal judgments only to the extent that the audience can reasonably regard them as valid.[120] That audience includes, at a bare minimum, the parties to the case. For most common law cases, and all cases in which a written opinion is produced, that audience also includes the professional and academic legal community.[121] For certain cases that touch on important social, policy, or constitutional questions, that audience might include the entire polity.[122]

Thinking of the polity as the audience for judgments about constitutional questions also helps us to consider the common law process of constitutional adjudication. Here, again, the judgment seeks a valid and legally defensible interpretation or construction of constitutional meaning. Fundamental as the text and the history are here, this form of judgment cannot be limited solely to the text and the history. A text alone cannot constitute a community; the community must also constitute the text. In other words, the text cannot be understood apart from the various processes the community uses to interpret it.[123] Each judgment helps to define the meaning of the community, and the community helps to define the meaning of the judgment. In this sense, a constitution is itself a form of legal judgment: it is a statement by and to the community and an expression of the community's image of itself.[124] Each judgment is a further expression of each judge's understanding of the community's relationship to its members and the standards according to which they have agreed to live.[125] Moreover, these communities are not just imagined.[126] Should the judgment require citizens and government to act in certain ways on the basis of the community's constitution, which the judgment helps to construct, then these communities are actualized through the process and result of the judgment.

The notion of a judgment that helps to construct a community's constitution and the judgment as a statement by an individual judge as a member of that community are often mischaracterized. Paul Campos offers an evocatively stated and commonly made mistake about this claim:

> The meaning of a text can change because people disagree about its meaning if and only if we assume that the different beliefs about the text's meaning which constitute this disagreement also constitute that meaning. Indeed, several contemporary constitutional theorists have advocated this account of interpretation. From this 'reader response' perspective, the meaning of the constitutional text is equivalent to some interpretive community's beliefs about the text's meaning. But whether or not a theorist holds this position explicitly is less important than the fact that anyone who subscribes to the view that the meaning of the constitutional text changes must either accept some version of it or be placed in the untenable position of the theorist who holds that the actual height of Mount Everest alters in response to the plurality of beliefs that exist on that particular question.[127]

There are two problems with Campos's criticism here. First, he equates legal validity with objective truth. Laws are not like mountains. The meaning of a constitutional text and the height of Mount Everest cannot be compared in the way Campos suggests for the reasons I explained earlier in this chapter and in the previous one.[128] Second, Campos seems to assume that the contemporary constitutional theorists he criticizes must believe that all proposed interpretations are equally valid or that these theorists cannot engage in normative evaluation of competing interpretations. But again, for reasons I have explained, this familiar criticism is entirely unfounded.[129] Finally, in relation to the last point, the reality of competing interpretive judgments does not and need not devolve into an "anything goes" free-for-all in legal interpretation.[130] The criteria of legal validity place genuine constraints on the legitimate judgments that are available to a judge.[131]

The relationship between the judge as the expositor of a judgment and the community as the collective evaluator of that judgment also helps us to appreciate a correspondence between Kantian aesthetic theory, on the one hand, and the common law and common law constitutionalism, on the other. On Kant's account of aesthetics, there are two instances when we should not place particular importance on judgments: (1) if there is no one to whom the judgment can be communicated, or (2) if there is no especial ability or capacity afforded to the communicator. In the absence of a community to whom a judgment can be communicated, experiences of isolated aesthetic pleasure are possible, but instances of intersubjective aesthetic judgment are not. And if a community lacks judges who possess the capacity to formulate and communicate judgments of taste, then the process of aesthetic judgment as a form of public discourse is impossible. Similarly, the common law tradition places judges in a position of central importance precisely because the common law system emphasizes both the audience to whom judicial decisions are communicated and the authority and unique position of judges as interpreters and expounders of the law. The communication of legal judgments to the parties, the profession, and the public is probably the most enduring contribution judges make as members of the judicial institution and of the legal community and is also the judicial institution's most enduring contribution to government and the polity.

A final point in relation to community also serves as a segue to the discussion of disinterestedness in the next section. Each judge knows that his judgment's validity depends upon its evaluation by the community, and so the judge knows that his judgment's intersubjective validity depends in part upon his ability to claim that his judgment is valid for others and not just for himself alone. In this way, the community frames the context for the judgment's validity and force:

> Kant holds that it is because your aesthetic judgment is not conditioned upon any private interest that you are entitled to claim that others ought to share your judgment. Impure judgments of taste void their claim to universality because they are based on private conditions. . . . I propose that we should reconsider . . . the sort of universality that we should expect from aesthetic judgment. . . . Advocates of aesthetic and cognitive claims appeal to a background of aesthetic and cognitive commitments already shared with those to whom the claims are made. . . . Only having already agreed on many things (implicitly or explicitly) can we demand that others agree with something more. . . . But this means, as we have seen, that the claims of interpretive understanding are only *conditionally* valid (when valid at all): *If* we share this sense of how things are, *then* you may insist that I agree with your judgment of an artist, because that should be my judgment also. . . . [N]ormativity is restricted by the bounds of the community of inquirers to which the claim is addressed. I suggest that we call this limited normativity a 'localized universality'.[132]

This quotation helps us appreciate the connection between community and disinterestedness in Kant's theory of aesthetic judgment. Our aesthetic reactions cannot accurately be claimed as intersubjective judgments if they are based exclusively or excessively on personal interests or biases. Instead, we must understand that we make our judgments, and claim them as intersubjectively valid, only because we make those judgments within a community that has, in a meaningful sense, already precommitted itself to a process and form of judgment. The reach of our aesthetic judgment depends on the range of our defined interpretive community. And to claim that other members of that community should endorse our judgments as valid, we must ensure that our judgments are faithful to its background commitments.

Disinterestedness

Kant tells us that aesthetic judgments must be distinterested.[133] He sometimes seems to indicate that this disinterest should be conceived as "indifference,"[134] which might suggest that we should be disengaged sensorily and intellectually when making judgments of taste. This is not the case. By indifference, Kant means that we should formulate our aesthetic judgments without being motivated by any concern for the "real existence of the object."[135] In other words, we should attempt to make our aesthetic judgments based on our response to the object, rather than any possible interest in the object itself. So, in fact, Kantian "indifference" in this connection is better understood as disinterest.[136] If indifference in Kantian aesthetics were understood as entire and holistic, then aesthetic judgment would be autonomic rather than autonomous. That is to say, we must possess some sort of interest in the object to judge it—our judgments are not supposed to be entirely disengaged—but our reactions and judgments must be free of any external or internal interest in reaching a specific result in the case of a specific object.[137] At the same time, however, this account of disinterest should not lead us to believe that we should attempt to make our aesthetic judgments in some rarified sphere of recondite taste, entirely detached from our human selves. Judging requires volition, and volition requires identity. As with the rest of Kant's aesthetic theory, where disinterest is concerned, the key is the conjunction between the subjective and the intersubjective. We must bring our individual humanity to the task of judging, and we must also view our humanity in connection with others as prospective judges of the artistic object, and of our judgment of that object:

> The normativity of interpretive understanding cannot depend on a purely disinterested evaluation of its products, and so this reading of Kant's theory of aesthetic judgment cannot accommodate the proposed disinterestedness of his pure judgment of taste. One might hold that the aesthetic dimension of human understanding can only be impure, motivated indeed by specific interests, but attempt to preserve Kant's judgment of taste in some noncognitive realm of pure aestheticism. But there is little reason to imagine that such a land of untrammeled aesthetic value actually exists and little reason to wish for it. Few philosophers working in the field of aesthetics today . . . take strict disinterestedness seriously as a requirement of cultivated aesthetic judgment. They would allow that taste is stunted when made merely the lapdog of unreflective prejudice, and they would encourage us to approach new work with an open mind. But they would reject the quite implausible notion that we are somehow to set aside the interests that make us who we are when we enter the hallowed sphere of art.[138]

Put differently, our judgments should be informed by our perspectives without being influenced by our prejudices. But to reach a judgment that can be claimed as valid for others, we must be able to claim that others can and will reach the same judgment. This claim cannot fairly be made for a judgment that reflects a personal bias. Our judgments are, again, subjective and intersubjective. They reflect who we are as judges and help to contribute our individual perspectives through our judgments as members of a community. In fostering a claim of intersubjective validity, disinterestedness allows other members of our community to evaluate a judgment's validity on its own merits, and ultimately to share that judgment.[139]

Applying Kant's account of disinterest in aesthetic judgment to the broader themes of this book, it is helpful to consider the linguistic distinction between disinterestedness and uninterestedness.[140] Simply put, someone is uninterested if she does not care at all about something.[141] Someone is disinterested if she has no personal stake in the outcome, which is the definition of impartiality that I discussed earlier.[142] For Kant, judgments of taste should be disinterested but judges need not be uninterested in art or aesthetics or judging.[143] Indeed, conflating uninterested and disinterested judgments in this manner might seem to render the entire project of aesthetic judgment futile or pointless. After all, why would an uninterested judge bother to undertake the careful and personal response, reflection, and expression necessary to render a meaningful artistic judgment?

The distinction between disinterested judgments and uninterested judgments corresponds to the distinction in this book between impartiality and objectivity and parallels Kant's own use of the term impartiality to describe the absence of interest that gives rise to judgments of taste.[144] Kant's use of impartiality in aesthetic judgment translates directly to impartiality as *the* core value of common law judging. Judicial decisions should be impartial and disinterested in the sense that judges must not have a personal desire to see one party win or lose. But judges need not be objective in the sense that is captured by the term "uninterested."[145] It is not necessary, in other words, that judges have no feelings whatsoever about the cases they decide. They need not and should not be uninterested, so long as they are disinterested.[146]

Disinterestedness and its contrast with uninterestedness help us to see another connection between Kant's aesthetic theory and the theory and practice of common law judging. I mentioned earlier that an individual's assessment of an object's beauty consists of a subjective response together with the reflective and expressive process that results in a full and final judgment.[147] To this point, I have focused principally on the second part of this equation, the communication of the judgment to the community as establishing its intersubjective validity through its claim to agreement. Now I want to highlight some aspects of the subjective response in relation to disinterestedness.[148]

According to Kant, aesthetic judgment begins with a subjective response to an artistic object. But the judge must feel assured that his subjective response can legitimately be claimed on behalf of other judges. Kant believed that disinterest contributed to aesthetic judgment: as long as a judge can honestly claim that his subjective response is not tainted by any improper bias toward the object, the judge may reasonably claim the judgment as intersubjectively valid. Kant did not seek to deny the importance of our subjective response or its relationship to the feelings generated by our response to the artistic object. At the same time, however, if a judge were concerned that his reaction and judgment might be motivated by an improper interest in the object, the judgment could not reasonably be claimed on behalf of others.[149]

In this regard, Kant's aesthetic theory mirrors the role of disinterest in common law judging. In the same way that Kantian aesthetic judgment leaves room for subjective, felt responses, so long as those responses are not biased or unduly invested in the object,[150] the common law allows and expects that the responses of its judges will play a role in the formulation of legal judgments, so long as those responses are not tainted by undue bias or interest in the case. In both Kantian aesthetic judgment and common law legal judgment, the ultimate defect of a judgment tainted by bias is its inability to claim the assent of future judges. The fact that a judge is biased does not necessarily ensure that his judgment was incorrect,[151] but it does ensure the appearance of impropriety. For Kantian aesthetics and common law judging, such an appearance is enough to undermine the validity of the judgment.[152]

Judging Art and Law

For those who see the ideal of judging as objectivity and disengagement, acknowledging the subjective element in judging may be discomfiting. But as I have already explained, the value of a judge's individual responses in the process of adjudication and deliberation is central to the common law tradition. The values and viewpoints of judges are absolutely necessary in the process of judicial reasoning, in the production of judicial decisions, and in the development of the law. From this perspective, the role of taste in Kantian aesthetic judgment parallels the sense of justice in legal judgment. The cultivation of a faculty of taste refines one's capacity to judge works of art. The development of one's sense of justice hones one's capacity to judge the content and application of law. In both aesthetic and legal judgments, a felt response is combined with reflective evaluation that is informed by reason and experience and expressed through a form of interpersonal communication to produce an authentic judgment about art or law.[153] This judgment makes a claim to the assent of other subjects through an appreciation and expression of our shared human faculties. For Kant and the common law, judgments are expressed and defended not in reference to an abstract conception of beauty or justice but in relation to other cases that have already been judged, and on the expectation of others' agreement with the judge's own determination.

The combination of a decision reached individually and independently, which is communicated and thereby claimed as intersubjectively valid for all members of the judge's community, animates both Kantian aesthetic judgment and legal judgment in the common law tradition. Each element of the process of aesthetic and legal judging is illuminated by considering the relationships between the processes of judgment. Subjectivity and intersubjectivity are integral to the process of judging and the value of each must be fully appreciated for the process to be fully understood.

Considering Kantian aesthetic judgment and common law legal judgment together, we find that Kant and the common law do not seek judgments that are objective either in the sense that the judge must disengage or suppress his subjective responses or that the judgment must state or seek the truth. Instead, the Kantian and common law processes of judging require that judges combine their subjective response with a reflective judgment that is claimed as valid by virtue of the form of its reasoning and expression according to the methods and sources of the community in which and to which the judgment is rendered. Provided that the judge can perform the adjudicatory function impartially and independently, without any improper interest or influence tainting the decision-making process, the judge remains free to decide for herself. That is the sort of judgment that is recognized by the community as intersubjectively valid and which best contributes to the perpetual process of understanding art and law.

In this chapter and the previous one, I argued for the conception of judicial decision making that is most authentic to the common law. This conception distinguishes objectivity from impartiality and from intersubjectivity. It recognizes that impartiality and intersubjective validity are necessary to the legitimacy of the process and the product of judicial reasoning and decision making. And it rejects strong objectivity as the means or the goal of common law judging. In the next chapter, I explore this conception in more detail by analyzing legal judgments that help clarify the relationship between subjectivity and intersubjectivity in common law decision making.

4 Making Law

> [W]hether it is desirable that the judges' power and practice of making Law should be concealed from themselves and the public by a form of words, is a matter into which I do not care to enter. The only thing I am concerned with is the fact. Do the judges make Law? I conceive it to be clear that, under the Common Law system, they do make Law.[1]
>
> —John Chipman Gray

Legislating from the Bench

In the common law tradition, judges make law.[2] This may seem a fairly innocuous, if not self-evident, statement, yet somehow it remains controversial.[3] Nevertheless, for purposes of this chapter and this book, I assume, as Gray did, a basic level of agreement that a fundamental part of a common law judge's institutional role is to create and alter legal standards in the course of resolving legal disputes.[4] In this chapter, I focus on the way that law is made in the course of the judicial process and the role of the judge as an individual in that process.[5] To do so, I concentrate on a few cases in which the law-making function of judges as individuals may be observed in practice.

The familiar concerns about judges "legislating from the bench," in all their various forms, are unfounded for one of two reasons. If the concern about "judicial" legislation is meant to express the view that judges do not or should not make law, then it is an argument against the common law as a legal system, not an argument against judges operating within that system.[6] If the concern about judicial "legislation" is meant to express the view that judges do not or should not make law in the same way that legislatures do, then it is tautologically true.[7] It is not only true that judges should not make law in this fashion, as I discussed in chapter 2,[8] judges cannot make law in this fashion. Judges can only establish legal norms in the course of resolving legal disputes in the context of legal cases through the articulation of legal conclusions justified by universalizable expressions of legal doctrine.[9] A judicial decision must be expressed and justified in legal form as a legal source grounded in legal argument. The formal and institutional constraints that govern judges mean that where judicial law making is concerned, "developing the law is a different thing from making it in the legislative sense, and one which is subject to rationally persuasive argument using materials from established law."[10]

Judges and legislators function in entirely different institutional contexts and under entirely different institutional constraints. Legislators are not supposed to be impartial; they are supposed to act on behalf of the constituents who elected them.[11] There are many reasons legislators may vote for legislation that do not necessarily indicate their approval of the substance of the legislation,[12] and many ways legislators are expected to be directly accountable to the electorate. In contrast, when a judge writes or signs a judicial opinion, it is understood to be his approval of the substance of the opinion he signed. And judicial independence assumes that judges must be responsive to the parties in a case and responsible to the public in rendering legal judgments, but judges are not supposed to be accountable to the electorate in the manner of legislators.[13]

More generally speaking, many of the institutional constraints that govern judicial decision making do not apply to legislators or legislation.[14] For example, the constraints of jurisdiction, justiciability, and the judicial obligation to decide cases in legal form by reference to legal sources are significant institutional restrictions on judges.[15] None of these constraints applies to legislators,[16] and they function to ensure that judges cannot and will not decide cases simply on the basis of their own subjective preferences. But this also should not lead us to assume that the subjective element in judicial decision making is illegitimate or undesirable.[17]

Changing Law

The common law judicial process involves resolving legal disputes in accordance with preexisting legal forms and sources, but also through a process that requires judges to reach and express their judgments in a manner that is both subjective and intersubjective. This dynamism derives from the circumstances in which common law judges function as institutional actors and the nature of the common law judicial process. The problem is not that there is a subjective element to judging. The problem is that we *think* this is a problem.

In an effort to analyze more fully the role of subjectivity in the formulation of legal judgments, this chapter involves sustained consideration of some judicial decisions. In seeing these cases as examples of the subjective and intersubjective dynamics of common law adjudication, and in relating the discussion of this chapter to the different forms of objectivity discussed in chapter 2, it is helpful to consider common law judging as a form of nonergodic decision making.[18]

In an ergodic system, there is a discoverable underlying structure to the system that will allow us to develop an analytic or theoretical model that can systematically and consistently explain and predict the operation of the system.[19] In the world of the physical sciences, ergodicity is usually assumed and accepted. For reasons I have explained in connection with legal objectivity and various attempts to model judicial decision making, it is a mistake to view the common law as an ergodic system.[20] The common law is nonergodic because through the course of resolving legal disputes by reference to existing legal sources, judges' efforts "to render their environment intelligible result in continual alterations in that environment and therefore new challenges to understanding that environment."[21] So through the process of making law as they decide cases, judges concurrently attempt to understand their legal world as they find it and, through some of their judgments, develop and change the law that will be understood in the future.

An important point to see here, which the ergodic/nonergodic distinction helpfully underlines, is that there may be ergodic processes that function within a nonergodic system.[22] Connecting this observation to the discussion of the previous chapters, we find the functionally effective and formal elements of the judicial process recur consistently and serve as a mode of normalizing and translating the structure, language, and outcomes of judicial decisions in the common law tradition. Judicial decisions recognizably and predictably exhibit these properties, which allow them to be evaluated by the appropriately constituted community.[23] These serve as ergodic elements of the broader system.

The broader common law system is nonergodic, however, because an intrinsic aspect of that system is its designed capacity to change through the evolution of innovative doctrinal norms initiated and improved through judicial decisions.[24] These innovative decisions through which these norms develop often begin with the subjective response of a judge responding to the case before her and rendering a judgment that then changes the law through the intersubjective process of evaluation and reception.[25] The adaptive capacity[26] of the common law allows the law to respond to changing social and political circumstances through a reasonably and reliably stable form of decision making, grounded in authoritative sources and modes of reasoning, so that case outcomes are recognizably legal, even when the outcome is that the law has changed.[27]

This chapter looks at examples of these cases. I limit myself to examining just three changes of existing law prompted by the responses of judges to entrenched legal rules: (1) the rejection of caveat emptor in favor of a duty on the part of sellers in real estate transactions to disclose latent material defects, (2) the recognition of a civil claim for racial discrimination in public accommodations, and (3) the elimination of the so-called marital exemption from prosecution for rape. In each of these cases, judges were confronted with legal doctrines that came to be understood over time as substantively indefensible. Each of these cases involves a reaction by judges to the unfairness of the law they were asked to apply, and the expression of a new legal norm through a judgment that was then adopted generally by the relevant legal community. The examples can easily be multiplied.[28]

Weintraub v. Krobatsch: The Duty to Disclose

Natalie Weintraub was selling her house and Donald and Estella Krobatsch wished to purchase it. The Krobatsches walked through the home, liked it, and signed a contract on June 30, 1971, to buy it from Mrs. Weintraub for $42,500. In accordance with the contract, the Krobatsches paid a 10 percent deposit to Mrs. Weintraub and indicated that they "had inspected the property and were fully satisfied with its physical condition, that no representations had been made and that no responsibility was assumed by the seller as to the present or future condition of the premises."[29]

On August 25, 1971, in the evening, the Krobatsches entered the house after Mrs. Weintraub had moved out but prior to closing on the sale. They were horrified "to see roaches literally running in all directions, up the walls, drapes, etc."[30] The Krobatsches immediately sought rescission of their contract with Mrs. Weintraub.

Mrs. Weintraub refused to rescind the agreement and sued the Krobatsches for the amount of their deposit ($4,250) as damages for breach of contract. The Krobatsches and Mrs. Weintraub then filed cross-motions for summary judgment.[31] At oral argument, the Krobatsches' attorney argued that the extent of the infestation belied any claim by Mrs. Weintraub that she was unaware of the infestation. The Krobatsches argued that this amounted to a fraudulent concealment or nondisclosure, which justified their rescission of the contract.

For her part, Mrs. Weintraub argued that any obligation she might have had as the seller of the property was obviated by the plain language of the contract signed by the parties. According to that contract, the Krobatsches manifested their acceptance of the property in its then-existing physical condition. Mrs. Weintraub argued that once the contract was executed, the venerable principle of caveat emptor shifted all legal responsibility for the condition of the property onto the Krobatsches.

The trial court denied the Krobatsches' motion and granted Mrs. Weintraub's motion for summary judgment, and the Appellate Division affirmed. In the lower courts' view, it did not matter if Mrs. Weintraub was aware of the roach infestation of the home she sold because the Krobatsches assumed all responsibility for the condition of the home when they signed their contract with Mrs. Weintraub.

The Supreme Court of New Jersey reversed the lower courts' ruling. That court accepted the Krobatsches' argument that they were entitled to a trial on the issue of whether Mrs. Weintraub was aware that her home was infested and fraudulently failed to disclose the infestation to the Krobatsches. In doing so, the court first cited existing New Jersey precedent establishing that "silence may be fraudulent" and may impose an obligation of disclosure on a party to a contract.[32] The court then addressed Mrs. Weintraub's argument that even if she had been aware of the infestation, she had no duty to disclose this condition of the home, or any other, to the Krobatsches because the obligation to discover property defects rested entirely on the purchaser.[33]

In addressing Mrs. Weintraub's argument, which rested on long-established principles of property and contract law, the Supreme Court of New Jersey extensively reviewed existing precedent from New Jersey and several other jurisdictions. One aspect of this analysis is particularly pertinent to my argument. The court considered the Massachusetts Supreme Judicial Court's decision in *Swinton v. Whitinsville Savings Bank*.[34] In *Swinton*, the Massachusetts court held that a seller could not be held responsible for failing to disclose to a buyer that his home was infested with termites.[35] Since the case involved a seller's deliberate silence but no affirmative misrepresentation, the Massachusetts court concluded that the burden rested with the buyer to locate any hidden defects in the property he was planning to purchase. The *Swinton* court based its reasoning upon the familiar distinction between what might be morally right and what was legally required.[36] William Prosser described the *Swinton* ruling as "singularly unappetizing."[37]

In its analysis of *Swinton*, the *Weintraub* court questioned whether it still represented the view of the Massachusetts Supreme Judicial Court and, even more important to my argument, expressly rejected the principle of the *Swinton* decision: "we are far from certain that it [*Swinton*] represents views held by the current members of the Massachusetts court. In any event we are certain that it does not represent *our sense of justice or fair dealing* and it has understandably been rejected in persuasive opinions elsewhere."[38] In rejecting the *Swinton* doctrine, the New Jersey Supreme Court replaced a rigid caveat emptor rule with an affirmative duty to disclose material latent defects. *Weintraub* established that in New Jersey, a seller is now "under a duty to disclose a material latent condition, known to him but unobservable . . . [to the buyer, where] in the circumstances 'it would be a wholly inequitable application of caveat emptor to charge her [the buyer] with knowledge of it.'"[39]

The broader legal community's intersubjective reception and validation of *Weintraub* can be seen in several ways. The duty to disclose was widely adopted in place of caveat emptor by other state courts after *Weintraub* was decided,[40] the ruling has been expanded particularly in residential cases to cover implied warranties of habitability for leaseholds and new construction,[41] and the decision has been widely praised by commentators.[42]

Weintraub exemplifies the importance of judicial responses to the law as a fundamental element of the common law process in which judges sometimes change and make law through the issuance of judgments that are then evaluated by the larger legal community. The language used by the *Weintraub* court in expressing its rejection of *Swinton*'s caveat emptor standard is, in this respect, simultaneously striking and familiar. But even though this language is not unusual, it should not go unnoticed. These choices of language are useful indicators of the individual reactions and values of the judges who make up the courts. And the use of this sort of language in judicial decisions evinces the intrinsic relationship between the personal reactions and perspectives of individual judges and the incorporation of these reactions and perspectives within the formal articulation of legal standards in their judgments.

Browning v. Slenderella Systems of Seattle: Discrimination in Public Accommodations

The Civil Rights Act of 1964[43] is widely perceived as finally establishing that private owners of public accommodations[44] cannot discriminate against customers on the basis of their race.[45] The 1964 Act is also widely perceived as "the greatest legislative achievement of the civil rights movement."[46] The

1964 Act was not, however, the first effort to respond through the law to racial discrimination in public accommodations. Prior to 1964, some state court judges began to recognize a civil claim against businesses that discriminated on the basis of race. An excellent example of this judicial response is *Browning v. Slenderella Systems of Seattle.*[47]

Ola Browning entered Slenderella salon on March 5, 1956, gave her name, and was asked to take a seat and wait for her appointment. After waiting almost two hours and watching women repeatedly arrive and be waited on before her, Mrs. Browning asked the salon manager if she would be served. The manager replied, "We have never served anybody but Caucasians and I just know you won't be happy here." When Mrs. Browning asked why she was given an appointment, the manager replied, "Well, you know by phone we have no way of knowing you were colored."[48]

Mrs. Browning sued Slenderella for "embarrassment, humiliation, mental anguish and emotional shock" that she suffered as a result of being refused service by the salon due to her race. Sitting *en banc*, the Supreme Court of Washington affirmed the judgment in favor of Mrs. Browning. The court determined that the salon and its actions were covered by the Washington public accommodation statute: "Every person who denies to any other person because of race, creed, or color, the full enjoyment of any of the accommodations, advantages, facilities or privileges of any public resort, accommodation, assemblage, or amusement, shall be guilty of a misdemeanor."[49]

The *Browning* decision is a notable judicial innovation in antidiscrimination law. First, and most obviously, the terms of the applicable statute create only criminal penalties for a violation. Nevertheless, the Washington Supreme Court determined that the statute "while penal in form, is remedial in its nature and effect and gives to the person wrongfully discriminated against a civil remedy against the person guilty of wrongful discrimination."[50] The court reached this conclusion while acknowledging that "a civil action for damages for such discrimination is rarely resorted to in this state" due to the existence of administrative remedies and criminal penalties.[51]

Second, the *Browning* court also explained that in the absence of any physical harm, a judgment for civil damages resulting from the tort of intentional infliction of emotional distress requires "severe emotional distress."[52] To determine whether the defendant's conduct was sufficiently likely to cause sufficiently severe distress, the appropriate inquiry was whether "the prohibited conduct is conduct which in the eyes of decent men and women in a civilized community is considered outrageous and intolerable."[53] Although the court observed that Mrs. Browning was not publicly humiliated because no one else was aware that she was denied service, and even though the employees of the salon "were courteous" to Mrs. Browning "at all times,"[54] the majority of the court ruled that "we have no difficulty in finding that the conduct of the defendant was 'outrageous.'"[55] Although the individual distress that results from this conduct is, as the court said, "subjective," the court went on to conclude that "knowledge of human nature tells one" that there are predictable and shared responses to conduct of this kind.[56] The judges in the *Browning* majority concluded that the salon's act of racial discrimination itself (no matter how courteously or privately inflicted) was sufficient to establish a civil claim for damages under Washington's public accommodation statute (despite its criminal form) because that conduct is outrageous, as a matter of law, when engaged in by a business that falls within the bounds of the statute.[57] The judges' shared knowledge of human nature was sufficient for them to understand the distress that this discrimination caused Mrs. Browning.

Three members of the Washington Supreme Court dissented in *Browning*. In his dissenting opinion, which was joined by Justice Ott, Justice Mallery stated that "the majority opinion violate[d] the thirteenth amendment to the United States constitution. . . . When a white woman is compelled against her will to give a negress a Swedish massage, that too is involuntary servitude."[58] Mallery held the view that private discrimination was a constitutionally protected liberty and he concluded that Slenderella was a private business and not a public accommodation:

> No public institution or public utility is involved in the instant case. The Slenderella enterprise was not established by law to serve a public purpose. . . . There is a clear distinction between the nondiscrimination enjoined upon a public employee in the discharge of his official duties, which are prescribed by laws applicable to all, and his unlimited freedom of action in his private affairs. . . . This right of discrimination in private businesses is a constitutional one.[59]

Although he did not articulate the legal basis for his opinion, in determining that Slenderella could not be penalized for its racial discrimination, Mallery seems to have maintained the traditional state action/private action distinction that is traced to the *Civil Rights Cases*.[60]

Mallery's dissent helps accentuate the importance of the majority's opinion in *Browning*. Prior to the 1964 Act and the United States Supreme Court rulings upholding it, many people shared Mallery's view. In fact, Mallery's dissent in *Browning* was cited by Strom Thurmond as support for his opposition to the 1964 Act.[61] Nevertheless, the majority of the justices of the Supreme Court of Washington were willing to recognize the harm of and claim for emotional distress caused by a business that serves the public but refuses to serve a black customer simply because she is black. And the justices in *Browning* based their ruling on an interpretation of the public accommodations statute that was informed by their shared response to the discrimination Mrs. Browning suffered.[62] They incorporated and translated that subjective response through a legal judgment that provided a remedy for the legal wrong of intentionally inflicting emotional distress. The *Browning* majority also distinguished between shared responses to the defendant's actions that informed their legal judgment and shared sympathies with the plaintiff that were an inappropriate basis for determining the amount of damages she should be awarded.[63]

The *Browning* judgment developed the legal doctrine of their jurisdiction and anticipated and supported broader developments in the law of the United States. Neither the fact that the *Browning* judgment was innovative nor the fact that the judgment was grounded on the shared subjective responses of the judges undermines the contribution the court made to the law. As the Supreme Court of Washington did in *Browning*, the Supreme Court of the United States rejected the "involuntary servitude" argument with respect to the 1964 Act[64] and rejected the notion that private ownership creates an absolute constitutional "right" to discriminate against customers on the basis of their race.[65] And as support for its ruling, the United States Supreme Court referenced the thirty-two states that had enacted public accommodations laws, including the Washington statute enforced in *Browning*.[66]

R. v. R.: The Marital Rape Exemption

In the same way that the importance of *Weintraub* and *Browning* cannot be fully appreciated without considering the law that they addressed and altered, the impact of *R. v. R.* can be best understood by beginning our discussion with *R. v. J.*[67] In *R. v. J.*, which was decided less than a year before *R. v. R.*, the Crown Court was asked to consider whether a husband could be guilty of raping his wife after the couple had separated but before they were formally divorced or judicially decreed to be separated. The specific legal question raised by the defendant in *R. v. J.* was whether the inclusion of the word "unlawful" in section 1(1)(a) of the Sexual Offences (Amendment) Act of 1976 should be taken to indicate Parliament's intention to maintain the marital rape exemption in British criminal law. The statutory provision read: "[A] man commits rape if he has *unlawful* sexual intercourse with a woman who at the time of the intercourse does not consent to it."[68] The exemption was traditionally derived from Matthew Hale's statement in *History of the Pleas of the Crown*: "[T]he husband cannot be guilty of rape committed by himself upon his lawful wife, for by their mutual matrimonial consent and contract the wife hath given herself up this kind unto her husband which she cannot retract."[69]

In effect, the defendant's argument in *R. v. J.* was that the court had to assume that Parliament included the word "unlawful" in the 1976 Act for a reason, and the only possible reason Parliament could have for including that word was to distinguish the actions criminalized by the statute from acts of nonconsensual sex that were historically exempted as "lawful," which could only involve the rape of a wife by her husband. The Crown argued in response that even if Hale's characterization of the law was accurate at the time it was made, the understanding of the marital relationship had developed in the intervening centuries and could no longer be taken as an adequate basis for maintaining the marital exemption in English law.[70]

The Crown Court accepted the defendant's argument in *R. v. J.*, with evident reluctance. The court determined as a matter of statutory interpretation that "There is a presumption against surplusage in a statute. The defence urge that there is no other situation to which the word 'unlawful' could possibly refer. One only has to read the subsection and ask what circumstances could make sexual intercourse with a woman who did not consent to it lawful, and there can be only one answer."[71] In addition, the court was strongly influenced by a paper on "Rape within Marriage" in which the Law Commission had just recently indicated that the marital exemption had been preserved in the 1976 Act. In the court's view, "The position is crystallised as at the making of the Act and only Parliament can alter it. . . . I would wish to add my voice to those who urge that Parliament should take steps to abrogate the general rule, as it is already being urged to do, but that at present I feel bound by authority to come to the decision I have since I have to interpret the law as it is."[72]

Judges have different views of their own ability to make and change the law, of course. *R. v. J.* was decided by a trial court. *R. v. R.* was decided by the highest court in the UK judicial system. The House of Lords[73] took a very different view from the Crown Court of its independent authority and responsibility to develop the law through its decision in *R. v. R.*[74]

The facts of *R. v. R.* can be summarized briefly. The couple were married in August 1984. They had a son in 1985. On October 21, 1989, after marital difficulties and a prior two-week separation, the wife moved with their son to her parents' home and left a letter for her husband indicating her intention to file a divorce petition. Two days later, the husband spoke with the wife on the phone and stated that he, too, would investigate divorce proceedings. On November 12, 1989, the husband forcibly entered the home of his wife's parents (who were out of the house) and forcibly attempted to have sexual intercourse with his wife. He choked her with both hands, but was unable to rape her. He was arrested, charged with rape and assault, tried, and then pled guilty to the attempted rape of and assault on his wife.

On appeal, the husband argued that § 1(1)(a) of the 1976 Act precluded, as a matter of law, a criminal charge against him of raping his wife. The Court of Appeal sustained his conviction. In upholding the Court of Appeal's ruling, the House of Lords eliminated the marital rape exemption from English law. Lord Keith summarized the House's judgment in this passage:

> It may be taken that the proposition [of Hale] was generally regarded as an accurate statement of the common law of England. The common law is, however, capable of evolving in the light of changing social, economic and cultural developments. . . . [O]ne of the most important changes is that marriage is in modern times regarded as a partnership of equals, and no longer one in which the wife must be the subservient chattel of the husband. . . . On grounds of principle there is now no justification for the marital exception in rape.[75]

Lord Keith's reference to the adaptive capacity of the common law might not seem all that remarkable. He was, however, writing in a legal system that traditionally treats absolute legislative supremacy as the fundamental principle of its constitution.[76] Consequently, the House's decision to alter or deviate from the established meaning of a fairly recent legislative enactment is noteworthy.[77] Lord Keith concluded his judgment by stating that the Act did not prevent the House from eliminating the marital exemption:

> The fact is that it is clearly unlawful to have sexual intercourse with any woman without her consent, and that the use of the word in the subsection adds nothing. . . . I am therefore of the opinion that s 1(1) of the 1976 Act presents no obstacle to this House declaring that in modern times the supposed marital exception in rape forms no part of the law of England. . . . 'The remaining and no less difficult question is whether, despite

that view, this is an area where the court should step aside to leave the matter to the parliamentary process. This is not the creation of a new offence, it is the removal of a common law fiction which has become anachronistic and offensive and we consider that it is our duty having reached that conclusion to act upon it.'[78]

In the United Kingdom, much more than in the United States, judges are reticent about asserting their authority to change the law, particularly in cases, such as *R. v. R.*, in which a UK court declines to enforce a parliamentary statute. This judicial reticence results from the doctrine of parliamentary sovereignty and the correlative assumption that judicial review permits UK courts only to ensure the effectuation of parliamentary intentions in administrative action rather than the evaluation of parliamentary legislation for compliance with the British constitution.[79] Nevertheless, the House of Lords determined in *R. v. R.* that it possessed an independent institutional authority to eliminate a manifestly outdated and unjust rule from English law, and Lord Keith described issuing the judgment as the duty of the judges who heard the case.[80] Moreover, their Lordships recognize the judgment in *R. v. R.* as developing or making new law,[81] and this judgment was widely welcomed and intersubjectively validated by the legal community[82] and the broader community.[83]

According to Nicholas Barber, *R. v. R.* represents a "clear example" of a case in which UK "judges have changed a statute because the statute conflicts with their own moral convictions."[84] He observes that even "though the judges may be unable to admit that the law had changed, commentators at the time had little doubt that *R v R* was an example of judicial lawmaking, and that a statute had been changed contrary to the will of the enacting Parliament."[85]

Law in the Making

In *Weintraub* and *R. v. R.*, judges responded to the unfairness of the existing rules they were asked to enforce by changing the law; in *Browning* the judges responded to the absence of a civil remedy for discrimination in public accommodations by developing the law. In all three cases, the judges determined that long-standing doctrines were inconsistent with the judges' understandings of fairness and equitable treatment under the law. In the three cases, caveat emptor, public accommodations, and the marital exemption insulated the respective defendants from any legal accountability for their wrongdoing. In each case, the existing legal rules operated as absolute bars against claims by people harmed as a result of the defendants' actions. In all three cases, judges changed the law by adopting new rules that allowed those harmed by a seller's deliberate failure to disclose a material latent defect in her property, a business's racial discrimination, and a husband's sexual assault of his wife to pursue their claims. And in all three cases, the defendants were held legally responsible for their actions.

In each of these cases, the judges' individual sense of justice comes through in the expression of new legal standards in property, tort, and criminal law. These cases support my argument for three reasons. First, these cases demonstrate that common law judges routinely make law in the modification of existing legal standards and in the formulation of new legal principles. Second, particularly in *Browning* and *R v. R.*, the judges did not understand themselves to be precluded from contributing to the development of the law as a result of legislative enactments. Third, these cases are useful examples of the incorporation of judges' values and perspectives within formal legal judgments that were communicated to the communities in which these courts functioned. In all three cases, the decisions demonstrate, in language and tone, the personal reactions and convictions of the judges who decided the cases. Far from undermining the validity or efficacy of these opinions, these reactions and convictions were central to the improvements each court made to the law of its jurisdiction and to the lives of those who were governed by these decisions.[86]

Judges writing individually or on behalf of a panel conventionally refer to themselves as "the court." But the relationship between the court as a legal institution and the court as an institution constituted by individual judges should always be kept in mind. It is valuable for judges to speak in an institutional voice in articulating legal standards and in resolving legal disputes. It is also important to recognize when judges speak in an individual voice in reacting to a defect in the law and in acting to correct it through the development of the law. *Weintraub*, *Browning*, and *R. v. R.* represent revealing, and not at all unique, instances in which the courts spoke both in an institutional and in an individual voice, by articulating new legal standards as a response to the unfairness of the law as the judges found it. By referring expressly to "our sense of justice and fair dealing," "knowledge of human nature," and "our duty," the judges in these cases expressed their shared subjective responses within their formal judgments, which were then evaluated and validated by their legal communities, and they transformed the law.

5 Judicial Individualism and Judicial Independence

> The heart of judicial independence, it must be understood, is judicial individualism.[1]
> —Irving Kaufman

The prior chapters of this book have explored the subjective responses of judges in the process of judicial decision making by examining the translation of those responses through modes of legal reasoning in the formulation of legal judgments that are communicated to a wider community, which then evaluates the validity of those judgments. In this chapter, I explore the process of judicial decision making by considering the structural protections of that process.[2] I argue in this chapter that the institutional independence of the judiciary cannot be understood fully as separate from the individual independence of its judges. More specifically, I examine some legislative attempts to interfere with or influence the judicial decision-making process as threats to judicial independence, and I examine them as a means of improving our understanding of the relationship between the institutional independence of the judiciary and the individual independence of judges. By analyzing legislation and judicial decisions from the United States and the United Kingdom, I consider the institutional protections of the judicial process as the Anglo-American constitutional method of ensuring that individual judges may decide for themselves what they believe the law says and how it should be applied in their courts.

Legislative interference with judicial independence can take many forms.[3] In this chapter, I focus on two types of legislative interference that strike closely at a judge's ability to act in accordance with her own independent perspective: legislative efforts to preclude judges from considering certain sources or evidence they might wish to consult and legislative efforts to require judges to consider evidence that they might wish to exclude.[4] In both of these instances, legislative interference with the judge's individual autonomy threatens the judiciary's broader institutional independence. I argue here that a judge cannot decide independently if she cannot decide as an individual, and a judge cannot decide individually if she cannot determine what legal sources and reasoning should inform her judgment independent of any external interference or pressure.

I discuss here only legislative attempts to interfere with the judicial decision-making process itself. I will not discuss legislation that challenges the finality of judicial rulings, although these statutes also raise significant separation of powers concerns.[5] All these forms of legislative interference are unified by their goal of subjecting judicial decisions and decision making to nonjudicial control. Consequently, as the Supreme Court has emphasized, all these forms of legislative interference challenge the independence of the judiciary by threatening the power of judges to decide cases autonomously:

> Article III establishes a 'judicial department.' . . . The record of history shows that the Framers crafted this charter of the judicial department with an expressed understanding that it gives the Federal Judiciary the power, not merely to rule on cases, but to *decide* them, subject to review only by superior courts in the Article III hierarchy—with an understanding, in short, that 'a judgment conclusively resolves the case' because 'a judicial Power is one to render dispositive judgments.'[6]

As the Court fully understood, the power to decide cases, to adjudge them, requires not just an arid ability to enter a judicial order but the full authority to decide for oneself what the proper judgment should be.[7]

Individual and Institutional Independence

Judicial independence in the Anglo-American tradition is usually described in terms of the individual, or decisional, independence of judges and the institutional independence of the judiciary.[8] Decisional independence means that each judge must be able to determine, individually and impartially, the proper legal ruling and reasoning in a given case, and institutional independence means that the decisions and decision-making processes of courts must be respected by and protected from the elected branches of government:

> Decisional independence concerns the impartiality of judges—the capacity of individual judges to decide specific cases on the merits, without 'fear or favor.' Branch or institutional independence, on the other hand, concerns the general, non-case specific separation of the judicial branch—the capacity of the judiciary to remain autonomous, so that it might serve as an effective check against the excesses of the political branches.[9]

Despite a familiar and widely shared understanding of the meaning of decisional and institutional independence, the relationship between the independence of judges and the independence of the judiciary is not well understood.

I begin by examining legislative efforts in the United States to constrain judges' decisional independence, such as the proposed Constitution Restoration Act (CRA) and the Sentencing Reform Act of 1984 (SRA). I argue that legislative interference with the decisional autonomy of individual judges through the SRA, the CRA, and similar initiatives represents a genuine challenge to the institutional independence of the judiciary envisioned by Article III.[10]

Some scholars disagree. They believe that as a general and practical matter, Congress poses little threat to judicial independence. For example, John Ferejohn argues that Congress will almost never possess the collective motivation to interfere with the independence of the federal courts:

> I shall argue here that an organization or person is a potential political threat to judicial independence if the entity or individual: (1) has reason to get a judge or court to reach a decision on grounds irrelevant to law; (2) has sufficient resources—political, social and/or economic—to influence or intimidate the judge; and (3) is capable of forming a will or intention to act in a way that interferes with judicial independence. . . . In the United States, I think that Congress will occasionally satisfy the first condition, always satisfy the second condition, and will rarely satisfy the third condition.[11]

The first prong of Professor Ferejohn's description of potential threats to judicial independence is problematic. An entity need not be motivated to impel judges to decide on grounds "irrelevant to law" to threaten judicial independence. The entity may simply be motivated to preclude judges from considering certain legally relevant grounds or to prevent judges from deciding for themselves which legally relevant grounds are worthy of consideration.

As I will explain in this chapter, I believe Professor Ferejohn also underestimates the will of Congress to challenge the decisional independence of judges, in part because Professor Ferejohn (like many others) overlooks the importance of the relationship between individual and institutional independence. Ferejohn believes that the individual independence of judges is actually more secure than institutional independence.[12] And he is probably correct, at least historically, concerning congressional threats to individual judges' legal judgments; the time when Congress attempted to impeach judges for their legal rulings seems to have passed.[13] But the threat to individual judicial independence that Ferejohn overlooks is the threat to the process of judicial decision making. For example, by making judicial reliance upon foreign sources an impeachable offense,[14] the CRA threatens to revisit the unhappy chapter in US constitutional history when Congress attempted to hinder judicial independence by penalizing judges for their legal decisions, in this instance not for the judgments they reached but rather for the reasoning they used to reach their judgments. The CRA indicates that Congress does still sometimes possess the will to threaten the ability of judges to decide—autonomously, individually, and independently—which sources they find persuasive when reasoning about the law and formulating legal judgments.[15]

Even more fundamentally, Ferejohn's argument proceeds from the assumption that we need to determine whether individual or institutional independence is more central to the US constitutional framework. I see no reason to make that assumption. Institutional and individual independence share the same constitutional groundwork and are mutually reinforcing. Institutional independence exists so that individual judges can reach their own judgment in evaluating and articulating the law. Conversely, individual independence allows the judiciary to fulfill its institutional role in ensuring that legislative and executive power are exercised only within constitutional and other legal constraints upon the government.

Judicial and scholarly discussions of judicial independence usually concentrate on institutional independence. In fact, it is not unusual for scholars to assume that institutional independence is really what judicial independence is all about. As Stephen Burbank put it, "Federal judicial independence is also first and foremost an institutional value, designed to protect the separation of powers and the rule of law. Article III of the Constitution vests judicial power in courts, not judges."[16] The problem with this view is that it is a bit like saying that the current standings of a sports league are statements about teams rather than players. In an important sense, that is undeniable. In an equally important sense, the players play the games, and it is misguided to conceive of a team's performance as somehow disconnected from the players themselves. The players *are* the team, and their efforts define the team's success. Similarly, judicial independence is without question an institutional value. As I mentioned at the end of the previous chapter, judges frequently refer to themselves as the court, and the courts have an institutional identity apart from the judges who are on the court at any point in time. Moreover, the courts' institutional identity is importantly connected to their institutional independence. Institutional independence positions judges in an institution that allows them to reach impartial judgments, and the process of individual judicial decision making reflects and reinforces the institutional autonomy and integrity of the judiciary. That is to say, the institutional value of judicial independence exists for a purpose, which is to allow the judges who comprise the judiciary to decide cases based upon their own judgment of the law.[17] Article III vests judicial power in courts. But Article III courts do not exist without judges. And Article III also says that "The *Judges*, both of the supreme and inferior Courts, shall hold their Offices during good Behaviour."[18]

Burbank bases his understanding of judicial independence on his understanding of US constitutional development. In his view, "a judge-centered view of judicial independence is problematic from a historical perspective, and it is demonstrably inadequate given conditions in, and the needs of, contemporary American society. . . . The primary goal of the architects of federal judicial independence was to enable the separation of powers and thereby to enable the judiciary to exercise the power of judicial review."[19] Taking the historical point first, it is difficult to see how the "primary goal" of judicial independence was enabling the exercise of judicial review, given the vehement disagreements and uncertainty surrounding the exercise of that power at the time of the framing. I am not arguing that judicial review was not anticipated at the time of the framing[20] or that there is no implicit support for the power in the text and structure of the Constitution.[21] I am simply noting that it cannot be considered a *fait accompli* during and following the drafting and ratification of Article III.[22] Burbank puts the institutional cart before the constitutional horse by suggesting that in the minds of the framers, the primary goal of judicial independence was to allow the courts to exercise judicial review.

Like Professors Ferejohn and Burbank, the Supreme Court of the United States usually concerns itself primarily with the judiciary's institutional independence in the constitutional design of the federal system. Here is a good example from the Court's *Northern Pipeline* decision, which held that Congress was not empowered to assign Article III judicial powers to an Article I court:

> Basic to the constitutional structure established by the Framers was their recognition that '[the] accumulation of all powers, legislative, executive, and judiciary, in the same hands, whether of one, a few, or many, and whether hereditary, self-appointed, or elective, may justly be pronounced the very definition of tyranny.' . . . The Federal Judiciary was therefore designed by the Framers to stand independent of the Executive and Legislature—to maintain the checks and balances of the constitutional structure, and also to guarantee that the process of adjudication itself remained impartial. . . . As an inseparable element of the constitutional system of checks and balances, and as a guarantee of judicial impartiality, Art. III both defines the power and protects the independence of the Judicial Branch. . . . In sum, our Constitution unambiguously enunciates a fundamental principle—that the 'judicial Power of the United States' must be reposed in an independent Judiciary. It commands that the independence of the Judiciary be jealously guarded, and it provides clear institutional protections for that independence.[23]

The Court in *Northern Pipeline* emphasized in this passage the relationship between judicial independence and judicial impartiality. As the Court pointed out, the function of the federal courts in the separation of powers structure and dynamics of the US constitutional system depends upon a judicial institution whose impartiality is protected by its independence from external influences. But the Court also recognized, although it takes a bit more effort to find in its opinion, that judicial independence and impartiality depend equally upon the autonomy and authority of judges to decide as individuals: "The independence from political forces that they [the life tenure and fixed salary provisions of Article III] guarantee helps to promote public confidence in judicial determinations. . . . The guarantee of life tenure insulates the individual judge from improper influences not only by other branches but by colleagues as well, and thus promotes *judicial individualism*."[24]

Decisional Autonomy and Judicial Independence

In the face of repeated threats and attempts to impose penalties upon judges for referring to foreign legal sources when interpreting the US Constitution,

Justice Scalia encouraged Congress to keep its legislative hands off of the judiciary's business:

> No one is more opposed to the use of foreign law than I am, but I'm darned if I think it's up to Congress to direct the court how to make its decisions. . . . [It] is like telling us not to use certain principles of logic. . . . Let us make our mistakes just as we let you make yours.[25]

One of the legislative initiatives to which Justice Scalia was responding was the Constitution Restoration Act (CRA), which was introduced in the Senate in 2004 and 2005.[26] Here is a provision from that proposed legislation:

> In interpreting and applying the Constitution of the United States, a court of the United States may not rely upon any constitution, law, administrative rule, Executive order, directive, policy, judicial decision, or any other action of any foreign state or international organization or agency, other than English constitutional and common law up to the time of the adoption of the Constitution of the United States.[27]

Another provision of the CRA indicated that any judge who chose to rely upon a foreign source of law when interpreting and applying the US Constitution would be subject to impeachment.[28] More recently, state legislatures and electoral initiatives have pursued similar goals in restricting the decisional autonomy of judges by precluding them from referring to foreign sources when rendering judgments. For example, the Oklahoma legislature approved a proposed amendment to Article VII, Section 1 of the Oklahoma state constitution that would preclude judges in Oklahoma from referring to international legal sources: "[I]in making judicial decisions[,] [t]he courts shall not look to the legal precepts of other nations or cultures. Specifically, the courts shall not consider international or Sharia Law."[29] This proposed amendment was approved on November 2, 2010, by more than 70 percent of Oklahoma voters.[30] The measure was ultimately enjoined by the United States Court of Appeals for the Tenth Circuit as an Establishment Clause violation due to its disfavored treatment of Islam.[31]

I am not discussing here whether it is a good idea for judges to refer to foreign sources when interpreting US law.[32] Although a great deal has been written about the propriety of judges citing foreign legal sources when interpreting the US Constitution, and about the efforts of Congress to intervene in this matter, surprisingly little attention has been paid to this issue as it relates to judicial independence.[33] This chapter considers congressional intervention in the process of judicial decision making as a threat to judicial independence. More specifically, this chapter attempts to answer this question: How can the various attempts by legislatures to intervene in the decision-making process of judges help us to understand the relationship between individual judicial independence and institutional judicial independence? Despite his strong opposition to US judges citing foreign sources when interpreting the US Constitution,[34] Justice Scalia was even more concerned by congressional attempts to dictate which sources individual justices may refer to in their reasoning and opinion writing.

Long before the introduction of the CRA, members of Congress had repeatedly attempted to interfere with judicial independence by, for instance, summoning a federal judge to testify regarding confidential grand jury proceedings.[35] More recently, Congress passed the 1984 Sentencing Reform Act (SRA),[36] which established the United States Sentencing Commission and ultimately led to the United States Sentencing Guidelines.[37] The purpose of the Guidelines was to address the disparity among the sentences imposed by courts upon individuals convicted of the same or similar criminal violations; different judges were imposing different sentences for the same crime.[38] Although the SRA largely replaced the perceived problem of judicial discretion with prosecutorial discretion,[39] and even though the Guidelines have been subjected to extensive criticism on constitutional and policy grounds,[40] my concern here is with the inability under the Guidelines of individual judges to decide for themselves what an appropriate sentence should be for an individual defendant.[41]

The Supreme Court ruled in *Mistretta v. United States* that the creation of the Commission through the SRA was not an unconstitutional violation of separation of powers and judicial independence.[42] An important factor in the Court's decision was the placement of the Commission "within the Judicial Branch."[43] Ironically, the majority in *Mistretta* also emphasized that the Commission "is not a court and does not exercise judicial power"[44] even though "the legislative history of the Act makes clear that Congress's decision to place the Commission within the Judicial Branch reflected Congress's 'strong feeling' that sentencing has been and should remain 'primarily a judicial function.'"[45] This view somehow led the Court to conclude that the placement of the Commission within the judicial branch did not "vest[] within the Judiciary responsibilities that more appropriately belong to another Branch, [but instead] simply acknowledge[d] the role that the Judiciary always has played, and continues to play, in sentencing."[46]

The majority gets the issue in *Mistretta* exactly backwards. The concern is not whether the creation of the Sentencing Commission grants to the judiciary a "non-judicial" authority that more appropriately belongs in another branch of government.[47] The concern is whether the creation of the Commission grants to the Commission a distinctively judicial authority that cannot properly be transferred to a "non-judicial" authority.[48] The Court had already observed that the Commission is not a court and does not exercise judicial authority. Then the Court observed that the power of sentencing is an authority "the judiciary always has" exercised. And then the Court decided that transferring the authority to determine sentences for criminal offenses from federal judges to the Sentencing Commission was not violative of judicial independence or separation of powers because Congress placed the Commission "within the judicial branch."

The majority's reasoning in *Mistretta* fails because it equates judicial independence entirely or predominantly with institutional independence. The Court's preoccupation with the independence of the judicial branch led it to conclude that depriving judges of their authority to fashion sentences for defendants in cases over which they presided was not an impermissible infringement upon judicial independence because the Commission was placed by Congress within the judicial branch of government. The majority therefore concluded that no one from outside the judicial branch was interfering with the judiciary's institutional authority. But of course the institutional independence and authority of the judiciary is virtually meaningless without the decisional independence of its judges to determine for themselves what the proper legal outcome of the trial process should be.

Justice Scalia dissented in *Mistretta*. In contrast with the majority's focus on the judicial branch, Scalia addresses in the second sentence of his opinion the impact of the Guidelines on the decisional independence of judges: "A judge who disregards them will be reversed."[49] Scalia devotes a substantial amount of the discussion in his dissent to issues of congressional delegation, institutional authority, and separation of powers. Throughout his analysis, though, he returns to the relationship between the institutional independence of the judiciary and the decisional autonomy of its judges:

> It is already a leap from the proposition that a person who is not the President may exercise executive powers to the proposition we accepted in *Morrison* that a person who is *neither* the President *nor* subject to the President's control may exercise executive powers. But with respect to the exercise of judicial powers (the business of the Judicial Branch) the plat-

> form for such a leap does not even exist. For unlike executive power . . . [a] judge may not leave the decision to his law clerk, or to a master. . . . Thus, however well established may be the 'independent agencies' of the Executive Branch, here we have an anomaly beyond equal: an independent agency exercising governmental power on behalf of a Branch where all governmental power is supposed to be exercised *personally* by the judges of courts.[50]

Given his concern with legislative incursions into the judicial process, Scalia's response to Congress's interfering with a judge's ability to reach independent legal determinations—whether in the form of the criminal sentences that should be imposed or the legal sources that should be considered—is consistent with respect to the Sentencing Reform Act and the Constitution Restoration Act. Scalia understands judicial independence to require that judges be allowed to determine for themselves what their judgments should be and how they should reason toward those judgments.

Judicial resistance to the Guidelines was powerful and predictable.[51] Unsurprisingly, prior to the Court's decision in *Mistretta*, over two hundred district court judges ruled that the SRA was unconstitutional.[52] More surprisingly, circuit and district judges voiced their opposition to the Guidelines in their published opinions.[53] And perhaps most surprisingly, even after *Mistretta*, district courts continued to rule the Guidelines unconstitutional, particularly after the enactment in 2003 of the so-called Feeney Amendment, which further curtailed the ability of federal judges to depart downward from the Guidelines.[54] In addition, the Feeney Amendment eliminated the requirement that at least three of the seven members of the Sentencing Commission be federal judges[55] and required "that the House and Senate Judiciary Committees, and the Attorney General, be notified each time a judge departs downward . . . [and] the report must include the 'identity of the sentencing judge.'"[56] Relying upon the Feeney Amendment, Attorney General John Ashcroft directed federal prosecutors, in a signed memorandum, to identify to the Department of Justice any federal judge who departed downward in sentencing in a manner not supported by the Guidelines.[57]

District court judges viewed the Feeney Amendment and the Ashcroft Memorandum as impermissibly interfering with the independence of judges: "The chilling effect resulting from such reporting requirements is sufficient to violate the separation of powers limitations of the United States Constitution. . . . There is no legitimate purpose served by reporting individual judges'[] performance to Congress. Congress does not have any direct oversight of the Judiciary."[58] These judges recognized that judicial independence does not mean simply that judges may not be penalized or punished for their legal judgments; it also means that they must be able to reason toward and reach their judgments without improper interference or intimidation. Intimidation can take the form of reporting to Congress under the Feeney Amendment or the threat of impeachment by Congress under the Constitution Restoration Act, and interference can take the form of impeding the ability of judges to reach what they believe is an appropriate criminal sentence or inhibiting the ability of judges to refer to what they believe are appropriate legal sources when interpreting the Constitution.

In holding the post–Feeney Amendment Guidelines unconstitutional, the US District Court for the District of Oregon returned to the rationale of *Mistretta* and to Justice Scalia's dissent:

> We are thus left with a strange creature that is nominally lodged within the Judicial Branch, and purports to be performing duties of a judicial nature, yet need contain no judges, does not answer to anyone in the Judicial Branch, and into which the Judicial Branch is assured no input. . . . The alterations to the Sentencing Commission effected by the Feeney Amendment require re-examination of a fundamental premise of *Mistretta*, namely, that the Sentencing Commission is part of the Judicial Branch. . . . I see no principled basis on which to distinguish the Sentencing Commission, post-Feeney, from the . . . other administrative agencies that populate the Executive Branch. . . . For such statutory purposes, Congress can define the term as it pleases. But since our subject here is the Constitution . . . the Court must . . . decide for itself where the Commission is located for purposes of separation-of-powers analysis.[59]

The District Court concluded that the Commission could no longer, even in a nominal or formal sense, be considered a part of a judicial branch that was meaningfully independent of the executive branch of government.[60] The importance of the Commission as a threat to judicial independence is determined by what it does rather than where it is, by Congress interposing the Commission in the judicial branch with the authority to interfere with the traditional role and responsibility of independent Article III judges.

After sustained academic and judicial criticism of the Guidelines and the Court's decision in *Mistretta*,[61] the Supreme Court ruled in 2005 that the Sixth Amendment right to a jury trial is violated by provisions in the Guidelines that impose enhanced sentences on the basis of facts determined by a judge rather than a jury, and that the Guidelines cannot be applied in accordance with the congressional intent underlying the SRA unless the Guidelines are deemed advisory rather than mandatory.[62]

Although the Supreme Court did link institutional and individual independence (inconspicuously) in *Northern Pipeline*, other courts have actually resisted this point. For example, in *McBryde v. Committee to Review Circuit Council Conduct and Disability Orders*, the United States Court of Appeals for the District of Columbia Circuit reviewed the determination by the Conduct Review Committee that Judge McBryde had engaged in abusive behavior toward attorneys and other judges, which was "prejudicial to the effective and expeditious administration of the business of the courts."[63] Acting under the Judicial Conduct and Disability Act of 1980,[64] the Committee publicly reprimanded Judge McBryde, ordered that no new cases would be assigned to him for one year, and precluded him for three years from presiding in any case involving any of the twenty-three attorneys who participated in the investigation of his alleged misconduct.[65]

Judge McBryde then challenged the constitutionality of the Judicial Conduct and Disability Act. He argued that the Act violated the Constitution's due process and separation of powers guarantees and that the Act violated the First Amendment by preventing disclosure of the record in the Committee proceedings. The District Court concluded that the Act did function as a prior restraint upon Judge McBryde's speech in violation of the First Amendment, but it rejected the rest of his arguments.[66] On appeal, the D.C. Circuit ruled that Judge McBryde's challenges to the one-year moratorium and the three-year preclusion were moot because they had expired and that several of his other challenges to the Act were barred by the statute itself. For purposes of my argument, the court's discussion of McBryde's separation of powers argument is most important.

Judge McBryde argued that impeachment is the only constitutional avenue for disciplining federal judges[67] and that therefore the Act violated separation of powers. McBryde also argued that the judicial independence provided under Article III prevents judges from being disciplined for their actions while on the bench.[68]

In rejecting Judge McBryde's arguments, the D.C. Circuit construed judicial independence under Article III as limited solely to institutional independence:

> [T]he great bulwarks of judicial independence are the guarantees of life tenure and undiminished salary during good behavior. For Judge McBryde, the fact that individual judges are the direct beneficiaries of these

> guarantees proves that it is the individual judge that is the relevant unit of judicial independence. . . . That individual judges are direct beneficiaries of the tenure and salary protections of Article III by itself hardly shows that the overarching purpose of these provisions was to insulate individual judges against the world as a whole (including the judicial branch itself), rather than . . . to safeguard the branch's independence from its two competitors.[69]

Although federal judges may be involuntarily removed from office only via "Impeachment for, and Conviction of, Treason, Bribery, or other high Crimes and Misdemeanors,"[70] according to the *McBryde* court, Article III does not foreclose other forms of discipline for lesser forms of misconduct.[71]

The tendency even for courts to overlook the connection between institutional independence and individual independence is striking. And the question whether impeachment is the sole constitutional means of disciplining federal judges is a serious matter that has not been adequately addressed by courts or scholars. But I do not want that question to distract from my argument here. Whatever may be the case with respect to disciplining a judge for his demeanor on the bench or in his chambers, my focus is on decisional autonomy as the cynosure of individual judicial independence and on individual independence as a central feature of institutional independence. In its decision in *Chandler v. Judicial Council of the Tenth Circuit*, the Supreme Court insisted that individual judges must be free to render judgments independently: "There can, of course, be no disagreement among us as to the imperative need for total and absolute independence of judges in deciding cases or in any phase of the decisional function."[72] Whatever the merits may be of the D.C. Circuit's view of the constitutionality of disciplining federal judges for other behavior, the *McBryde* court's attempt to dissociate institutional independence entirely from individual independence was seriously misguided.[73]

Charles Gardner Geyh explains the relationship between the judge's independence and the judiciary's independence in this way:

> Thinking about judicial independence with reference to judges as individuals highlights the role independence plays in judicial decision making. It is said that if we want judges to decide cases on the basis of facts as they find them and law as they construe it to be written, we must insulate them from external influences that could corrupt their integrity or impartiality—hence the need for 'decisional' or 'decision-making' independence. On the

> other hand, thinking about judicial independence in terms of judges collectively, as a branch, shifts our focus toward the role of the judiciary in a representative democracy where the powers of government are separated. The argument goes that if the judiciary is to maintain its structural separation from the legislative and executive branches and to keep the other branches in check through the exercise of judicial review, it must be able to preserve its institutional integrity and resist encroachments—hence the need for 'institutional' or 'branch' independence.[74]

In discussing the relationship of institutional and individual judicial independence, we cannot lose sight of the fact that the constitutional and definitional obligation of individual judges and the judicial institution is to adjudicate: to decide cases and to render judgments. The central purpose of insulating the courts from external influence was so that each judge of those courts could reach her own judgment of what the law means and requires.[75]

Once we see the correlation between decisional independence and institutional independence, we can appreciate that this freedom of a judge to decide cases without external interference also requires that these cases be decided by a judge acting as a judge, within the distinctive forms and constraints of his institution. Jefferson Powell describes these interconnected aspects of judicial autonomy and obligation as the "Three Independences":

> Independence of position, then, is concerned with tangible, external threats to the courts' proper exercise of their constitutional function, and it is secured in the Founders' view by external structural protections for the individuals who exercise the power of the courts. But I want us to take note of the way in which Hamilton links these external factors to the internal subjectivities of the judges—to their 'temper' as he puts it. The second strand in the weave making up judicial independence is what I am calling independence of decision. The courts are only truly independent, our tradition has maintained, when the decisions of the judges take effect, are enforceable and enforced, without circumvention or defiance by legislatures and executive officers. . . . The third element that I believe is woven into the general concept of judicial independence is what I am calling independence of thought. The courts are only truly independent, our tradition has maintained, when the judges reach their conclusions through a process of thought and decision that is significantly different from the forms of decisionmaking the other branches of government employ. The function of adjudication involves by definition the exercise of a

> type of judgment that proceeds from different premises and operates within different constraints than those which characterize the activities of the legislature and the executive. . . . Judges who fail to maintain and respect the difference between judicial and extrajudicial reasoning are not independent in the American constitutional sense, no matter how secure their positions and how respected their judgments, for those judgments will then necessarily be subservient to something other than the people's law.[76]

In Powell's terms, judicial independence of position, decision, and thought create an institution that is constrained primarily from within, an institution that allows judges to act on their own best judgment of what the law requires so long as they can always demonstrate that they are acting in accordance with what their legal tradition requires of them. The independence of judges demands that they be independent as judges.

Attempts by Congress to curtail the sources or evidence to which judges may refer when deciding cases are, in fact, attempts to interfere with judicial independence. In relation to the distinction between institutional and decisional judicial independence, an unusual aspect of these legislative efforts to restrict decisional resources is that they attempt to reduce the courts' institutional independence by reducing the judges' decisional independence. The core value of decisional independence is that "judges must be free to decide individual cases according to the judge's view of the law."[77] These legislative efforts to limit the sources available to judges constrain the judges' ability to determine, independently and without external interference, their own understanding of the law. Judges who are limited in their individual capacity to determine for themselves what the law means are limited in their institutional capacity to operate apart from undue intrusions by coordinate branches of government.[78] Accordingly, these legislative incursions threaten judicial independence and require the courts to preserve their institutional integrity by protecting their decisional autonomy.[79]

Decisional Integrity and Judicial Independence

To this point, we have considered legislative attempts to prevent judges from considering sources and evidence that they might want to consider as a threat to the decisional independence of judges and, consequently, to the institutional independence of the judiciary. Now we will examine the converse problem: to what extent are legislative attempts to require judges to consider evidence that they might wish to exclude a threat to judicial independence? To answer this question, I will focus on an important judgment by the House of Lords, the predecessor to the Supreme Court of the United Kingdom.[80]

One year after it ruled in *A. v. Secretary of State for the Home Department* (hereafter *Belmarsh*) that the potentially indefinite detention of foreign nationals violated British[81] and EU[82] law, the House of Lords heard a subsequent appeal on behalf of the same group of detainees.[83] In this case, which I will refer to as *Belmarsh II*,[84] the House was asked to consider whether the Special Immigration Appeals Commission (SIAC)—the administrative tribunal authorized by Parliament to hear cases under the Anti-Terrorism Act[85]—could review evidence that might have been obtained through torture conducted without the participation or authorization of the British government.[86] When this issue was raised in the proceedings before the SIAC, the SIAC determined that the procurement of evidence through torture was a fact that went to the weight, but not to the admissibility, of the evidence.[87]

The House disagreed. Lord Bingham and Lord Nicholls underscored the common law's long-standing prohibition against torture of all types, for all purposes.[88] And although this prohibition was not always respected by the Crown, torture was consistently declared to be "totally repugnant to the fundamental principles of English law" and "repugnant to reason, justice, and humanity."[89] The legal proscription of torture in English law was formalized in 1640 and seems to have been followed faithfully (but not entirely without exception).[90]

In their argument before the House, the detainees relied upon the common law prohibition against torture as a legal foundation for their more specific claim that the use of evidence obtained via torture violates the principle that the government cannot introduce an involuntary confession as evidence against the defendant.[91] The Police and Criminal Evidence Act of 1984 codified this common law principle and required that where a defendant asserts that a confession was obtained improperly, the government must demonstrate beyond a reasonable doubt that the confession was not the result of oppressive conduct.[92] After examining the statutory and decisional law on this subject, the House concluded that the use of torture to obtain evidence goes to the admissibility of the evidence, rather than its weight. In other words, where the government cannot rebut the claim that evidence was obtained by torture, that evidence must be excluded.[93]

In addition to their argument that the use of evidence procured by torture is analogous to admission of an involuntary confession, the detainees argued that the use of evidence obtained by torture amounts to an abuse of the judicial process and the judicial institution. The detainees argued that common law principles protect against the use of evidence gathered through torture because "the infliction of torture is so grave a breach of . . . the rule of law that any court degrades itself and the administration of justice by admitting it. . . . [T]he court must exercise its discretion to reject such evidence as an abuse of its process."[94]

More than any other issue or argument in the *Belmarsh* cases, the abuse-of-process principle most directly and concretely recognizes that the judicial process itself—the individual challenge to government action raised before an independent judge—is intrinsic to the Anglo-American tradition of judicial independence and the rule of law. The central point, which the House endorsed and reaffirmed, is that the judiciary has an independent institutional authority to maintain the integrity of the judicial process even (or especially) when confronted with an apparent abuse of power by the executive or the legislature:

> [T]he judiciary [must] accept a responsibility for the maintenance of the rule of law that embraces a willingness to oversee executive action and to refuse to countenance behaviour that threatens either basic human rights or the rule of law. . . . [Where] it offends the court's sense of justice and propriety to be asked to try the accused in the circumstances of a particular case . . . the court, in order to protect its own process from being degraded and misused, must have the power to stay proceedings which have come before it and have only been made possible by acts which offend the court's conscience as being contrary to the rule of law.[95]

The court's sense of justice is a judge's sense of justice and the court's conscience is a judge's conscience. The formal language should not distract us from the functional reality that the offense in permitting evidence obtained through torture is an offense to the conscience and sense of justice of the judge who is asked to allow that evidence to be used in her court. The House's conclusion is that individual judges must protect the judicial process in which they participate. As in other instances where a sense of justice and conscience figure into a determination of the legality of government action, it is the subjective sense and conscience of individual judges on which this determination ultimately rests.[96]

Lord Bingham concluded that this principle authorized the judiciary to exercise its "jurisdiction to prevent abuse of executive power."[97] Lords Nicholls, Hoffmann, and Brown reinforced this point by highlighting explicitly the different institutional functions and responsibilities of the executive and the judiciary.[98] And Lord Hoffmann went on to recognize that preservation of the integrity of the judicial process by the judiciary itself helps to demonstrate that this is the most fundamental basis for excluding improperly obtained evidence:

> [What is] the purpose of the rule excluding evidence obtained by torture[?] . . . Is it to discipline the executive agents of the state by demonstrating that no advantage will come from torturing witnesses, or is it to preserve the integrity of the judicial process and the honour of English law? If it is the former, then of course we cannot aspire to discipline the agents of foreign governments. Their torturers would probably accept with indifference the possibility that the work of their hands might be rejected by an English court. If it is the latter, then the rule must exclude statements obtained by torture anywhere, since the stain attaching to such evidence will defile an English court whatever the nationality of the torturer. I have no doubt that the purpose of the rule is not to discipline the executive, although this may be an incidental consequence. It is to uphold the integrity of the administration of justice.[99]

The House recognized in *Belmarsh II* that allowing evidence obtained by torture to be introduced in court would threaten the integrity and independence of the judiciary as an institution and the rule of law as a core value of Anglo-American constitutional government.[100] To preserve the nature of their institution and of their constitution, judges are understood in the common law tradition to possess the authority to disavow acts of the government that violate legal principle. This authority becomes acutely important when the acts of the government threaten the judicial process itself. That process is frequently the means by which the legality of the government's actions are challenged and determined, and this is why, in the United Kingdom and the United States, judges occupy the institutional position between the government and the governed, to enforce the legal limitations on government action that define constitutionalism.[101]

This substantive and structural principle—that certain government acts are irretrievably inconsistent with the rule of law and that judges are obliged to say so—unifies the analysis of the various judicial opinions and statements discussed in this chapter. In protecting the process of judging, by deciding which sources and evidence they find convincing, or by determining what an appropriate sentence should be for a criminal violation, or by ensuring that the integrity of the judicial process not be tarnished through the consideration of evidence obtained by torture, the independence of the judicial institution depends upon the responses of individual judges. Where acts of the legislative or executive branch threaten to undermine the integrity of the judicial process, the judges' obligation is to preserve their institution by ensuring that they as independent judicial officials cannot be used to violate the constitutional principles that define and limit their government. This is also why several justices of the Supreme Court of the United Kingdom reaffirmed in *R. (on the application of Evans) v. Attorney General* the constitutional principle that neither legislative enactments nor executive action may exempt a government official from compliance with a court's legal judgment or permit that official to override the court's judgment:

> A statutory provision which entitles a member of the executive (whether a Government Minister or the Attorney General) to overrule a decision of the judiciary merely because he does not agree with it would not merely be unique in the laws of the United Kingdom. It would cut across two constitutional principles which are also fundamental components of the rule of law. First, subject to being overruled by a higher court or (given Parliamentary supremacy) a statute, it is a basic principle that a decision of a court is binding as between the parties, and cannot be ignored or set aside by anyone, including (indeed it may fairly be said, least of all) the executive. Secondly, it is also fundamental to the rule of law that decisions and actions of the executive are, subject to necessary well established exceptions . . . reviewable by the court at the suit of an interested citizen. . . . The proposition that a member of the executive can actually overrule a decision of the judiciary because he does not agree with that decision is equally remarkable, even if one allows for the fact that the executive's overruling can be judicially reviewed. Indeed, the notion of judicial review in such circumstances is a little quaint, as it can be said with some force that the rule of law would require a judge, almost as a matter of course, to quash the executive decision.[102]

In fact, the inability of government actors to disregard or repudiate a court's judgment is encompassed by the fundamental rule of law commitment that the government is bound by the law. In *Evans*, Lord Neuberger accordingly emphasized the "constitutional importance" of the principle and presumption that the legality of government action must be subject to review by the judiciary.[103]

Indeed, if judges were to stand silently by in the face of government acts that would, for all practical purposes, create a space in which government could act without any reference to or constraint of the law, this would create what Lord Steyn called a "legal black hole,"[104] because rule of law values require that government action must always be limited by law and a legal black hole is a condition or circumstance in which government is empowered to act lawlessly.[105] For purposes of this chapter, the most significant threat posed by lawless government action is the tension between a legal black hole and the judicial role. This tension troubled Lord Steyn in relation to US and UK courts:

> The United States has a long and honourable commitment to the Magna Carta and allegiance to the rule of law. In recent times extraordinary deference of the United States courts to the executive has undermined those values and principles. As matters stand at present the United States courts would refuse to hear a prisoner at Guantanamo Bay who produces credible medical evidence that he has been and is being tortured. They would refuse to hear prisoners who assert that they were not combatants at all. They would refuse to hear prisoners who assert that they were simply soldiers in the Taliban army and knew nothing about Al-Qaeda. They would refuse to examine any complaints of any individuals. The blanket presidential order deprives them all of any rights whatever. As a lawyer brought up to admire the ideals of American democracy and justice, I would have to say that I regard this as a monstrous failure of justice.[106]

As Lord Steyn emphasized in this passage, whatever government actors may attempt to do in interrogation rooms, there are certain things they cannot do in courtrooms. In the common law tradition, judges have an obligation to ensure that the judicial process operates as it was meant to, by ensuring that the government must demonstrate the legality of its actions before an independent judge. That shared constitutional commitment of the Anglo-American tradition probably best explains the similar resistance among judges in the United Kingdom and the United States to attempts by other government actors to limit their ability to decide for themselves what their legal judgments should be or to degrade the integrity of the judicial process.

6 Conclusion

[T]he danger is not that judges will bring the full measure of their experience, their moral core, their every human capacity to bear in the difficult process of resolving the cases before them. It seems to me that a far greater danger exists if they do not.[1]

—Judith Kaye

The Ideal Judge?

We need to move beyond thinking of the ideal judge as someone who suspends her own personal experiences and values and perspectives so that she can judge from a place of abstract neutrality and objectivity. We need to move beyond a place where judges say things like these at their confirmation hearings so that they can navigate through the political process of being appointed:

> Judges are like umpires. Umpires don't make the rules, they apply them.[2]
>
> [M]y fundamental commitment, if I am confirmed, will be to the greatest extent possible to totally disregard my own personal belief.[3]

Common law judges are not umpires. It is neither possible nor desirable for judges to disregard their beliefs when they are judging. These statements assume that a judge's role is to apply the law without regard to what the judge may believe about the law and that the content of the law exists wholly apart from what a judge may believe about it. This is the view I have called strong objectivism.

Strong objectivism, which I have also called "mind-independence," is the idea that an object exists and has meaning in the world apart from our beliefs about that object. For instance, the fact that people used to believe that the Earth is flat did not make the Earth flat; the fact of this planet's shape exists apart from what people may think or say about it. I refer to this form of objectivism as "mind-independence." Applied to law, strong objectivism requires the meaning of law to exist apart from what we may believe about the law. Applied to judging, strong objectivism means that the role of judges is to find (or make their best effort to find) the true meaning of the law and to apply it in the cases they are asked to decide. This view of law and judging also means that a judge should decide cases on the basis of the objective law rather than the judge's subjective values or perspectives. This view is found frequently in public and political comments about the courts: "judges should not legislate from the bench," "judges should not impose their own values in place of the law," and so on.

But judges disagree about how certain cases should be decided. In part, this is because who a judge is as an individual—that person's experiences, values, and perspectives—influences that judge's response to a case and understanding of the law. The recognition that different judges may decide the same case in different ways, in part because of their different perspectives and values, has led some people to claim that the law does not genuinely determine judicial decision making at all. On this view, judging is simply the projection of a judge's subjective preferences into a judicial decision (followed by the camouflaging of those subjective preferences in the language of legal reasoning). I have called this view subjectivism. Subjectivism is commonly known today as legal realism, and it is found in comments like: "[J]udges pick and choose among these facts and the precedents they support in order to produce a decision most compatible with their policy preferences, while asserting—of course—that the chosen ones most accord with the facts of the case for decision."[4]

Subjectivism and strong objectivism are typically taken to be the opposite of one another, and we can see why. Strong objectivism means that judicial decisions should be determined only according to the law rather than a judge's subjective beliefs. Subjectivism means that judicial decisions are determined only by a judge's subjective beliefs rather than the law. This book offers a response and an alternative to these views. I began by explaining the inadequacy and inaccuracy of strong objectivism and subjectivism as approaches for attempting to understand law and judging. My argument is not that objectivity is irrelevant to an accurate conception of the judicial process. My argument is that strong objectivism cannot help us understand the law or the judicial process because the law and the judicial process are human creations, not natural objects. The meaning of the law simply cannot be perceived in the same manner as the shape of the Earth and cannot properly be understood according to the same mode of objectivism that may apply to the natural world.[5] Similarly, the meaning of the judicial process should not be conceived as an endeavor to locate a legal truth. As with strong objectivism as mind-independence, this notion of legal truth is misplaced. There is a meaningful understanding of truth that applies to the judicial process, but it is a legal truth that is produced through that process rather than an objective truth that is discovered by that process.[6]

Strong objectivism and subjectivism are equally inaccurate and implausible visions of law and judging. Once we have moved past them, we can begin to focus on alternative conceptions of objectivity that more accurately cohere with the common law tradition. I considered two of these alternative conceptions of objectivism, minimal and modest, and suggested another form, which I called mediated objectivism.[7] The common law creates additional complexities for these accounts of objectivism, however, because whichever conception of objectivism we prefer, we are still left with an unavoidable distinction between our conception of the objectivity of law and our conception of objectivity in judging.[8] As Connie Rosati has explained, thinking of law as minimally objective entails a conception of judging that she calls judicial majoritarianism (the law is what the majority of judges say it is).[9] But as Rosati observes, that view is reductive and distorts critical distinctions between existing law and adjudicated law.[10] Minimal objectivism also seems to gloss over the relationship between judges who issue judgments as members of a community and the community that then evaluates and instantiates the judgment's full meaning. Minimal objectivism does not seem to address the process of determining the "legal facts" in a jurisdiction, which consist of existing legal sources but are not fully determined by them.[11]

This leads to a further point about the dynamics of a judge and a community in presenting and evaluating judgments. As I discussed in the introduction, the core concern about subjectivity in judging—and the concomitant effort to argue for objectivity as the ideal of law and judging—is that judges will substitute their personal values for preexisting legal rules. I explained in chapter 2 that this concern is motivated by a mistaken conception of objectivity in law that has generated a false dichotomy between the subjective values of judges and the objective qualities of law. I argued that we need a more precise understanding of legal objectivity, and we need to distinguish objectivity from impartiality, so that we can arrive at a more accurate notion of legal validity.

As an alternative to the conventional approach, I argued for an understanding of judging that emphasizes the dynamics of an individual judicial response to a case that is communicated through recognized forms of legal argument to a larger community, which then evaluates and validates the judgment. To explain this dynamic, I drew parallels in chapter 3 between judging law in the common law tradition and judging art in Kantian aesthetic theory and argued for replacing the concepts of objectivity and truth with intersubjectivity and validity. I focused on four elements of Kant's theory: judgment, communication, community, and disinterestedness. As with Kant's aesthetic theory, common law judging involves a subjective and an intersubjective aspect. Common law judgments are an individual judge's considered assessment of the law's meaning and are claimed by that judge to be correct, not in the abstract sense of objective truth, but in the functional sense of shared modes of reasoning and expression that will lead other judges to the same conclusion. The judge who issues the judgment cannot make that determination for other judges, however. The judge communicates the judgment to the community and the community determines the judgment's meaning and status as a legal source through an intersubjective process of evaluation and validation.

Once we stop seeing subjectivity and objectivity as opposed to one another and instead begin to understand the relationship of a subject to an object, we can see that the process of judgment requires a judge's communication of a judgment of art or law to a community that shares the capacity to respond similarly. The judgment is a statement about the object being judged that must be communicated so that the community can evaluate the judgment. That process of intersubjective communication and evaluation is what determines the meaning of the judgment over time.

For example, we perceive this intersubjective process when a judge and a community begin to view a judgment that invalidates a law precluding two people of different races from marrying as a legal basis for a judgment that invalidates a law preventing two people of the same sex from marrying.[12] As Justice Kennedy explained in his *Obergefell* judgment, a judge's understanding of a constitutional right cannot be entirely excised or abstracted from his community's understanding of what it means to be denied that right:

> The limitation of marriage to opposite-sex couples may long have seemed natural and just, but its inconsistency with the central meaning of the

> fundamental right to marry is now manifest. With that knowledge must come the recognition that laws excluding same-sex couples from the marriage right impose stigma and injury of the kind prohibited by our basic charter. . . . If rights were defined by who exercised them in the past, then received practices could serve as their own continued justification and new groups could not invoke rights once denied. [R]ights come not from ancient sources alone. They arise, too, from a better informed understanding of how constitutional imperatives define a liberty that remains urgent in our own era.[13]

And judges occasionally acknowledge, as Kennedy did in *Obergefell*, the evolution of legal meaning that informs their judgments through their own responses, and the responses of other judges, to this evolution:

> The ancient origins of marriage confirm its centrality, but it has not stood in isolation from developments in law and society. The history of marriage is one of both continuity and change. That institution—even as confined to opposite-sex relations—has evolved over time. . . . Indeed, changed understandings of marriage are characteristic of a Nation where new dimensions of freedom become apparent to new generations, often through perspectives that begin in pleas or protests and then are considered in the political sphere and the judicial process. This dynamic can be seen in the Nation's experiences with the rights of gays and lesbians. Until the mid-20th century, same-sex intimacy long had been condemned as immoral by the state itself in most Western nations, a belief often embodied in the criminal law. . . . In the late 20th century, following substantial cultural and political developments, same-sex couples began to lead more open and public lives and to establish families. This development was followed by a quite extensive discussion of the issue in both governmental and private sectors and by a shift in public attitudes toward greater tolerance. As a result, questions about the rights of gays and lesbians soon reached the courts, where the issue could be discussed in the formal discourse of the law.[14]

The point here is not that proper judging (or judges) would require holding these observations in abeyance while making legal rulings. The point is that their legal judgments about concepts such as equal protection or due process (or, as I discussed in chapter 4, fair dealing or racial discrimination or marital relationships[15]) cannot possibly be reached in the absence of their subjective responses to the operation of these principles in the lives of litigants through the facts of the cases they decide. Indeed, one of the best demonstrations of this may be found in the fact that other judges who disagree with the interpretation or extension of these principles were able to anticipate the arc that the law would take through their courts' judgments. Justice Scalia's dissent in *Lawrence v. Texas* is perhaps the clearest prediction of the law's development on this point.[16]

To be sure, some judges believe that their favored approach to judging permits the courts to maintain their ostensibly proper role "of assuring, as neutral observer, that the democratic rules of engagement are observed."[17] My argument is not that judges should always simply follow an evolving understanding of social issues. My argument is that judges cannot reach judgments that do not involve a response, in one fashion or another, to that evolving understanding and to the law's operation in relation to it. In other words, Justice Kennedy and Justice Scalia are both incorporating their own understanding of the law's proper operation in regulating the intimate lives of certain individuals, regardless of whether they believe the Constitution prohibits or permits differentiating and disadvantaging people on the basis of their sexual orientation or gender expression. And Scalia, like Kennedy, incorporated into his judgments his assessment of broader social views toward the legal regulation of the intimate lives of gay people.[18]

The meaning of liberty and equality in constitutional law does not exist apart from what judges and their community understand these principles to mean in their application to the lives of those governed by these principles. Their meaning is developed through the process of judges communicating their understanding of these concepts in reasoned legal judgments and the community's evaluation and reception of these judgments. As I discussed in chapter 3, this process of communication and validation is dynamic and collaborative. Rather than viewing this process as an effort to locate the objective truth about constitutional principles, we need to recognize that the meaning of judgments in the common law tradition is developed through this interactive and intersubjective process. Together, judges and their communities determine the substantive content of judgments that explicate the fundamental legal principles that govern their lives and their society.[19]

The Subject and Object of Judging: Affirmative Action in Life and Law

The expectation that the ideal judge is one who eliminates her personal experiences and beliefs from her judging is, in fact, a claim that we can view the world without a viewpoint. As I have argued, even if this were possible, we should not desire it of our judges.[20] More to the point, though, I have argued that Kant's theory of aesthetic judgment and the common law's process of legal judgment help us to understand—as individual judges or as members of a community that validates judgments through a shared capacity to judge—the relationship between our world and our worldview.[21] Our understanding of the object (art or law) we are judging cannot exist apart from ourselves or the object; we help to determine the object's meaning, and the object helps us, through the process of reflective judgment, to understand ourselves. The concepts, terms, experiences, and perceptions that are invoked by the individual who judges are shared, in some important sense, by the community that evaluates the judgment. These frames help to constitute the objects for us as individuals and our community's shared understanding of them. The subject and the object, or the subjective and the objective, should be understood in their relationship to one another, rather than in opposition. Through this intersubjective process of judgment, communication, and validation, we construct the meaning of law or art and the standards according to which those judgments may properly be made, communicated, and validated.[22]

Comparing the experiences and judgments of Clarence Thomas and Sonia Sotomayor with regard to affirmative action will help us to explore this process of judgment as it operates in the decision making of judges. Justice Thomas has expressed his explicit disapproval of affirmative action in higher education admissions. His goal at Yale Law School, he wrote, was "to vanquish the perception that [he] was somehow inferior to his white classmates. . . . But it was futile for [him] to suppose that [he] could escape the stigmatizing effects of racial preference, and [he] began to fear that it would be used forever after to discount [his] achievements."[23] And Justice Thomas's concerns that affirmative action may reinforce stereotypes and undermine the achievements of minority students who benefit from the program are shared by others.[24]

Justice Thomas's personal experience with affirmative action has influenced his legal judgments. In his *Grutter* opinion, Thomas expresses the theme of the previous passage that affirmative action actually harms those it is meant to help: "The Law School is not looking for those students who, despite a lower LSAT score or undergraduate grade point average, will succeed in the study of law. The Law School seeks only a facade—it is sufficient that the class looks right, even if it does not perform right. And this mismatch crisis is not restricted to elite institutions."[25]

Thomas went on in *Grutter* to discuss his concern about affirmative action's possible stigmatizing effects in a passage that presages the thought expressed in his memoir:

> It is uncontested that each year, the Law School admits a handful of blacks who would be admitted in the absence of racial discrimination. Who can differentiate between those who belong and those who do not? The majority of blacks are admitted to the Law School because of discrimination, and because of this policy all are tarred as undeserving. This problem of stigma does not depend on determinacy as to whether those stigmatized are actually the "beneficiaries" of racial discrimination. When blacks take positions in the highest places of government, industry, or academia, it is an open question today whether their skin color played a part in their advancement. The question itself is the stigma—because either racial discrimination did play a role, in which case the person may be deemed "otherwise unqualified," or it did not, in which case asking the question itself unfairly marks those blacks who would succeed without discrimination.[26]

Thomas's view that affirmative action actually injures minorities through entrenched stigmatization of their abilities and achievements runs through his *Grutter* opinion, his other affirmative action opinions, and his extracurial writing.[27] Justice Thomas reiterated these same concerns in his concurring opinion in *Fisher*:

> [T]he University's discrimination 'stamp[s] [blacks and Hispanics] with a badge of inferiority.' It taints the accomplishments of all those who are admitted as a result of racial discrimination. And, it taints the accomplishments of all those who are the same race as those admitted as a result of racial discrimination. In this case, for example, most blacks and Hispanics attending the University were admitted without discrimination under the Top Ten Percent plan, but no one can distinguish those students from the ones whose race played a role in their admission. . . . Although cloaked in good intentions, the University's racial tinkering harms the very people it claims to be helping.[28]

Like Justice Thomas, Justice Sotomayor graduated from Yale Law School.[29] Like Thomas, Sotomayor acknowledges that her admission to Yale (and to Princeton for her undergraduate education) was due in part to affirmative action.[30] Like Thomas, Sotomayor describes an experience of sometimes feeling out of place at elite schools due to her less-privileged background.[31] Like Thomas, Sotomayor felt less well-prepared academically for the educational environment in which she found herself.[32] Like Thomas, Sotomayor was confronted with others' assumption that her admission was not earned and with her own anxiety that she might not succeed:

> *The Daily Princetonian* routinely published letters to the editor lamenting the presence on campus of "affirmative action students," each one of whom had presumably displaced a far more deserving affluent white male and could rightly be expected to crash into the gutter built of her own unrealistic aspirations. . . . The pressure to succeed was relentless, even if self-imposed out of fear and insecurity. For we all felt that if we did fail, we would be proving the critics right.[33]

And like Justice Thomas, Justice Sotomayor was confronted in her professional life with people who discounted her accomplishments by attributing them solely to affirmative action. In fact, they describe remarkably similar experiences in this regard.[34]

Nevertheless, Justice Sotomayor's view of affirmative action is entirely different from Justice Thomas's. Where Thomas sees an inescapable badge of inferiority, Sotomayor sees a worthwhile window of opportunity:

> I had no need to apologize that the look-wider, search-more affirmative action that Princeton and Yale practiced had opened doors for me. That was its purpose: to create the conditions whereby students from disadvantaged backgrounds could be brought to the starting line of a race many were unaware was even being run. I had been admitted to the Ivy League through a special door, and I had more ground than most to make up before I was competing with my classmates on an equal footing. But I worked relentlessly to reach that point.[35]

Informed by her experiences, the view of affirmative action Justice Sotomayor expresses in her memoir is echoed in her judicial opinions on the subject and is most evident in her dissenting opinion in *Schuette v. Coalition to Defend Affirmative Action*.[36] After the Court's *Grutter* decision, a majority of voters in Michigan approved an amendment to the state constitution that prohibited, among other things, any public college or university in Michigan from "discriminat[ing] against, or grant[ing] preferential treatment to, any individual or group on the basis of race, sex, color, ethnicity, or national origin."[37] This provision was challenged as an equal protection violation under the United States Constitution.

In *Schuette,* the majority of the Court[38] upheld the amendment to the Michigan constitution. In his opinion for a plurality of the Court, Justice Kennedy emphasized that *Schuette* was "not about the constitutionality, or the merits, of race-conscious admissions policies in higher education. . . . The question here concerns . . . whether, and in what manner, voters in the States may choose to prohibit the consideration of racial preferences in governmental decisions, in particular with respect to school admissions."[39] With that qualification, the Court ruled that the US Constitution did not prohibit voters from setting policy parameters in this fashion, provided that the political process is not used "to encourage infliction of injury by reason of race."[40] The Court did not view the electoral preclusion of affirmative action to be an injury.

Justice Sotomayor dissented. Joined by Justice Ginsburg, she drew upon the political-process doctrine established in *Hunter v. Erickson*[41] and *Washington v. Seattle School Dist. No. 1.*[42] As developed in *Hunter* and *Seattle,* the political-process doctrine prevents states not just from excluding or restricting the participation of racial minorities in the political process, but also from acting in a manner that will effectively "suppress the minority's right to participate on equal terms in the political process. Under this doctrine, governmental action deprives minority groups of equal protection when it (1) has a racial focus, targeting a policy or program that 'inures primarily to the benefit of the minority,' and (2) alters the political process in a manner that uniquely burdens racial minorities' ability to achieve their goals through that process."[43]

In Sotomayor's view, both prongs of the political-process doctrine were met in *Schuette.* First, the amendment to the Michigan constitution has a racial focus that is evident in the text itself.[44] Second, the amendment "establishes a distinct and more burdensome political process for the enactment of admissions plans that consider racial diversity."[45] The amendment therefore violates the political-process doctrine and denies equal protection to racial minorities in Michigan. To explain the practical effect of the amendment's alteration of the political process in Michigan, Sotomayor compares the relative advantages that (white) legacy applicants have in the admissions process to the relative challenges faced by other (minority) applicants who ask to have their racial diversity considered. The effective result of the amendment is "that a white graduate of a public Michigan university who wishes to pass his historical privilege on to his children may freely lobby the board of that university in favor of an expanded legacy admissions policy, whereas a black Michigander who was denied the opportunity to attend that very university cannot lobby the board in favor of a policy that might give his children a chance that he never had and that they might never have absent that policy."[46] In violation of *Hunter* and *Seattle*, the amendment "subtly distorts governmental processes in such a way as to place special burdens on the ability of minority groups to achieve beneficial legislation."[47] As things stand in Michigan, the only way for advocates of race-sensitive admissions to achieve their goal through the political process is an amendment of the state constitution.[48]

Justices Sotomayor and Thomas have explained their experiences with affirmative action and the divergent perspectives toward affirmative action that these experiences engendered. As a result of these experiences and perspectives, they disagree in their legal judgment regarding the constitutionality of affirmative action. Justice Sotomayor begins with "the common-sense reality that race-sensitive admissions policies benefit minorities."[49] This reality matters to her constitutional judgment because all state-implemented racial differentiations must satisfy strict scrutiny to be upheld as constitutional,[50] and increasing racial diversity among students at institutions of higher education has been held to satisfy the compelling state interest requirement of this test.[51] As a result of the Court's precedent with respect to determining the constitutionality of race-sensitive admissions processes, Justice Sotomayor's understanding of the benefits of affirmative action is linked to her judgment of its constitutionality. According to the Court's judgment in *Grutter*, affirmative action benefits the minority students who have the opportunity to attend a particular college or university as well as the white students who attend that college or university.[52] Applying the Court's precedent in light of her own experience, Sotomayor concludes that the benefits of diversity justify the race-sensitive admissions practice and satisfy the strict scrutiny standard: "race-sensitive admissions policies further a compelling state interest in achieving a diverse student body precisely because they increase minority enrollment, which necessarily benefits minority groups."[53]

Justice Thomas does not share Justice Sotomayor's reality. He disagrees with her about the benefits of race-sensitive admissions for minorities. In Thomas's view, as he expressed in his *Fisher* and *Grutter* opinions, affirmative action actually harms minority students by undermining the achievements of those students who would be admitted in the absence of the admissions program and by placing unprepared students in a competitive academic environment in which they are unable to succeed:

> I must contest the notion that the Law School's discrimination benefits those admitted as a result of it. . . . [N]owhere in any of the filings in this Court is any evidence that the purported "beneficiaries" of this racial discrimination prove themselves by performing at (or even near) the same level as those students who receive no preferences. . . . The Law School tantalizes unprepared students with the promise of a University of Michigan degree and all of the opportunities that it offers. These overmatched students take the bait, only to find that they cannot succeed in the cauldron of competition.[54]

Just as Sotomayor's application of the political-process doctrine in *Schuette* derives from her belief in the benefits of affirmative action as a result of her personal experiences and values, Thomas's conclusion in *Grutter* and *Fisher* that affirmative action is unconstitutional derives from his belief in the harms of affirmative action as a result of his personal experiences and values.

In relation to this book's argument, the disagreement between Justice Sotomayor and Justice Thomas concerning affirmative action usefully illuminates the relationship between a judge's personal experiences and legal judgments. Justices Sotomayor and Thomas have developed different and defensible understandings of the constitutional principle of equal protection as a result of their experiences as racial minorities in the United States. Broadly speaking, Sotomayor regards the principal value of equal protection as antisubordination, while Thomas sees the principal value of equal protection as anticlassification.[55] Rather than fixate upon the experiences that inform their judgments, or valorize a conception of judging that is abstracted from personal experiences and values, we should instead recognize that the judgments themselves are their contribution to the law's meaning and development. These varying understandings of the underlying value of equal protection are translated through Thomas's judgments in *Grutter* and *Fisher* and through Sotomayor's judgment in *Schuette*. And the merits of their respective judgments can be determined only after their evaluation and reception by a larger community. As I mentioned in chapter 3, the intersubjective validity of a judgment ultimately depends upon a judge's ability to claim that others will agree with her reasoning and share her assessment. As a considered articulation of a legal conclusion, a judge who bases her ruling on personal biases rather than on careful reasoning cannot reasonably claim the assent of other judges and has thereby preemptively sacrificed her own ability to contribute to our shared understanding of our law.[56] At the same time, the recognition that the subject who authors a judgment must draw upon her experiences and values in articulating the judgment does not defeat the object of producing a judgment that can be evaluated and validated as an abiding contribution to our community's law.

Reading Judges and Reading Judgments

The same is true for the community that evaluates and validates the judgment. It must be evaluated in accordance with the concepts, terms, and processes of reasoning of the relevant legal tradition and culture and not the prejudices or biases of particular members of the community. Again, Justices Thomas and Sotomayor provide useful examples. Just as the black community (or the politically conservative community) does not think with one mind or in one way about racially charged issues, Justice Thomas's views of these constitutional questions cannot simply be itemized and categorized. He opposes affirmative action. He also views cross burning as a form of racial intimidation that is not protected by the First Amendment.[57] His understanding of these legal issues cannot be disconnected completely from his experiences and values.

During her time on the United States Court of Appeals for the Second Circuit, Justice Sotomayor decided a case involving a claim that a promotion test administered by the New Haven Fire Department had a disparate negative impact on black firefighters. In that case, *Ricci v. DeStefano*,[58] Sotomayor joined two colleagues in upholding the District Court's ruling that the promotion exam "results showed a racially adverse impact on African-American candidates for both the Lieutenant and Captain positions."[59] *Ricci* became a flashpoint during Sotomayor's confirmation hearings before the Senate Judiciary Committee. The allegation at those hearings was that as a Latina, Sotomayor was partial to the African American firefighters because they were racial minorities. Here are Senator Jeff Sessions' comments at the hearings on the *Ricci* case:

> [A]s a lower court judge, our nominee has made some troubling rulings. I am concerned by *Ricci*, the *New Haven Firefighters* case—recently reversed by the Supreme Court—where she agreed with the City of New Haven's

> decision to change the promotion rules in the middle of the game. Incredibly, her opinion consisted of just one substantive paragraph of analysis. Judge Sotomayor has said that she accepts that her opinions, sympathies, and prejudices will affect her rulings. Could it be that her time as a leader in the Puerto Rican Legal Defense and Education Fund, a fine organization, provides a clue to her decision against the firefighters? . . . It seems to me that in *Ricci*, Judge Sotomayor's empathy for one group of firefighters turned out to be prejudice against another.[60]

What Senator Sessions chose to overlook, and what was far less widely discussed during Justice Sotomayor's hearings, was that Sotomayor wound up ruling against a Latino firefighter in *Ricci*.[61] And, of course, Sotomayor's legal judgment was shared by the other two judges on the Second Circuit panel, the District Judge whose opinion they upheld, the other six Second Circuit judges who voted to deny an *en banc* rehearing of the case, and the four Supreme Court justices who would have upheld the Second Circuit ruling. Moreover, one of the judges who voted with Justice Sotomayor against the *en banc* rehearing in *Ricci*, Barrington Parker Jr., is black and was nominated to the Second Circuit by President George W. Bush,[62] and one of the judges who voted to rehear the case as an *en banc* panel, José Cabranes, is Latino and was nominated by President Bill Clinton (and is regarded by Justice Sotomayor as "the first person [she] can describe as a true mentor"[63]).

In the introduction, I explored Justice Sotomayor's now familiar "wise Latina" comment and the intense reaction and discussion it provoked during her confirmation hearings before the Senate Judiciary Committee. Justice Sotomayor recognized that who she is as a person would influence who she is as a judge. Controversial as her comment may be, it is true of every judge. As I explained in chapter 2, it is true of Justice Ginsburg, and as I explained here, it is just as true of Justice Thomas as it is of Justice Sotomayor. Justice Thomas's personal experiences and values have led to his broader perspective as a politically conservative black man,[64] and this perspective informs his view of the constitutionality of affirmative action. The same is true of Justice Sotomayor's experiences and values as a Latina informing her view of affirmative action. Their experiences have been translated into individual perspectives and opinions concerning the meaning and scope of equal protection under the law of the Constitution. Counting judges' votes, or categorizing their race, are inadequate means of attempting to understand fully the judges or their votes. We would be better served by carefully analyzing their judgments.

Common Law Judgment

Discussions of objectivity in law and judging ultimately result in efforts to place law, judging, and judges in some designated category rather than to help us understand the relationship of a judge to the law in the process of formulating a judgment. The preoccupation with identifying the correct form of objectivity for law assumes there is only one form that is correct, and it fails to account for the distinction between the existing sources of law and the law that is made through judicial interpretation and application of these sources. The law that exists at the start of the adjudicative process and the law that is made, interpreted, or applied through that process are determined, in part, by the judge's subjective beliefs, values, and perspectives toward the law as expressed to a community through the form of a legal judgment. The meaning of that legal judgment is then constructed by the community through a process of evaluation and reception. Objectivity is not the best concept for attempting to capture this dynamic, because the law's meaning cannot be identified without reference to the judge's values and the community's evaluation.

Attempting to fit law into a form of objectivity leads us to ask whether the meaning of law is "judgment-dependent" (minimal or modest objectivism) or "judgment-independent" (strong objectivism).[65] Inevitably, this requires us to debate the meanings of objectivity rather than the meaning of law or the process of judging. Moreover, framing the debate in these "either-or" terms has led people for generations to ask whether the meaning of the judgment is "law-dependent" (formalism) or "law-independent" (realism). And the well-worn path of this debate quickly brings us back around to the strong objectivism of formalism and the subjectivism of realism.

In arguing for an understanding of common law adjudication through a process of intersubjective communication and validation, this book challenges the paired views that objectivity is the goal of judging and that subjectivity threatens the integrity of the judicial process. Rather than assume that judges should disengage or disregard their personal values and perspectives when they write their judgments, I have argued that a subjective element in common law judging is inescapable and is in fact one of the central values of a legal tradition that expects its judges to contribute to the law's development. We need to see that the meaning of the law depends upon the identifiable content of the legal sources and upon the meaning of those sources to judges who bring different experiences, values, and perspectives to their reading and application of the sources. The content of the law is neither determined by the judge's values alone nor can it be fully understood as sequestered entirely from those values. Likewise, the meaning of a judgment is neither fully determined apart from the content of the existing law nor can it be fully understood in the absence of its communication to and evaluation by a larger legal and political and social community.

We need to consider the difference between the law that a judge considers in formulating her judgment and the law that is made through the process of issuing her judgment. Judges occupy the unique institutional and individual position in the common law tradition of defining the law in the course of reaching their judgments and making or altering the law once their judgments are expressed. Indeed, the common law process does not end with the issuance of the judgment to the community. The community constitutes itself as a community governed by law through an intersubjective process of evaluating the judgment and determining its lasting validity as a legal source. The rule-of-law values of the common law tradition require that a legal system's constitutional principles are never wholly encompassed by a constitution, even if that constitution is written.

The common law attempts to protect the constitutional values of its tradition by protecting the institutional and individual independence of its judges. The common law tradition of judicial independence ensures that judges may determine for themselves what the law means and how it should be applied, which also necessitates that a judge's values and perspectives will influence what she understands the law to mean and how she believes it should be applied. I argued in chapter 5 that the institutional independence of the judiciary exists to ensure this individual independence of judges in determining for themselves which sources they will consider in rendering their judgments, and I examined some judgments that changed and developed the law in the United States and the United Kingdom. In developing property, tort, criminal, and constitutional law, these cases serve as concrete examples of legal judgments that express the individual responses of the judges who decided them.

Whatever a judge's experiences may be, as a wise Latina or as a black man who was raised by his grandfather in Georgia or as a Jewish woman who lived through World War II, those experiences will influence the way that judge understands the facts and the law of any case. Every judge's values are created by means of experiences that inform the perspective through which that judge understands the law. We should therefore select our judges carefully. But we should not deny the cumulative value of these experiences in the judicial process by which judges contribute to a shared understanding of the legal values that help to constitute our community and the standards by which we govern ourselves.

Table of Authorities

Cases Cited

UNITED KINGDOM

UNITED STATES

Statutes Cited

UNITED KINGDOM

Other Sources

Notes

Chapter 1

1. David Bell, *The Art of Judgement*, 96 Mind 221, 222 (1987).

2. Sonia Sotomayor, *A Latina Judge's Voice*, 13 Berkeley La Raza L.J. 87, 92 (2002).

3. The question whether empathy is a quality we should seek or avoid in our judges was triggered by President Obama's comment concerning the individual he would wish to appoint to replace Justice Souter: "I view that quality of empathy, of understanding and identifying with people's hopes and struggles, as an essential ingredient for arriving at just decisions and outcomes." For the full text of President Obama's comment, *see* David Jackson, "Obama's Friday Remarks on Souter and the Court," *USA Today*, May 1, 2009. For an interesting discussion and defense of a role for empathy in judicial decision making, *see* Lucia Corso, *Should Empathy Play Any Role in the Interpretation of Constitutional Rights?*, 27 Ratio Juris 94 (2014). Corso differentiates an "epistemic view" of empathy from a "moral view," explains that genuine empathy requires an individual who is neither indifferent to the experiences of others nor overly emotional about them, and concludes that "empathy may be seen as a quality of good judgment, for it allows a more profound understanding of the needs put forward in the legal claims and hence a better insight into the factual/legal issues [of a case]." *Id.* at 100.

4. Nomination of Sonia Sotomayor to be an Associate Justice of the Supreme Court of the United States: Confirmation Hearing Before the S. Comm. on the Judiciary, 111th Cong. (2009) [Sotomayor Hearings], 16–17, 18.

5. *See, e.g., Id.* at 8 (Sen. Jeff Sessions: "Judge Sotomayor has said that she accepts that her opinions, sympathies, and prejudices will affect her rulings."); *Id.* at 13 (Sen. Orrin Hatch: "Must judges set aside or may judges consider their personal feelings in deciding cases? Is judicial impartiality a duty or an option? Does the fact that judicial decisions affect so many people's lives require judges to be objective and impartial? Or does it allow them to be subjective and sympathetic?"); *Id.* at 23 (Sen. Jon Kyl: "Judge Sotomayor clearly rejected the notion that judges should strive for an impartial brand of justice. She has already accepted that her gender and Latina heritage will affect the outcome of her cases."); *Id.* at 39 (Sen. Tom Coburn: "[I]t shouldn't matter which judge you get. It should matter what the law is and the facts are. . . . And if we disregard objective consideration of facts, then all rulings are subjective. . . . [Y]our questioning of whether the application of impartiality in judging, including transcending personal sympathies and prejudices, is possible in most cases or is even desirable is extremely

troubling to me."). Senators Coburn, Grassley, Hatch, Kyl, and Sessions voted against confirming Justice Sotomayor.

6. *See, e.g.*, Nomination of Samuel A. Alito, Jr. to be an Associate Justice of the Supreme Court of the United States: Confirmation Hearing Before the S. Comm. on the Judiciary, 109th Cong. (2006), 475 ("[W]hen a case comes before me involving, let's say, someone who is an immigrant, and we get an awful lot of immigration cases and naturalization cases, I can't help but think of my own ancestors because it wasn't that long ago when they were in that position. And so it's my job to apply the law. It's not my job to change the law or to bend the law to achieve any results, but I have to, when I look at those cases, I have to say to myself, and I do say to myself, this could be your grandfather. This could be your grandmother. They were not citizens at one time and they were people who came to this country. When I have cases involving children, I can't help but think of my own children and think about my children being treated in the way that children may be treated in the case that's before me. And that goes down the line. When I get a case about discrimination, I have to think about people in my own family who suffered discrimination because of their ethnic background or because of religion or because of gender, and I do take that into account. When I have a case involving someone who's been subjected to discrimination because of disability, I have to think of people who I've known and admired very greatly who had disabilities and I've watched them struggle to overcome the barriers that society puts up, often just because it doesn't think of what it's doing, the barriers that it puts up to them. So those are some of the experiences that have shaped me as a person.") Justice Alito was responding to this question from Senator Coburn: "This booklet is design to protect the weak, to give equality to those who might not be able to do it themselves, to protect the frail, to make sure that there is equal justice under the law. . . . Can you comment just about Sam Alito and what he cares about and let us see a little bit of your heart and what is important to you and why?"). *Id.* at 474–75. Senators Coburn, Grassley, Hatch, Kyl, and Sessions voted in favor of confirming Justice Alito.

7. Sotomayor Hearings, 545, 546 (Statement of Professor Neomi Rao).

8. For an excellent study of this issue, *see* Christopher L. Eisgruber, *The Next Justice: Repairing the Supreme Court Appointments Process* (Princeton University Press, 2007).

9. A statement by Justice Sotomayor (which was joined by Justice Breyer) serves as an example of what I mean here. Justice Sotomayor joined a unanimous vote of the Supreme Court to deny certiorari, despite racially inflammatory comments made by a federal prosecutor during cross-examination of a defendant, because the defendant's attorney did not challenge those comments at trial and then failed to raise the issue on appeal. Justice Sotomayor agreed that given the posture in which the case was presented to the Court, the Court could not properly review (or reverse) the outcome, due to the proceedings in the lower courts. But she still wrote separately "to dispel any doubt whether the Court's denial of certiorari should be understood to signal our tolerance of a federal prosecutor's racially charged remark" and to reaffirm that a prosecutor may not "attempt to substitute racial stereotype for evidence, and racial prejudice for reason." *Calhoun v. United States*, 133 S. Ct. 1136, 1136, 1137 (2013).

10. *See* Richard A. Posner, *How Judges Think* (Harvard University Press, 2008), 106 ("Indignation at a wrong is consistent with corrective justice; sympathy for a litigant

is not. The character of an emotional reaction . . . does not make emotion always an illegitimate or even a bad ground for a judicial decision. . . . Emotion can be a form of thought, though compressed and inarticulate. It is triggered by, and more often than not produces rational responses to, information."). Judge Posner's comments are helpful in seeing the difference between improper bias toward an individual litigant and appropriate individual responses to the facts and issues raised in a case. *See also* Martha C. Nussbaum, *Emotion in the Language of Judging*, 70 St. John's L. Rev. 23, 30 (1996) ("[E]motion that is tethered to the evidence and free from reference to one's own personal goals and situation is not only acceptable, but actually essential to public judgment.").

11. *See* Matthew H. Kramer, *Objectivity and the Rule of Law* (Cambridge University Press, 2007), 38–41. *See also* H. L. A. Hart, *The Concept of Law* (3rd ed.) (Oxford University Press, 2012), 161 ("[T]o apply a law justly to different cases is simply to take seriously the assertion that what is to be applied in different cases is the same general rule, without prejudice, interest, or caprice.").

12. *See, e.g.*, William N. Eskridge, Jr., *The New Textualism*, 37 UCLA L. Rev. 621, 646 (1990) ("[J]udicial interpreters can and should be tightly constrained by the objectively determinable meaning of a statute; if unelected judges exercise much discretion in these cases, democratic governance is threatened.") (Eskridge is characterizing formalism). As I will explain in more detail in the next chapter, the notion that the objective meaning of a law is determined by its written language is a point that is easily misunderstood. Many people assume that the writing of the law must constrain its meaning (which it often does). But as Tara Smith has explained, the writing of the law also allows the law to function as an external constraint precisely because its linguistic meaning is open-ended. *See* Tara Smith, *Originalism's Misplaced Fidelity: "Original" Meaning Is Not Objective*, 26 Const. Comment. 1, 34, 35 (2009) ("I would readily agree that the fact that our constitution is written, as well as what is written, must constrain contemporary judges. Given the objective character of concepts, however, we must interpret the written law accordingly. The point of writing law is to make the law knowable to all. That purpose could not be achieved if the written words were understood subjectively, as, in effect, a private code that referred only to the contents of particular individuals' heads. . . . [I]n applying the law, we do not employ subjective criteria of meaning. Laws do not govern only those people who share the exact same experiences and beliefs as the authors of a law. My misunderstanding of a particular law neither exempts me from the obligation to obey that law nor alters what it is that I must obey. In practice, that is, we routinely recognize that the written law's meaning is objective. Indeed, it is the objective, open-ended character of concepts that enables the law to govern prospectively. The application of a law written in the 18th century to disputes in the 21st rests on the premise that language refers to a greater number of instances than a law's authors may have experienced or imagined. Far from posing a threat to the objectivity of law . . . the open-endedness of concepts is what allows the law to be applied objectively.").

13. *Marbury v. Madison*, 5 U.S. (1 Cranch) 137, 163 (1803). It is no small irony that this canonical statement of Anglo-American rule-of-law values, which is so often quoted as countervailing unbridled judicial authority, appears in the most seminal claim of judicial authority by a judge in a judicial opinion in Anglo-American legal

history. It is also worth noting that all governments of laws are also governments of men and women, because all human laws are made by human beings. *See, e.g.*, John Gardner, *Law as a Leap of Faith: Essays on Law in General* (Oxford University Press, 2012), 85, 86 ("All three of the types of law I discussed here are types of positive law. They are all made by somebody and we know that they count as law only when we know who made them. Legislated law is made by legislators. Case law is made by judges. Customary law is made by (official or non-official) populations. . . . [T]here is no such thing as non-positive law. There are no legal norms that come into existence without being brought into existence by someone."); Thomas Aquinas, *The Treatise on Law* (R. J. Henle, ed.) (University of Notre Dame Press, 1993), 38 ("Positive law (variously called 'human law,' 'man-made law,' 'civil law,' 'municipal law') is the law produced by human legal institutions.") (this quote is from Henle, not from Aquinas himself).

14. *See, e.g.*, Joseph Isenbergh, *Activists Vote Twice*, 70 U. Chi. L. Rev. 159, 160 (2003) ("By judicial activism I mean the decision of cases according to the judges' preferences. Its opposite, for present purposes, is adjudication according to neutral principles without regard for preference. An activist judge, in other words, gives effect to preference over the objective meaning of the law when they conflict.")

15. *See, e.g.*, John W. Salmond, ed., *The Science of Legal Method* (Macmillan, 1921), lxxv ("[T]he law presents itself primarily and essentially as a system of rigid rules in accordance with which justice is administered . . . to the exclusion of the unrestricted judicial discretion of the judges . . .").

16. *See, e.g.*, Laura Kalman, *The Strange Career of Legal Liberalism* (Yale University Press, 1996), 5 ("Once the legal realists had questioned the existence of principled decision making, academic lawyers spent the rest of the twentieth century searching for criteria that would enable them to identify objectivity in judicial decisions.").

17. *See, e.g.*, Mark A. Graber, *Resolving Political Questions Into Judicial Questions: Tocqueville's Thesis Revisited*, 21 Const. Comment. 485, 502 (2004) ("The central creed of much judicial behaviorism [is] that judicial decisions are made on the basis of judges' political preferences rather than legal rules.").

18. *See, e.g.*, Michael J. Gerhardt, *The Power of Precedent* (Oxford University Press, 2008), 80 ("[A]ttitudinalists and rational choice theorists generally claim the Court primarily functions as a cipher for justices' expressions of their individual preferences.").

19. *See, e.g.*, Antonin Scalia, *Originalism: The Lesser Evil*, 57 U. Cin. L. Rev. 849, 863, 864 (1989) ("Now the main danger in judicial interpretation of the Constitution—or, for that matter, in judicial interpretation of any law—is that the judges will mistake their own predilections for the law. . . . Originalism . . . establishes a historical criterion that is conceptually quite separate from the preferences of the judge himself.").

20. *See, e.g.*, Antonin Scalia, *A Matter of Interpretation: Federal Courts and the Law* (Princeton University Press, 1997), 25 ("[T]o abandon textualism . . . [is] to render democratically adopted texts mere springboards for judicial lawmaking.").

21. *See generally* Hart, *The Concept of Law*, 129–36 (describing legal formalism's response to the "open texture" of legal language as an overemphasis on the ability of preexisting legal rules to resolve legal disputes).

22. *See* Hart, *The Concept of Law*, 136–47.

23. *See generally* W. Preston Warren, *Modes of Objectivity*, 39 Phil. & Phenomenological Res. 74, 77–78 (1978) ("[S]tructure is a mode of objectivity. . . . Social structures are diversely institutional. . . . Social structures afford clear examples of two modes of existential objectivity. They are communally transindividual, and they are in certain ways, directly functional. . . . Communication indeed can be primarily suggestive, inducing feeling tones and appropriate responses but also inducing what intelligence discovers to be very inappropriate responses. . . . But the process of feedback may soon bring correction. Here we have the basis for intersubjectivity but through objective channels grounded in other objective conditions."). I explain in chapters 2 and 3 that the objective conditions and channels of the judicial institution create the constraints within which the individual judge's decision is communicated and received. And I explore the ways these objective conditions and channels create and constrain the intersubjective process of evaluating the individual judgment.

24. *See* Nicos Stavropoulos, *Objectivity in Law* (Oxford University Press, 1996), 6 ("The central questions of jurisprudence are domain-specific, not global. Arguments against the possibility of objectivity in law are not to do with the concept of truth *in abstracto*, but with the nature of law in particular. . . . I shall argue for a kind of objectivity that is consistent with the anti-realist slogan that 'meaning depends on use', and that needs no fact in virtue of which a judgment that a concept applies to a case is true, other than the ordinary theoretical support such a judgment must rely on.").

25. Barbara Herrnstein Smith, *Belief and Resistance: Dynamics of Contemporary Intellectual Controversy* (Harvard University Press, 1997), 22. Smith discusses legal judgment specifically, although her arguments range far more broadly. For my purposes, however, I mean to limit my reference to her work to a legal context.

26. President George W. Bush, State of the Union Address (Jan. 31, 2006).

27. Todd E. Pettys, *Judicial Discretion in Constitutional Cases*, 26 J. L. & Politics 123, 129 (2011) (Pettys is not describing his own view in the quotation).

28. Jonathan R. Macey, *Promoting Public-Regarding Legislation Through Statutory Interpretation: An Interest Group Model*, 86 Colum. L. Rev. 223, 239 (1986).

29. Tom Dannenbaum, *Nationality and the International Judge: The Nationalist Presumption Governing the International Judiciary and Why It Must Be Reversed*, 45 Cornell Int'l L. J. 77, 109 (2012).

30. I address this point in detail in chapter 4.

31. *See* Kent Greenawalt, *Discretion and Judicial Decision: The Elusive Quest for the Fetters that Bind Judges*, 75 Colum. L. Rev. 359 (1975) (discussing and debunking critiques of judicial legislation).

32. *See* below at 77–78.

33. *See, e.g.*, Anke Freckmann and Thomas Wegerich, *The German Legal System* (Sweet & Maxwell, 1999), 182–84 (describing the German jury system); Doris Marie Provine, "Courts in the Political Process in France," in Herbert Jacob, *et al.*, *Courts, Law, and Politics in Comparative Perspective* (Yale University Press, 1996), 213–15 (describing the French jury system).

34. The German Federal Constitutional Court is probably the best-known example of a court in a civil law nation that was created to employ broader powers of legal interpretation and exposition. *See generally* Donald P. Kommers and Russell A. Miller, *The Constitutional Jurisprudence of the Federal Republic of Germany* (3rd ed.) (Duke Uni-

versity Press, 2012), chap. 1 (providing a thorough and accessible description of the origins and functions of the Court). *See also* John Henry Merryman and Rogelio Pérez-Perdomo, *The Civil Law Tradition: An Introduction to the Legal Systems of Europe and Latin America* (3rd ed.) (Stanford University Press, 2007), 157–58.

35. *See* Merryman and Pérez-Perdomo, *The Civil Law Tradition*, 36–37. As Merryman and Pérez-Perdomo indicate, the traditional understanding of the civil law judicial function is incomplete but pervasive. *See id.* at 46–47.

36. *See* Konrad Zweigert and Hein Kötz, *Introduction to Comparative Law* (3rd ed.) (Oxford University Press, 1998), 69–70, 181; H. Patrick Glenn, *Legal Traditions of the World: Sustainable Diversity in Law* (5th ed.) (Oxford University Press, 2014), 152–55.

37. I do not want to oversimplify what is not overly simple even within the civil law tradition. For example, the German Civil Code emphasizes exactitude and certainty while the French Code was meant to permit some space for judicial interpretation. *See* Zweigert and Kötz, *Introduction to Comparative Law*, 89–93, 262–63.

38. *See* Merryman and Pérez-Perdomo, *The Civil Law Tradition*, 62–65. An element of this feature of the civil law tradition, as it evolved in Germany, was the effort to locate the law's political morality wholly within the law's text and proper application. Judicial decisions were meant to be validated solely by reference to the posited content of the law. As it happened, however, this may have resulted in the substitution of judicial values that are, by definition, external to the law's content in place of (and contrary to) the scientifically derived meaning of the law. *See* Roger Berkowitz, *The Gift of Science: Leibniz and the Modern Legal Tradition* (Harvard University Press, 2005), 156–57 ("Against all previous scientific codes that sought to actualize an ideal of reasoned justice, the BGB offers a wholly technical *Recht* in the service of equally allotted social and economic values. . . . *Recht* is not, as it was for Leibniz and Savigny, a product of necessary scientific knowing of the ethical world. And yet *Recht* continues to be known as a product of science. . . . *Recht*, in other words, is the means for the achievement of the ends adopted by the jurists who form and administer the scientifically constructed legal order."). *See also id.* at 107–8. In Berkowitz's view, the "relentless pursuit of truth" envisioned by thinking of law as science ultimately leads to the submission of law to political ends. *See id.* at 158. In terms of the argument of this book, we might say that the truth in the law's application through judicial reasoning cannot be located beyond the communication and validation of the judgment itself as a source of law. Put differently, in creating space for judicial values *within* a process of legal reasoning we allow for a method of legal development through legal judgments that engage the dynamics of political morality along with the distinctive authority of legal sources.

39. *See* Zweigert and Kötz, *Introduction to Comparative Law*, 258–59.

40. *See* Zweigert and Kötz, *Introduction to Comparative Law*, 264–65.

41. *See* Freckmann and Wegerich, *The German Legal System*, 97–98.

42. *See* Kommers and Miller, *The Constitutional Jurisprudence of the Federal Republic of Germany*, 46–47.

43. *See, e.g.*, Glenn, *Legal Traditions of the World*, 238 ("The only avenue for a Norman legal order, common to the realm, was through a loyal judiciary. This immediately marks off a common law tradition from all others.").

44. *See* Robert P. Burns, *A Theory of the Trial* (Princeton University Press, 1999), 14 nn. 16–17, and accompanying text. *See also id.* at 129–31.

45. *See* below at 29–30.

46. *See* R. C. van Caenegem, *European Law in the Past and the Future: Unity and Diversity over Two Millennia* (Cambridge University Press, 2002), 44–45. Of course, some judges rely on their clerks to draft their opinions. These opinions also reflect their author's personality.

47. *See generally* Jeffrey A. Segal, Harold J. Spaeth, and Sara C. Benesh, *The Supreme Court in the American Legal System* (Cambridge University Press, 2005), 16 ("Given (1) that different courts and judges do not reach a common decision about a given case, (2) that appellate court decisions—especially those of the Supreme Court—commonly contain dissents, and (3) that a change in a court's membership not atypically produces a different result, why do so many persist in believing that judicial decisions are objective, dispassionate, and impartial?").

48. R. Kent Newmyer, *The Supreme Court under Marshall and Taney* (Crowell, 1968), 16.

49. *See* Timothy R. Johnson, *Oral Arguments and Decision Making on the United States Supreme Court* (State University of New York Press, 2004), 14–17.

50. For an early statement of this point by an individual who truly appreciated its importance, *see* Edward Coke, "Preface to Part Nine of the *Reports*," in 1 *The Selected Writings of Sir Edward Coke*, ed. Steve Sheppard (Liberty Fund, 2003), 307 ("For it is one amongst others of the great honours of the Common Laws, that Cases of great difficulty are never adjudged or resolved *in tenebris* [in darkness] or *sub silentio suppressis rationibus* [in silence suppressing the reasons]; but in open Court, and there upon solemn and elaborate Arguments, first at the Bar by the Counsel learned of either party . . . and after at the Bench by the Judges . . . declaring at large the authorities, reasons and causes of their Judgments and Resolutions in every such particular Case.") (footnote omitted).

51. *See, e.g.*, Lewis F. Powell, Jr., "What Really Goes On at the Supreme Court," in David M. O'Brien, ed., *Judges on Judging: Views from the Bench* (4th ed.) (CQ Press, 2013), 129 ("It is fortunate that our system, unlike that in many other countries, invites and respects the function of dissenting opinions. The very process of dissent assures a rigorous testing of the majority view within the Court itself, and reduces the chance of arbitrary decision making . . . the forceful dissent of today may attract a majority vote in some future year."); Benjamin N. Cardozo, *The Nature of the Judicial Process* (Yale University Press, 1921), 79 ("It is the dissenting opinion of Justice Holmes [in *Lochner v. New York*, 198 U.S. 45, 25 S.Ct. 539, 49 L.Ed. 937 (1905)], which men will turn to in the future as the beginning of an era. In the instance, it was the voice of a minority. In principle, it has become the voice of a new dispensation, which has written itself into law."). *See* below at 172–73n198, 186n68, 187n77.

52. *See* Richard A. Posner, *The Problems of Jurisprudence* (Harvard University Press, 1990), 79–80; Louis L. Jaffe, *English and American Judges as Lawmakers* (Oxford University Press, 1969), 45–46; Richard A. Posner, *Legal Reasoning From the Top Down and From the Bottom Up: The Question of Unenumerated Constitutional Rights*, 59 U. Chi. L. Rev. 433, 447 (1992).

53. And any judge might get something wrong. *See Buck v. Bell*, 274 U.S. 200, 207 (1927) ("We have seen more than once that the public welfare may call upon the best citizens for their lives. It would be strange if it could not call upon those who already sap the strength of the State for these lesser sacrifices, often not felt to be such by those

concerned, in order to prevent our being swamped with incompetence. It is better for all the world, if instead of waiting to execute degenerate offspring for crime, or to let them starve for their imbecility, society can prevent those who are manifestly unfit from continuing their kind. The principle that sustains compulsory vaccination is broad enough to cover cutting the Fallopian tubes. Three generations of imbeciles are enough.") (Holmes, J.) (footnote and citation omitted).

54. *See, e.g.*, Benjamin N. Cardozo, *Law and Literature and Other Essays and Addresses* (Harcourt, Brace and Co., 1931), 36 ("More truly characteristic of dissent is a dignity, an elevation, of mood and thought and phrase. Deep conviction and warm feeling are saying their last say with knowledge that the cause is lost. The voice of the majority may be that of force triumphant, content with the plaudits of the hour, and recking little of the morrow. The dissenter speaks to the future, and his voice is pitched to a key that will carry through the years.").

55. *See* Jules L. Coleman and Brian Leiter, *Determinacy, Objectivity, and Authority*, 142 U. Pa. L. Rev. 549, 601–7 (1993).

56. *See* Coleman and Leiter, *Determinacy, Objectivity, and Authority*, 607–21.

57. *See, e.g.*, John Bell, "The Acceptability of Legal Arguments," in Neil MacCormick and Peter Birks, eds., *The Legal Mind: Essays for Tony Honoré* (Oxford University Press, 1986), 51–57 (discussing the use of "a set of criteria against which the acceptability of legal arguments can be judged," which Bell calls a canon, and describing the "legal audience" or a smaller "sub-group of the legal profession" as the community that ultimately determines the acceptability and meaning of legal judgments); Dennis Patterson, *Normativity and Objectivity in Law*, 43 Wm. & Mary L. Rev. 325, 328–29 (2001) ("I want to replace the conventional understanding of objectivity with an account of the notion that grows out of the actual practice of law. My claim is that the normativity and objectivity of legal judgment is a function not of the way the world is, but is forged in community agreement over time. . . . Law exhibits an argumentative framework employed by participants in legal practice to show the truth of legal propositions. . . . Objectivity is a product of the recursive use of this argumentative framework."). *See also* Kramer, *Objectivity and the Rule of Law*, 123 ("[T]he clarity of legal language is not to be gauged principally by reference to an ordinary person's understanding and knowledge. . . . Instead, the chief touchstone for the understandability of the formulations of legal norms is the competent legal expert's comprehension.").

58. *See* Brian Leiter, *Objectivity and the Problems of Jurisprudence*, 72 Tex. L. Rev. 187, 194–95 (1993). *See also* Kramer, *Objectivity and the Rule of Law*, 47 ("[E]pistemic objectivity . . . is a scalar property rather than an all-or-nothing property. Things partake of it to varying degrees. An area of enquiry can be epistemically more objective or less objective than any number of other areas of enquiry.").

59. *See, e.g.*, S. L. Hurley, *Natural Reasons: Personality and Polity* (Oxford University Press, 1989), 14–15 ("Of all the possible objectivist positions available in the logical space left by the denial of subjectivism, [strong objectivity] is one of the least tempting. Hardly anyone holds it, there is little point in arguing against it, and there is not very much to say about it. Any subjectivists who take it to be their most serious opposition are wasting their time on a straw man, and underestimating the strength of their objectivist opposition.").

60. *See, e.g.*, Michael Moore, *Moral Reality*, 1982 Wis. L. Rev. 1061 (1982); Michael Moore, *A Natural Law Theory of Interpretation*, 58 S. Cal. L. Rev. 277 (1985); Michael S. Moore, "Law as a Functional Kind," in Robert P. George, ed., *Natural Law Theory: Contemporary Essays* (Oxford University Press, 1992). Moore's metaphysical realism is motivated by his commitment to natural law theory and natural law theory's metaethical commitment to moral realism.

61. Moore, *A Natural Law Theory of Interpretation*, 300–301.

62. *See* Michael Moore, *Moral Reality Revisited*, 90 Mich. L. Rev. 2424, 2492 (1992); Michael Moore, *The Interpretive Turn in Modern Theory: A Turn for the Worse?*, 41 Stan. L. Rev. 871, 878–79, 882 (1989); Moore, *A Natural Law Theory of Interpretation*, 294.

63. *See, e.g.*, Dennis Patterson, *Law and Truth* (Oxford University Press, 1996), 46–50; Brian Bix, *Law, Language, and Legal Determinacy* (Oxford University Press, 1993), 140–57.

64. I use the term "legal realist" to refer to a contemporary view and a conventional understanding, but I should mention, as Brian Tamanaha has meticulously demonstrated, that this subjectivist view of law was not the view of the first scholars and judges who called themselves realists. *See* Brian Z. Tamanaha, *Beyond the Formalist-Realist Divide: The Role of Politics in Judging* (Princeton University Press, 2010), chaps. 5–6. In addition to Tamanaha's careful historical dismantling of the current version of realism, H. L. A. Hart offered a powerful theoretical criticism of the view (which he called rule-skepticism). *See* above at 136n22.

65. *See* David O. Brink, "Legal Interpretation, Objectivity, and Morality," in Brian Leiter, ed., *Objectivity in Law and Morals* (Cambridge University Press, 2001), 14–16.

66. *See, e.g.*, Segal, Spaeth, and Benesh, *The Supreme Court in the American Legal System*, 96 ("[T]he rules governing civil procedure—as with those applicable to legal fields generally—not only do not admit of mathematical precision, but do not even bear a modicum of objectivity. . . . [T]he eye of the beholder determines their applicability. The fact that many of the law's rules and tests are labeled *objective* no more evinces their truth, or their correspondence with reality, than it does the figments of one's imagination. . . . [W]ords mean what courts, judges, and attorneys choose them to mean.") (emphasis in original).

67. It is worth noting that legal realists (as they actually thought and wrote and not as they have been appropriated and caricatured) usually accepted this. Steven Winter explains this in his discussion of Karl Llewellyn. *See* Steven L. Winter, *A Clearing in the Forest: Law, Life, and Mind* (University of Chicago Press, 2001), 221 ("His [Llewellyn's] reconception of legal certainty captures a profound truth about the social and operational reality of law. . . . Law functions most of the time because it has a 'this-is-how-these-things-are-done' quality to it. If it did not, no legal system could survive without the constant exercise of raw, repressive power. . . . A legal rule that is motivated—i.e., that embodies situation-sense—will seem 'natural' or 'right' to those governed by it because they will see the rule as a reflection of the objective qualities of the social world in which they live. The operational success of a legal system (as distinct from its justice or legitimacy) depends upon the institutionalized meaning that precedes the promulgation of the rule.") For a concise discussion of this point, *see* Tamanaha, *Beyond the Formalist-Realist Divide*, 6–7, 87–98. For a reasonably brief and reasonably clear exposition by Llewellyn of his own view, *see* "Appellate Judging as a

Craft of Law," in Karl Llewellyn, *The Common Law Tradition: Deciding Appeals* (Little, Brown & Co., 1960), 213–35.

68. Beverly B. Cook, *Public Opinion and Federal Judicial Policy*, 21 Am. J. Pol. Sci. 567, 571 (1977).

69. *See* Barry Friedman and Andrew D. Martin, "Looking for Law in All the Wrong Places: Some Suggestions for Modeling Legal Decision-making," in Charles Gardner Geyh, ed., *What's Law Got To Do With It?: What Judges Do, Why They Do It, and What's at Stake* (Stanford University Press, 2011), 157–65; Owen Fiss, *The Law as It Could Be* (New York University Press, 2003), 154–55 ("The disciplining rules may vary from text to text. . . . Even within the law, there may be different rules depending on the text—those for contractual interpretation vary from statutory interpretation, and both vary from those used in constitutional interpretation. Though the particular content of disciplining rules varies . . . they furnish the standards by which the correctness of the interpretation can be judged. These rules are not simply standards or principles held by individual judges but, instead, constitute the institution (the profession) in which judges find themselves and through which they act.").

70. Friedman and Martin, "Looking for Law in All the Wrong Places," in Geyh, *What's Law Got To Do With It?*, 163, 164. *See also* Linda Meyer, *"Nothing We Say Matters":* Teague *and New Rules*, 61 U. Chi. L. Rev. 423, 424 (1994) ("[I]n the common law tradition, the Court has declined to limit the 'holding' of a precedent to any explicit statement of a rule in the language of that case. Instead, a holding includes the 'material' facts and result of the prior case, and the appropriate level of generality at which to capture and to describe those material facts is not predetermined by anything the prior court has said."); Stephen R. Perry, *Judicial Obligation, Precedent and the Common Law*, 7 Oxford J. Leg. Stud. 215, 252 (1987).

71. Charles Gardner Geyh, *Straddling the Fence Between Truth and Pretense: The Role of Law and Preference in Judicial Decision Making and the Future of Judicial Independence*, 22 Notre Dame J. L. Ethics & Pub. Pol'y 435, 444, 446 (2008). *See also* Charles L. Black, Jr., *The People and the Court: Judicial Review in a Democracy* (Macmillan, 1960), 165–67.

72. Geyh, *Straddling the Fence Between Truth and Pretense*, 443.

73. Geyh, *Straddling the Fence Between Truth and Pretense*, 437.

74. Charles Gardner Geyh, *When Courts and Congress Collide: The Struggle for Control of America's Judicial System* (University of Michigan Press, 2006), 281.

75. As I indicated a few paragraphs ago, my argument against subjectivist views of judging takes legal realism as the most prominent expression of that view. Not all subjectivists are legal realists, however, where theoretical analysis of judging is concerned. For a thoughtful subjectivist defense of judicial authority, *see* Dale Smith, *Can Anti-Objectivists Support Judicial Review?*, 31 Austl. J. Leg. Phil. 50, 62 (2006) ("Even if we view our moral beliefs as simply reflecting our preferences, we may regard those preferences as sufficiently important that we would want to act on (some of) them even if this meant overriding the majority's preferences. The recognition that our moral beliefs are not *objectively* correct need not—indeed, is unlikely to—lead us to cease attaching importance to those beliefs.") (emphasis in original). For purposes of my argument against legal realism, Smith helpfully explains that the view of moral principles (or legal rules) as lacking objective truth or reality need not commit someone to a view of judging as morally or legally unconstrained or illegitimate.

76. Some might claim that the account of judging I will develop and defend here incorporates a form of "crypto-solipsism." *See* F. C. S. Schiller, *Solipsism*, 18 Mind 169, 171 (1909). According to Schiller, the label crypto-solipsism may be applied "to any view which needs Solipsism for its logical completion." *Id.* Given that I will argue for the indispensable component of subjective response in common law judging, and to the extent that this form of subjective response depends on the individuated response of particular judges, Schiller's charge that this view is "crypto-solipsistic" may be unavoidable. In fact, though, I do not believe this label applies accurately to my argument, because of the relationship (which I will explain in detail in chapter 3) between subjectivity and intersubjectivity. As a result of this relationship, a common law judge cannot avoid asking "himself how his perceptions accord with those of others" and he cannot "suppress the opinions of those who disagree with him." *Id.* at 174, 178. Indeed, as I will explain in chapter 3, the validity of a common law judge's judgment actually depends upon the perceptions and possible disagreements of others.

77. *See* Patterson, *Normativity and Objectivity in Law*, 345–47 (explaining that a sole actor cannot usefully be said to apply a norm correctly or incorrectly because there is no social practice by which his action can be evaluated as correct or incorrect).

78. *See* John McDowell, *Mind, Value, and Reality* (Harvard University Press, 1998), 203–12, esp. 208–9. *Cf. Poe v. Ullman*, 367 U.S. 497, 542 (1961) ("Due process has not been reduced to any formula; its content cannot be determined by reference to any code. . . . If the supplying of content to this Constitutional concept has of necessity been a rational process, it certainly has not been one where judges have felt free to roam where unguided speculation might take them. The balance of which I speak is the balance struck by this country, having regard to what history teaches are the traditions from which it developed as well as the traditions from which it broke. That tradition is a living thing. A decision of this Court which radically departs from it could not long survive, while a decision which builds on what has survived is likely to be sound. No formula could serve as a substitute, in this area, for judgment and restraint.") (Harlan, J., dissenting).

79. *Cf.* Cass R. Sunstein, "Incommensurability and Kinds of Valuation: Some Applications in Law," in Ruth Chang, ed., *Incommensurability, Incomparability, and Practical Reason* (Harvard University Press, 1997), 244–45. As I indicate in the text, the goal here is not to defend a particular approach to evaluation or a preferred normative content for legal rules. But as Sunstein explains in his essay, the "expressive function of law" necessitates that law reach conclusions in disputed areas of valuation. And my argument here attempts to underscore the relationship between the judicial process of evaluation and legal conclusions about valuation.

80. *See generally* Tara Smith, *Judicial Review in an Objective Legal System* (Cambridge University Press, 2015), 241 ("The law is a body of conceptual instruction; as such, it is not reducible to a list of concrete commands that can be heard and followed with no intervening thought on the part of the person following it. . . . [T]he subject must act and contribute to the conclusion in a way that is not fully scripted by the material that he attempts to understand. . . . [T]o recognize the inescapable role of the subject in a process of thinking does not license subjectiv*ism*. The fact that the activity of judgment is *performed* by a subject does not render it subjectivist, for it does not entail that

the *standard* employed must be the subject's belief or preference.") (internal punctuation deleted) (emphasis in original).

81. *See* Brian Z. Tamanaha, *Law as a Means to an End: Threat to the Rule of Law* (Cambridge University Press, 2006), 242 ("The sophisticated modern recognition that judges' background views subconsciously influence their interpretation of the law at some deep level is correct. . . . Too often, however, a leap is made from these points to the conclusion that, therefore, judges are deluded, naïve, or lying when they claim that their decisions are determined by the law. To the extent that a judge is consciously rule-bound when engaging in judging, the judge is correct in claiming to be rule-bound *in the only sense that this phrase can be humanly achieved.* Since judging is a human practice, it is absurd to evaluate the decision-making of judges by reference to a standard that is impossible to achieve, inevitably finding them wanting.") (emphasis in original). Tamanaha illustrates this point with his contrast of a "Consciously [Rule-] Bound judge" and a "Consciously Ends-Oriented judge.") See *id.* at 241–45. This is also an "either-or" conception of judging ("either judges are rule-bound or ends-oriented") that may be slightly misleading. But I do not want this minor reservation to distract or detract from the force of Tamanaha's larger point, with which I entirely agree.

82. *See* Patterson, *Normativity and Objectivity in Law*, 327–28 ("Objectivity is often theorized as a relationship between an assertion and some state of affairs in virtue of which the assertion is 'objectively true.' The nub of the argument is that assertions or beliefs are true in virtue of the way things are (i.e., facts). Facts make assertions and beliefs true, and objectively so, for facts are not mere matters of mind: they are a function of the way things are. By conceptualizing objectivity in terms of a connection between a belief or assertion and a mind-independent state of affairs, proponents of objectivity all but guarantee creation of objectivism's opposite, subjectivism. Subjectivists deny the efficacy of the objectivist account of the relation between mind and world, locating the seat of truth and belief in the individual subject. The debate is intractable. I argue that the choice between objectivism and subjectivism is false. Just because we are free to describe a situation in a variety of ways (rejecting objectivism) does not dictate the conclusion that, within each vocabulary, there are no standards for correct and incorrect assertion (rejecting subjectivism). I propose to approach objectivity from the point of view of normativity. By 'normativity' I mean to identify the ways in which speakers of a language appraise assertoric utterances in terms of 'correct' and 'incorrect' or 'true' and 'false.'").

83. *See* Kent Greenawalt, *Law and Objectivity* (Oxford University Press, 1992), 197–216.

84. Fiss, *The Law as It Could Be*, 154.

85. Fiss, *The Law as It Could Be*, 154.

86. H. L. A. Hart, *The Ascription of Responsibility and Rights*, 49 Proc. Aristotelian Soc'y 171, 182 (1949) (emphasis in original). Hart later reconsidered the view of criminal responsibility he expressed in this article, but not the point discussed in the text. *See* H. L. A. Hart, *Punishment and Responsibility: Essays in the Philosophy of Law* (2nd ed.) (Oxford University Press, 2008), v.

87. *See, e.g, Fifth Third Bank of Western Ohio v. United States*, 402 F.3d 1221, 1225 (Fed. Cir. 2005) ("[T]he parties do not dispute basic issues of offer, acceptance, and

consideration, the essentials of contract formation."). In fact, of course, enforceable contracts require more than just these three elements.

88. In a metaphysically or epistemologically objective or realist sense.

89. What I have in mind here is the tradition of describing facts established to the satisfaction of the legal fact-finder as "legal truth." *See* Neil MacCormick, *Rhetoric and the Rule of Law: A Theory of Legal Reasoning* (Oxford University Press, 2005), 72 ("In effect, legal fact-finding processes transform brute facts into institutional facts. Whatever may have happened in the world, a jury's determination that *a* hit *b* on the head and caused *b*'s death makes that count as a legal truth, a proposition counted as true in a certain legal process."); Gary Goodpaster, *On the Theory of American Adversary Criminal Trial*, 78 J. Crim. L. & Criminology 118, 129–30 (1987) ("[L]aw is just one of a number of kinds of discourse about the world. As a discourse, the law has its own concepts, categories of thought, and ways of perceiving and processing information. Legal discourse may, in some respects, track the world in the same way that other kinds of discourse do, while in other respects it may not.").

90. *See* Marianne Constable, *Our Word Is Our Bond: How Legal Speech Acts* (Stanford University Press, 2014), 65–71. As Constable explains, a legal judgment is both a "locutionary act" in its stating of the law and an "illocutionary act" as a statement of law that is evaluated by a community. *See id.* at 29, 68. At this point, I am discussing the locutionary function of the judgment. I discuss its illocutionary aspects in chapter 3.

91. *See* below at 26–30, 60–62.

92. This point may be easier to see in certain tort cases, for example, where the physical evidence does not typically exist in the same way. In other words, there never is "negligence in the air." *Palsgraf v. Long Island R.R. Co.*, 248 N.Y. 339, 341 (1928) (Cardozo, J.) (quoting Frederick Pollock, *The Law of Torts* (11th ed.) (Stevens & Sons, 1920), 455).

93. *See, e.g.*, *U.S. WEST, Inc. v. Time Warner, Inc.*, 1996 Del. Ch. LEXIS 55 (Del. Ch. June 6, 1996), [*33] n. 11 ("I mention 'the existence of legal rights and duties . . .' in order to leave open the possibility that parties have failed to create any contract rights and duties despite their parallel intentions to do so.") (citing *Restatement (Second) of Contracts* § 201(3) and cmt. d (1981); Arthur Linton Corbin, *Corbin on Contracts: A Comprehensive Treatise on the Rules of Contract Law* (West Publishing Co., 1960), § 538).

94. *See, e.g.*, Oliver Wendell Holmes, *The Path of the Law*, 10 Harv. L. Rev. 457, 463–64 (1897) ("Nothing is more certain than that the parties may be bound by a contract to things which neither of them intended. . . . The parties are bound by the contract as it is interpreted by the court, yet neither of them [may have] meant what the court declares that they have said."); *Restatement (Second) of Contracts* § 21 ("Neither real nor apparent intention that a promise be legally binding is essential to the formation of a contract.").

95. *See* below at 78–80, 82, 85, 87–89.

96. For an example of this sort of understanding of objectivity, *see* below at 66–71.

97. *See, e.g.*, Barry Stroud, *The Quest for Reality: Subjectivism and the Metaphysics of Colour* (Oxford University Press, 1999), 12 ("In all these theories, there is a conception of the world or reality as being a certain way independently of the responses of any sentient beings. . . . Although this conception of reality and of the project of separating the 'subjective' from the 'objective' is a very old idea, it is by no means a thing of

the past."); Patricia Marino, *What Should A Correspondence Theory Be and Do?*, 127 Phil. Stud. 415, 419 (2006) ("objectivity . . . [is the idea] that snow is white is a fact independently of what we believe, how we see the world, and so on."). Objectivity and mind-independence are sometimes discussed in relation to the reference or correspondence theory of truth, according to which factually true statements accurately refer or correspond to mind-independent objects in the world.

98. *See, e.g.*, Greenawalt, *Law and Objectivity*, 12–13, 34–53; Kramer, *Objectivity and the Rule of Law*, 14–25. A related connection between objectivity and the rule of law is the idea that the answers to legal questions can be found in recognized legal sources, so the law meaningfully (though perhaps not entirely) determines the outcome of legal disputes (rather than mere judicial discretion).

99. Mind-independence itself can take various forms in relation to objectivity. The use of mind-independence in my argument is a weak form. *See* Kramer, *Objectivity and the Rule of Law*, 6 ("That most general legal norms are at least weakly mind-independent is quite evident. The existence of those norms does not stand or fall on the basis of each individual's mental activity.").

100. This is not limited to the legal positivist notion that a rule of recognition circumscribes the limited domain of authoritative legal sources. Natural law and interpretivist theories also recognize the distinctive function of legal sources in legal reasoning. *See* Hart, *The Concept of Law*, 94–95; Joseph Raz, *The Authority of Law: Essays on Law and Morality* (2nd ed.) (Oxford University Press, 2009), 47–52; John Finnis, *Natural Law and Natural Rights* (2nd ed.) (Oxford University Press, 2011), 319–20; John Finnis, "Natural Law and Legal Reasoning," in Robert P. George, ed., *Natural Law Theory: Contemporary Essays* (Oxford University Press, 1992), 142, 151; Ronald Dworkin, *Justice in Robes* (Harvard University Press, 2006), 6; Ronald Dworkin, *Law's Empire* (Harvard University Press, 1986), 88, 98–99. Of course, theorists who identify with one or another of these schools of thought may disagree about whether legal sources are the exclusive basis for legal reasoning and judicial decision making, or whether morality may (or must) be incorporated as a condition of validity when identifying sources of law. For the most part, I cannot engage these debates here. Since it bears directly on the discussion in the text, however, I should note that Dworkin is sometimes accused of denying the sources thesis. *See, e.g.*, Michael C. Dorf, *Legal Indeterminacy and Institutional Design*, 78 N.Y.U. L. Rev. 875, 914 (2003). Insofar as this might be taken to mean that Dworkin denies a significant place for legal sources in legal reasoning, it would be more accurate to say Dworkin accepts that legal sources play a central role in legal reasoning, but he does not believe that the content of the law can be fully identified through a rule of recognition (or is necessarily exhausted by the sources). In this respect, Dworkin is best understood as claiming that the sources thesis and the rule of recognition are not coextensive and as arguing for an alternative version of the sources thesis in which the content of the law is constructed through a process of legal reasoning rather than identified through a social practice of legal officials. *See* Stavropoulos, *Objectivity in Law*, 141–42.

101. This is not meant as a claim about the broader philosophical discussion of Kant's notion that there is an external world "in itself" about which we have necessarily partial access and understanding. For purposes of my discussion of Kant, the formulation of legal or aesthetic judgments can operate if we take preexisting legal or ar-

tistic sources to have a meaningful existence of their own or if we take the judgments of those legal or artistic objects to be their full and only representational existence. *Cf.* McDowell, *Mind, Value, and Reality*, 307 n. 21 ("My point is that we can have a position that is critical (in the same roughly Kantian sense: it acknowledges that world and mind are constitutively made for each other), but which, by dropping the 'in itself', precisely sheds any need to talk of such a contribution.").

102. *See, e.g.*, Segal, Spaeth, and Benesh, *The Supreme Court in the American Legal System*, 20–21 ("By ignoring certain aspects of reality in order to concentrate on those that allegedly explain the behavior in question, models provide a useful handle for understanding that more exhaustive and descriptive approaches do not. . . . [I]ncreasing a model's complexity also increases the number of idiosyncratic variables, lessens its coherence, and—most importantly—destroys its parsimony. Inasmuch as no model can, by definition, explain everything, the objective is to discover the most economic explanation that can account for the largest portion of the behavior in question. . . . A necessary feature of any model is that testing of its explanatory capability demands that it be falsifiable."). For more on the problems with this approach to studying judicial decision making, *see* Friedman and Martin, "Looking for Law in All the Wrong Places," in Geyh, *What's Law Got To Do With It?*, 154 ("The legal model is not falsifiable because it is not a model at all. . . . All one can say is that a model does a better or less good job at explaining or predicting what it set out to explain or predict."). *See also* below at 174nn207, 211.

103. *Cf.* below at 165–66n118.

104. Jerome Frank, *Courts on Trial: Myth and Reality in American Justice* (Princeton University Press, 1949), 148.

105. The notion of the judge-as-umpire is an effort in this direction. *See* below at 110. *But cf. Richmond Newspapers, Inc. v. Virginia*, 448 U.S. 555, 595 (1980) ("Under our system, judges are not mere umpires, but, in their own sphere, lawmakers—a coordinate branch of government. While individual cases turn upon the controversies between parties, or involve particular prosecutions, court rulings impose official and practical consequences upon members of society at large.") (Brennan, J., concurring); *Dep't of Pub. Works v. Lillard*, 33 Cal. Rptr. 189, 193 (Cal. Ct. App. 1963) ("The judge is obligated to conduct the trial in a fair and impartial manner. He may not, of course, choose sides. His function, however, is much more than that of a plate umpire at a baseball game calling balls and strikes."); *State v. Crittenden*, 38 La. Ann. 448, 450–51 (1886) ("A trial is not a mere *lutte* between counsel, in which the judge sits merely as an umpire to decide disputes which may arise between them.").

106. *See, e.g.*, Melinda Gann Hall, *Introduction to "An Analysis of the Rehnquist Court's Establishment Clause Jurisprudence: A New Marriage of Legal and Social Science Approaches,"* 1999 L. Rev. M.S.U.-D.C.L. 865, 867 (1999) ("Reduced to the most fundamental element, Segal and Spaeth argue that the justices' public policy preferences are the *only* influences on their votes on the merits of the cases decided by the Court.") (citing Jeffrey A. Segal and Harold J. Spaeth, *The Supreme Court and the Attitudinal Model* (Cambridge University Press, 1993)) (emphasis in original).

107. *Cf.* Hurley, *Natural Reasons*, 337 ("[Suppose] the nominee for Justice believes it is better to have an affirmative action policy in a particular context than not to. But under what circumstances would she not believe it was better? In order for a social

knowledge function to apply to an unrestricted domain of counterfactual situations in which her beliefs are different, it must have some way of ascertaining whether circumstances obtain in which her beliefs about alternatives of certain kinds vary independently of truths about them. It might, for example, want to distinguish cases in which, if the candidate were not to have family and friends who would benefit from affirmative action, she would not believe it was right, from cases in which if she had not had certain first-hand experiences of discrimination and its effects, she would not believe affirmative action was right. The social knowledge function might regard her beliefs about such issues as inappropriate to rely upon in the former case, but not in the latter."). *See* below at 117–20.

Chapter 2

1. Martha Minow, *Stripped Down Like a Runner or Enriched by Experience: Bias and Impartiality of Judges and Jurors*, 33 Wm. & Mary L. Rev. 1201, 1206 (1992).

2. Aharon Barak, *The Role of a Supreme Court in a Democracy*, 53 Hastings L.J. 1205, 1210 (2002). *See also* Aharon Barak, *The Judge in a Democracy* (Princeton University Press, 2006), 101–5; John Rawls, *Political Liberalism* (Columbia University Press, 1993), 236; Melvin Aron Eisenberg, *The Nature of the Common Law* (Harvard University Press, 1988), 9–10, 14–26; Harry H. Wellington, *Common Law Rules and Constitutional Double Standards: Some Notes on Adjudication*, 83 Yale L. J. 221, 244 (1973). This position is subtly but importantly different from the view that judges should engage in their own evaluation of the decision or interpretation that best expresses the public values of their society, government, and law (but may not yet be reflected in those public values). *See, e.g.*, Ronald Dworkin, *Law's Empire* (Harvard University Press, 1986), 167–68, 225–28, 255–56. Here it is less clear where the judge's own moral evaluation ends and where the incorporation of public morality, as understood by the judge, enters into the articulation of the law.

3. *See* above at 16.

4. *See* W. Preston Warren, *Modes of Objectivity*, 39 Phil. & Phenomenological Res. 74, 83 (1978). Functional effectiveness can also be thought of as "procedural objectivity." *See* Jules L. Coleman and Brian Leiter, *Determinacy, Objectivity, and Authority*, 142 U. Pa. L. Rev. 549, 596 (1993) ("Legal decision-making procedures are designed to forge compromises among conflicting interests as well as to establish ground rules on which individuals with conflicting all-encompassing theories or political and philosophical conceptions might agree. . . . [P]rocedural objectivists share the view that what justifies the outcomes of legal disputes is the fact that judges reach them by following objective procedures.").

5. *See, e.g.*, Paul Gewirtz, *On "I Know It When I See It,"* 105 Yale L.J. 1023, 1025 (1996) ("From this perspective, the exercise of judicial power is not legitimate if it is based on a judge's personal preferences rather than law that precedes the case, on subjective will rather than objective analysis, on emotion rather than reasoned reflection.").

6. *See* Richard A. Posner, *The Problems of Jurisprudence* (Harvard University Press, 1990), 37; George D. Braden, *The Search for Objectivity in Constitutional Law*, 57 Yale L.J. 571, 572 n. 5 (1948) ("By objectivity I mean that quality of a rule of law which

enables it to be applied to similar situations with similar results regardless of the identity of the judges who apply it.").

7. *See, e.g.*, David Lyons, *Open Texture and the Possibility of Legal Interpretation*, 18 Law and Phil. 297, 298–308 (1999).

8. A good example here is the work of scholars to apply Wittgenstein's approach to rule following to ascertain whether legal rules are being followed. *See* Brian Bix, *Law, Language, and Legal Determinacy* (Oxford University Press, 1993), ch. 2; Dennis Patterson, *Law and Truth* (Oxford University Press, 1996), 12–15. For an argument that philosophical disputes about language hold almost no relevance for the philosophy of law, *see* Michael Steven Green, *Dworkin's Fallacy, or What the Philosophy of Language Can't Teach Us about the Law*, 89 Va. L. Rev. 1897, 1942–46 (2003).

9. For excellent articulations of two sides in this debate, *compare* John Tasioulas, *The Legal Relevance of Ethical Objectivity*, 47 Am. J. Juris. 211 (2002) *with* Jeremy Waldron, "The Irrelevance of Moral Objectivity," in Robert P. George, ed., *Natural Law Theory: Contemporary Essays* (Oxford University Press, 1992).

10. One response to these criticisms is that the meaning of language, legal rules, and moral rules can be found in the shared use of those terms in the relevant linguistic community. *See, e.g.*, Simon Blackburn, "Rule-Following and Moral Realism," in Steven Holtzman and Christopher Leich, eds., *Wittgenstein: To Follow a Rule* (Routledge & Kegan Paul, 1981). In terms of objectivity, this is the view that law is minimally objective. *See* above at 10–11.

11. *See* Ludwig Wittgenstein, *Philosophical Investigations*, ed. P. M. S. Hacker and Joachim Schulte (4th ed.) (Wiley-Blackwell, 2009), §§ 143–242.

12. *See* Ernie Lepore and Kirk Ludwig, *Donald Davidson: Meaning, Truth, Language, and Reality* (Oxford University Press, 2005), 123–24, 271–76.

13. *See* Donald Davidson, *Subjective, Intersubjective, Objective* (Oxford University Press, 2001), 91 ("I do not think that, because the ultimate court of appeal is personal, therefore my judgements are arbitrary or subjective, for they were formed in a social nexus that assures the objectivity if not the correctness of my beliefs. Intersubjectivity is the root of objectivity, not because what people agree on is necessarily true, but because intersubjectivity depends upon interaction with the world. . . . It is here that each person, each mind or self, reveals itself as a part of a community of free selves. There would be no thought if individuals did not play the indispensable, and ultimately unavoidably creative, role of final arbiter.").

14. *See* Davidson, *Subjective, Intersubjective, Objective*, 83 ("The ultimate source (not ground) of objectivity is, in my opinion, intersubjectivity. If we were not in communication with others, there would be nothing on which to base the *idea* of being wrong, or, therefore, of being right, either in what we say or in what we think.") (emphasis in original). I will not address here the larger philosophical debate about whether Davidson's approach succeeds as a holistic theory of linguistic meaning. *See* Scott Soames, *Philosophy of Language* (Princeton University Press, 2010), 46–49.

15. *See* Barak, *The Judge in a Democracy*, 102 ("With impartiality comes objectivity. It means making judicial decisions on the basis of considerations that are external to the judge and that may even conflict with his personal view.") (footnotes omitted); Matthew H. Kramer, *Objectivity and the Rule of Law* (Cambridge University Press, 2007), 53 ("Another epistemic variety of objectivity is impartiality, which consists of disin-

terestedness and open-mindedness, and which can also be designated as 'detachedness' or 'impersonality.' It is to be contrasted with bias and partisanship."). One problem with this equation of objectivity and impartiality, as I have discussed in the text, is that it elides qualities in judges that should be distinguished. Thinking of objectivity as impartiality and impartiality as detachment (or, worse, "impersonality") only encourages the confusion of values with biases. Assuming that judges must be detached from the dispute they are deciding to decide that dispute impartially reinforces the misleading notion that it is improper for a judge's own values and perspectives to influence her judicial decisions. To be fair, Kramer acknowledges this and says that "although impartiality does consist in detachedness, it does not in any way entail a lack of empathetic understanding of human actions and intentions." Kramer, *Objectivity and the Rule of Law*, 63. It is not clear, then, what work detachment is doing to improve our understanding of impartiality (or objectivity). Moreover, even Kramer's less controversial connection of impartiality to open-mindedness is contested. *See, e.g.*, *Republican Party of Minn. v. White*, 536 U.S. 765, 778–79 (2002) ("[A] possible meaning of 'impartiality' (again not a common one) might be described as openmindedness. This quality in a judge demands, not that he have no preconceptions on legal issues, but that he be willing to consider views that oppose his preconceptions, and remain open to persuasion, when the issues arise in a pending case. This sort of impartiality seeks to guarantee each litigant, not an *equal* chance to win the legal points in the case, but at least *some* chance of doing so. . . . The problem is, however, that . . . [b]efore they arrive on the bench (whether by election or otherwise) judges have often committed themselves on legal issues that they must later rule upon.") (citation omitted) (emphasis in original). My point here is not that I disagree with Kramer's claim that open-mindedness is an aspect of impartiality (I do not) or even with his claim that detachment or impersonality is a necessary aspect of impartiality (although I do). My point is simply that all this just winds up extending an argument about what objectivity really means, which ultimately will not improve our understanding of the process of judging.

16. The first person I can recall suggesting this sort of distinction is Leslie Friedman Goldstein. I am grateful to her for starting me thinking about this issue.

17. *See White*, 536 U.S. at 775–76 ("'[I]mpartiality' in the judicial context—and of course its root meaning—is the lack of bias for or against either party to the proceeding. Impartiality in this sense assures equal application of the law."). *See also* Grant Hammond, *Judicial Recusal: Principles, Process and Problems* (Hart Publishing, 2009), 33 ("What we seem to be looking for is something that inappropriately affects the reasoning process in that it has nothing, or very little, to do with the actual merits of the case, but is somehow brought into play in the determination of it. . . . A failure to avoid this sort of error is said by the law to amount to a want of impartiality.").

18. *See, e.g.*, Lynda L. Butler, *The Politics of Takings: Choosing the Appropriate Decisionmaker*, 38 Wm. & Mary L. Rev. 749, 761 (1997) ("[T]he judiciary has the best chance of being objective and rendering decisions that are not affected by a judge's own political values."); John Stick, *Can Nihilism Be Pragmatic?*, 100 Harv. L. Rev. 332, 370 (1986) ("[L]egal theorists who prize objectivity seek to prevent judicial decisions that are based on the judge's own moral or political values.").

19. *See generally Laird v. Tatum*, 409 U.S. 824, 835 (1972) ("Since most Justices

come to this bench no earlier than their middle years, it would be unusual if they had not by that time formulated at least some tentative notions that would influence them in their interpretation of the sweeping clauses of the Constitution and their interaction with one another. It would be not merely unusual, but extraordinary, if they had not at least given opinions as to constitutional issues in their previous legal careers. Proof that a Justice's mind at the time he joined the Court was a complete *tabula rasa* in the area of constitutional adjudication would be evidence of lack of qualification, not lack of bias."). *See also Blank v. Sullivan & Cromwell*, 418 F. Supp. 1, 4-5 (S.D.N.Y. 1975) ("[I]f background or sex or race of each judge were, by definition, sufficient grounds for removal, no judge on this court could hear this case, or many others, by virtue of the fact that all of them were attorneys, of a sex, often with distinguished law firm or public service backgrounds.").

20. *See In re J.P. Linahan, Inc.*, 138 F.2d 650, 651 (2d Cir. 1943) ("Democracy must, indeed, fail unless our courts try cases fairly, and there can be no fair trial before a judge lacking in impartiality and disinterestedness. If, however, 'bias' and 'partiality' be defined to mean the total absence of preconceptions in the mind of the judge, then no one has ever had a fair trial and no one ever will. The human mind, even at infancy, is no blank piece of paper.") (Frank, J.).

21. *See generally Aetna Life Ins. Co. v. Lavoie*, 475 U.S. 813, 821–22 (1986) ("The record in this case presents more than mere allegations of bias and prejudice, however. Appellant also presses a claim that Justice Embry had a more direct stake in the outcome of this case. . . . More than 30 years ago Justice Black, speaking for the Court, reached a similar conclusion and recognized that under the Due Process Clause no judge 'can be a judge in his own case [or be] permitted to try cases where he has an interest in the outcome.'") (quoting *In re Murchison*, 349 U.S. 133, 136 (1955)); *Tumey v. Ohio*, 273 U.S. 510, 523 (1927) ("[I]t certainly violates the Fourteenth Amendment, and deprives a defendant in a criminal case of due process of law, to subject his liberty or property to the judgment of a court the judge of which has a direct, personal, substantial, pecuniary interest in reaching a conclusion against him in his case.").

22. *See* Mass. Const. Part I, art. 29 ("It is the right of every citizen to be tried by judges as free, impartial and independent as the lot of humanity will admit.").

23. *See* Joel Cohen, *Blindfolds Off: Judges on How They Decide* (American Bar Association, 2014), 83 ("I'm not sure 'objective' is the right word there. There's a set of values that they [other judges] apply that are just different than the values that I'm applying.") (remarks of former judge Nancy Gertner). *See also White*, 536 U.S. at 777 ("It is perhaps possible to use the term 'impartiality' in the judicial context (though this is certainly not a common usage) to mean lack of preconception in favor of or against a particular *legal view*. This sort of impartiality would be concerned, not with guaranteeing litigants equal application of the law, but rather with guaranteeing them an equal chance to persuade the court on the legal points in their case. . . . A judge's lack of predisposition regarding the relevant legal issues in a case has never been thought a necessary component of equal justice, and with good reason. For one thing, it is virtually impossible to find a judge who does not have preconceptions about the law.") (emphasis in original).

24. *Linahan*, 138 F.2d at 651–53 (citations omitted). The canons of judicial ethics do not assume or require that a judge's values will not play a role in his legal rulings.

But the canons do require a judge to act impartially. So, for example, Rule 2.2 of the American Bar Association Model Code of Judicial Conduct states that "A judge shall uphold and apply the law, and shall perform all duties of judicial office fairly and impartially." *ABA Model Code of Judicial Conduct* (2011), Rule 2.2. At the same time, one of the official comments explaining the operation of Rule 2.2 recognizes that "each judge comes to the bench with a unique background and personal philosophy." *ABA Model Code of Judicial Conduct*, Rule 2.2, cmt. [2]. The Model Code envisions judges who bring their own unique backgrounds and personal philosophies of judging to the bench and who can nevertheless adjudicate impartially and fairly.

25. *See* Shimon Shetreet and Sophie Turenne, *Judges on Trial: The Independence and Accountability of the English Judiciary* (2nd ed.) (Cambridge University Press, 2013), 212 ("The requirement for neutrality does not require judges to discount the very life experiences that may so well qualify them to preside over disputes.").

26. *See Caperton v. A.T. Massey Coal Co.*, 556 U.S. 868, 876 (2009) ("[T]he Due Process Clause incorporated the common-law rule that a judge must recuse himself when he has 'a direct, personal, substantial, pecuniary interest' in a case. This rule reflects the maxim that '[n]o man is allowed to be a judge in his own cause; because his interest would certainly bias his judgment, and, not improbably, corrupt his integrity.'") (quoting *Tumey*, 273 U.S. at 523 and *Federalist* No. 10).

27. *See* 28 U.S.C. § 144 ("Whenever a party to any proceeding in a district court makes and files a timely and sufficient affidavit that the judge before whom the matter is pending has a personal bias or prejudice either *against him or in favor of any adverse party*, such judge shall proceed no further therein, but another judge shall be assigned to hear such proceeding. The affidavit shall state the facts and the reasons for the belief that bias or prejudice exists.") (emphasis supplied); 28 U.S.C. § 455(b) (describing the reasons for judicial recusal as personal bias or prejudice toward a party, or prior professional knowledge of the matter in controversy, or a financial interest in the case or with respect to a party, or a family relationship with one of the parties or attorneys in the case). *See also Paschall v. Mayone*, 454 F. Supp. 1289, 1300 (S.D.N.Y. 1978) ("[T]he alleged bias must be 'personal' and 'stem from an extrajudicial source and result in an opinion on the merits on some basis other than what the judge learned from his participation in the case.'") (citations omitted).

28. *See, e.g., In re Mason*, 916 F.2d 384, 386 (7th Cir. 1990) (Easterbrook, J.) (party affiliation inadequate to support a claim of specific bias).

29. *See, e.g., Pennsylvania v. Local Union 542*, 388 F. Supp. 155, 163, 181 (E.D. Pa. 1974), *aff'd*, 478 F.2d 1398 (3d Cir. 1974), *cert. denied*, 421 U.S. 999 (1975) ("I concede that I am black. I do not apologize for that obvious fact. I take rational pride in my heritage, just as most other ethnics take pride in theirs. However, that one is black does not mean, *ipso facto*, that he is anti-white; no more than being Jewish implies being anti-Catholic, or being Catholic implies being anti-Protestant. As do most blacks, I believe that the corridors of history in this country have been lined with countless instances of racial injustice. . . . So long as Jewish judges preside over matters where Jewish and Gentile litigants disagree; so long as Protestant judges preside over matters where Protestants and Catholic litigants disagree; so long as white judges preside over matters where white and black litigants disagree, I will preside over matters where black and white litigants disagree.") (Higginbotham, J.).

30. *In re Union Leader Corp.*, 292 F.2d 381, 388 (1st Cir. 1961). *See also Ex parte Fairbank Co.*, 194 F. Supp. 978, 989–990 (M.D. Ala. 1912) ("'Prejudice or bias,' in the ordinary sense of the term, and not censurable in its character, may arise from innumerable conditions in life. A man ordinarily has a bias in favor of the political party to which he belongs, or a prejudice in some degree against its opponents. The same thing is true in a degree as to the church of which he is a member, and he is generally prejudiced or biased more or less about his race, his country, and its institutions. He cannot avoid forming to some extent bias or prejudice regarding men and affairs in nearly every matter as to which he has to inform his judgment or regulate his conduct in the walks of daily life. He must have neighbors, friends, and acquaintances, business and social relations, and be a part of his day and generation. Evidently the ordinary results of such associations and the impressions they create in the mind of the judge are not the 'personal bias or prejudice' to which the statute refers. The impressions, whether favorable or unfavorable, of men, which a judge receives, or his convictions about them growing out of his contact or acquaintance with them in the ordinary walks of life, cannot fall within the evil the statute designs to suppress, unless they are so strong that they result in personal bias or prejudice as to individual suitors.").

31. *See* Timothy J. Goodson, *Duck, Duck, Goose: Hunting for Better Recusal Practices in the United States Supreme Court in Light of* Cheney v. United States District Court, 84 N.C. L. Rev. 181, 189–90 (2005) ("[I]f judges were expected to recuse themselves based on irrational or unsupported conjecture of judicial bias, the parties in the litigation or a vindictive press would be able to control the assignment of judges. A judge whose participation is subject to unjustified removal by the parties or the press cannot be said to be neutral. In order to preserve judicial independence, the law of recusal constrains the policy of impartiality with the requirement that a charge of bias be supported by facts, or that appearance of impartiality be evaluated from the perspective of a reasonable observer."). Of course, a judge's assessment of his own bias might be clouded, which is why the judge's decision not to recuse himself may be appealed. *See Caperton*, 556 U.S. at 882–84.

32. *See* below at 209n13.

33. *See* below at 71–72, 103–4.

34. *See* Shetreet and Turenne, *Judges on Trial*, 4–5 ("[I]mpartiality is central to the independence of the individual judge. . . . It is *the* fundamental principle of justice . . . at common law. . . . It first entails a substantive independence, independence in the conduct of the judicial business—the judge's core activity being to decide cases. . . . Individual judges are subject to no other authority for their decisions than the appeal courts. A basic requirement for maintaining public confidence in the legal system is the court's duty to provide a reasoned judgment for its decisions.") (emphasis in original). For more on the relationship between judicial impartiality and judicial independence, *see* below at 91–92, 95.

35. In his attempts to locate the source of a text's meaning either in an individual reader or in an interpretive community of readers, Stanley Fish always misses part of the story, at least where legal texts are concerned. Fish wants to reject subjectivism while embracing antifoundationalism (the view that there is no individual perspective outside of the social and cultural prejudices through which we perceive and experience our world). Our individual interpretations are only meaningful insofar as they

can be understood by and within an interpretive community (of similarly situated, prejudiced, and socially conditioned individuals). *See, e.g.*, Stanley Fish, *Doing What Comes Naturally: Change, Rhetoric, and the Practice of Theory in Literary and Legal Studies* (Duke University Press, 1989), 323, 342–45. Fish seems to claim that the individual's interpretation is bounded by the community (or communities) of which he is a part; but at the same time, Fish also seems committed to the claim that the individual remains free to interpret without constraint. This is due, in part, to the fact that Fish never fully accounts for the formal and substantive constraints that legal sources place on the interpretations available to the individual and on the evaluations available to the community. To borrow Pierre Schlag's phrasing, within the law, not all discourses are equally authoritarian. *See* Pierre Schlag, *Normativity and the Politics of Form*, 139 U. Pa. L. Rev. 801, 822 n.58 (1991). *See also* Owen Fiss, *The Law as It Could Be* (New York University Press, 2003), 179–89.

36. 531 U.S. 98 (2000).

37. *See* Howard Gillman, *The Votes That Counted: How the Court Decided the 2000 Presidential Election* (University of Chicago Press, 2001), 175–76 ("More difficult to assess are those times when judges rule in a way that is consistent with their party affiliation without support from the other party. . . . However, this alone is not enough to prove partisan decision-making. Disagreements among judges of different political parties occur all the time, for understandable reasons, given what we know about the influence of political ideology on judicial decision-making. In such cases, the question becomes whether the decision seemed to be consistent with the judge's familiar pattern of decision-making or whether it seemed to be an ad hoc deviation from that pattern in order to accommodate the interests of a favored partisan.").

38. *See* David Margolick, Evgenia Peretz, and Michael Shnayerson, *The Path to Florida*, Vanity Fair (Oct. 2004), 310, 319–22, 355–59.

39. *Cf.* Neil MacCormick, *Institutions of Law: An Essay in Legal Theory* (Oxford University Press, 2007), 181 ("[T]his very non-partisanship of the judiciary is itself a precious achievement of politics when and to the extent that it is realized. . . . It is not then the case that judges and courts are in every sense non-political—of course they ought to be non-partisan, refraining from taking sides overtly in matters of inter-party dispute in the ongoing political struggles of the day. But achieving non-partisan impartiality is itself a particular political role. . . . It is by participating in this way that judges contribute most to sustaining the common good of the polity.").

40. *See* above at 9–14.

41. This need not be understood only in legal positivist terms.

42. *See* below at 58–59, 181–82n45.

43. Dennis Patterson, *Normativity and Objectivity in Law*, 43 Wm. & Mary L. Rev. 325, 356 (2001). Patterson is not arguing in favor of the scale's utility.

44. *See* Patterson, *Normativity and Objectivity in Law*, 358–59 ("As proof of this thesis, one might point to the fact that in matters arithmetic, consensus is far easier to come by than in law. Why is it that disagreement—which seems pervasive in law—is comparatively absent in arithmetic? Are we not permitted to say that arithmetic, or for that matter, science, is simply 'more objective' than law? Could it be that the appearance of objectivity in arithmetic and its comparable absence in law, is due not to the subject matter but to desiderata? In doing sums, there is universal agreement

about what counts as a correct answer. It is not the agreement as such which 'produces' objectivity, rather, universal agreement is the corollary of a prior consensus on criteria of correctness. In looking at practices like science and arithmetic, we are tempted to think the 'hardness' of these practices is a function of the objects of investigation. We are tempted to believe that rocks and theorems enjoy an ontological and epistemological status that is simply of a higher order than propositions of law or literary criticism.").

45. John McDowell, *Mind, Value, and Reality* (Harvard University Press, 1998), 160, 161. The specific concept that McDowell is discussing in this passage is humor. For reasons I will explain in the next chapter, I think McDowell's use of the term and concept "aesthetic" here is especially apt and his point relates equally well to the concepts of beauty and justice. *Cf. id.* at 187 ("[I]t is a mistake to think we cannot show proper respect for science unless we suppose that truth about disenchanted nature is the sole context in which the material good standing of an exercise of intellect can be directly apparent.").

46. McDowell, *Mind, Value, and Reality*, 162, 163.

47. *See* McDowell, *Mind, Value, and Reality*, 164 ("We have no point of vantage on the question what can be the case, that is, what can be a fact, external to the modes of thought and speech we know our way around in, with whatever understanding of what counts as better and worse execution of them our mastery of them can give us."). *See also* Tasioulas, *The Legal Relevance of Ethical Objectivity*, 220–21 ("[G]iven the self-understanding of a particular domain, a realist standing might be attributable to the entities and qualities invoked within it even though they are constitutively tied to the existence and experience of human beings. . . . [T]here is no explanatory priority either way between ethical property and its associated repertoire of ethical responses. . . . On this sort of view, ethical properties are constituted in part by their normative relation to human subjective responses (the relation is normative because the property has to merit the response, it is not enough that it bear some non-normative, e.g. purely causal, relation to it). But the latter responses can only be understood in terms of concepts of value properties that are there to be discerned independently of any individual or collective subjectivity. Moreover, these ethical qualities may be tied to modes of human response that are not natural endowments but rather the product of initiation into an ongoing tradition, its vocabulary, narratives and paradigms, all subject of course to endless refinement and revision in the light of a standing obligation to engage in critical reflection on one's intellectual inheritance.").

48. *See* above at 10. I do not want (or need) to press this point too strongly. In some of his writings, McDowell also seems to express his view in modestly objective terms. *See* McDowell, *Mind, Value, and Reality*, 146 ("Values are not brutely there—not there independently of our sensibility—any more than colours are: though, as with colours, this does not prevent us from supposing that they are there independently of any particular apparent experience of them.").

49. Gerald Postema describes the justification and evaluation of legal judgments as a form of objectivity he calls publicity. According to Postema, objectivity as publicity "is a methodological conception of objectivity. It is defined relative to a particular notion of correct normative judgments. This notion of correctness has an important procedural component built into it. It cannot be separated from the process of delib-

erative judging. Broadly speaking, a judgment is correct, on this view, if it is backed by sound reasons that are or can be articulated and assessed publicly. . . . First, correctness is . . . a relation between propositions and arguments or reasons that support them, and this relationship is embodied in the activity of making and assessing arguments offered in support of the proposition. Thus, to say that a proposition is correct is to assess it in terms of standards of argument drawn from the normative discourse in question. Second, the process of offering and assessing arguments for judgments is regarded as essentially interpersonal, public. Correctness is manifested in the process of reasonable persons offering reasons to *each other*." Gerald J. Postema, "Objectivity Fit for Law," in Brian Leiter, ed., *Objectivity in Law and Morals* (Cambridge University Press, 2001), 117 (emphasis in original). Postema's conception of objectivity is domain-specific and shares many features with McDowell's view. As with McDowell's view, Postema's is broadly supportive of the argument I make here. My one reservation is simply that Postema describes his view as a form of objectivity. As a result, he is driven to concede, due to the underlying philosophical debate, that certain functional realities of legal practice and legal reasoning fall "far short of the ideal of objectivity as publicity" and that their "objectivity-distorting effects" should be improved. *See id.* at 128. This is why I believe that differentiating objectivity from intersubjectivity is important. Postema treats the formulation of legal judgments by judges and the assessment of those judgments by a larger community together as publicity, and he refers to these processes as the objectivity of law. I argue, instead, that we should distinguish among the formulation of legal judgments by judges, the legal norms expressed in those judgments, and the evaluation and reception of those judgments by the community.

50. *See, e.g.*, Goodpaster, *On the Theory of the American Adversary Criminal Trial*, 121–27, 134–38 (differentiating the "truth-finding" theory of a trial from the "fair decision" theory and the "rights theory."). Of course, as Goodpaster explains, these theories are not mutually exclusive.

51. *See* below at 59–62.

52. *See* above at 148n4.

53. Some will argue that these are also flaws of the system.

54. *See* Goodpaster, *On the Theory of American Adversary Criminal Trial*, 130 ("[T]he law may also have both a different concept of truth and a different way of finding truth than do other systems of thought. A trial is an accusatory proceeding. As such, trials have no abstract interest in what happened independent of the accusation. In other words, the issue in a trial is the truth of the accusation, and the accusation is true if it is proven to be true within the rules of proof and persuasion. In this manner, a trial *produces* truth, rather than finds it. This truth is a 'legal' truth and is that which the system recognizes as true.") (emphasis supplied).

55. The variety of individual experiences and perspectives that different members of the jury bring with them to the jury box is one good example. *See, e.g.*, *Peters v. Kiff*, 407 U.S. 493, 503–4 (1972) ("[W]e are unwilling to make the assumption that the exclusion of Negroes has relevance only for issues involving race. When any large and identifiable segment of the community is excluded from jury service, the effect is to remove from the jury room qualities of human nature and varieties of human experience, the range of which is unknown and perhaps unknowable. It is not necessary to

assume that the excluded group will consistently vote as a class in order to conclude, as we do, that its exclusion deprives the jury of a perspective on human events that may have unsuspected importance in any case that may be presented."); *Ballard v. United States*, 329 U.S. 187, 195 (1946) ("The systematic and intentional exclusion of women, like the exclusion of a racial group, or an economic or social class, deprives the jury system of the broad base it was designed by Congress to have in our democratic society. . . . The injury is not limited to the defendant—there is injury to the jury system, to the law as an institution, to the community at large, and to the democratic ideal reflected in the processes of our courts.") (citations omitted). Obviously, some subjective perspectives amount to active biases that will disqualify a juror for an inability to be impartial. *See, e.g.*, *People v. McCray*, 57 N.Y.2d 542, 547 (1982), *cert. denied sub nom.*, *McCray v. New York*, 461 U.S. 961 (1983) ("[T]hose who admit to such prejudices or admit to membership in groups from which such prejudices may readily be inferred, obviously should be disqualified from sitting on juries where these prejudices could interfere with the attainment of a fair and just verdict. For example, fundamental fairness dictates that a member of the Ku Klux Klan be disqualified from sitting on a jury in a case in which a black man is accused of assaulting a white. These individuals can adequately be eliminated through the challenge for cause.").

56. For example, the legal rules that the parties and the court agree should be applied in a case. Objectivity here can be thought of in a rule of law sense and in a functional effectiveness sense. *See* above at 146n98, 148n4, and below at 163nn106–111. Part of the problem with the broad term objectivity is that these usages overlap, but not entirely. The parties and the court may agree that the rules exist and that they govern the process in certain ways, but may still disagree about how the rules should be applied or how they should govern the process.

57. In Scotland, jurors may return a verdict of "not guilty" to indicate their conclusion that the defendant did not commit the crime of which he was accused or of "not proven" to indicate their conclusion that sufficient doubt exists to preclude conviction. *See* Peter Duff, *The Scottish Criminal Jury: A Very Peculiar Institution*, 62 Law & Contemp. Prob. 173, 193 (1999).

58. *See* Neil MacCormick, *Practical Reason in Law and Morality* (Oxford University Press, 2008), 17–21.

59. For a sense of what I have in mind here, *see* Iris Murdoch, *Metaphysics as a Guide to Morals* (Penguin Books, 1993), 25–26 ("A misleading though attractive distinction is made by many thinkers between fact and (moral) value. Roughly, the purpose of the distinction . . . is to *segregate* value in order to keep it pure and untainted, not derived from or mixed with empirical facts. . . . This originally well-intentioned segregation then ignores an obvious and important aspect of human existence, the way in which almost all our concepts and activities involve evaluation.") (emphasis in original). *See also* above at 143n79.

60. Heidi Li Feldman's discussion of blend concepts is a helpful way of explaining the interaction between legal norms and factual circumstances when attempting to achieve the proper outcome in a given case. *See* Heidi Li Feldman, *Objectivity in Legal Judgment*, 92 Mich. L. Rev. 1187, 1194–99 (1994).

61. *See* Murdoch, *Metaphysics as a Guide to Morals*, 34–35.

62. *See* Linda Meyer, *"Nothing We Say Matters": *Teague* and New Rules*, 61 U. Chi. L.

Rev. 423, 472 (1994) ("The description that language—and by extension, law—will give to an action or thing will depend upon which aspect of it is important to human action at the moment. . . . Each description relates it to human action; which is relevant or important or 'material' depends upon the context or the purpose of the action. By extension, a fact in a case has analogical importance not intrinsically, but by reference to the point of the inquiry. The common law, by keeping the focus on the context, sees that the statement of any rule is always tied to the point to which we are attending.").

63. *Cf.* Alan Montefiore, "Objectivity, Impartiality and Open-Mindedness," in Alan Montefiore, ed., *Neutrality and Impartiality: The University and Political Commitment* (Cambridge University Press, 1975), 19 ("[N]o one can simply carve out the facts to suit himself merely by choosing some favoured or convenient description; it is in this sense, as a reminder of and as a way of expressing these constraining limits, that it may occasionally be worth insisting that the facts are what they are in themselves, independently of what anyone may think about them. But this in no way limits the truth or force of the 'fact' that the concepts, the descriptions and the categories that one has to use as soon as one starts to reflect on the facts of any situation, but above all one that is social or political, must themselves derive from, rest on and reflect a certain human experience.").

64. Richard Posner uses the term "priors" to describe the range of personal experiences, values and perspectives that any judge brings to any case he must decide, and he explains that different judges react differently to the same case as a result of their different priors. *See* Richard A. Posner, *Reflections on Judging* (Harvard University Press, 2013), 129–30. *See also* above at 133n2.

65. *See, e.g.*, Cohen, *Blindfolds Off*, 82 ("You come with your experience. . . . You're listening to someone in the context of your life, that's the only lens in which to view them. . . . [I]ssues of plausibility, credibility, all the weighing and balancing tests, even the procedural questions—how far to delve into a legal issue before you're satisfied that you understand it—require judgment, the judgment of human beings.") (remarks of former judge Nancy Gertner).

66. As I have explained, I focus on judges in the text, but this point may be even more evident when we consider a juror's response to the evidence and the applicable law. *See* Robert P. Burns, *A Theory of the Trial* (Princeton University Press, 1999), 144–45 ("Where the jury decides a case differently from the way in which a judge would decide it, this usually occurs because what social scientists blandly call 'values' have influenced the very fact-finding process itself, not usually because the jury has found the same 'facts' as the judge and then consciously applied different norms."). This is also why we should usually consider a judge's or juror's responses to the law and the facts as an individual whose full identity matters but not (simply) as a woman or a Latina or a sixty-one-year-old. *Cf. id.* at 143–44.

67. *See* Burns, *A Theory of the Trial*, 125–41, 188–204, 209–11.

68. *See* above at 9–14.

69. *See* Joseph Raz, *The Authority of Law: Essays on Law and Morality* (2nd ed.) (Oxford University Press, 2009), 46–48; Joseph Raz, *Ethics in the Public Domain: Essays in the Morality of Law and Politics* (rev. ed.) (Oxford University Press, 1994), 194–95.

70. *See* H. L. A. Hart, *Positivism and the Separation of Law and Morals*, 71 Harv. L. Rev.

593, 601 n. 25 (1958). It is important to recognize exactly what this claim means for positivism. Despite frequent misreadings, it is *not* the claim that there are no connections between morality and law, or even that none of these is ever necessary. *See* John Gardner, *Law as a Leap of Faith: Essays on Law in General* (Oxford University Press, 2012), 48–51. The separability thesis is the claim that morality is never necessary to the identification of law as law, unless, for inclusive positivists, a particular legal system has incorporated a moral determinant for identifying law within its rule of recognition. *See, e.g.*, H. L. A. Hart, *The Concept of Law* (3rd ed.) (Oxford University Press, 2012), 185–86, 204, 250, 269; H. L. A. Hart, *Essays in Jurisprudence and Philosophy* (Oxford University Press, 1983), 6, 361; Jules Coleman, "Authority and Reason," in Robert P. George, ed., *The Autonomy of Law: Essays on Legal Positivism* (Oxford University Press, 1996), 287–88, 295.

71. Hart, *Positivism and the Separation of Law and Morals*, 624.

72. *See, e.g.*, Benjamin C. Zipursky, *Legal Coherentism*, 50 SMU L. Rev. 1679, 1692 (1997) ("The positivist purports to explain what law is, and, in this sense, what makes legal statements true, by pointing to legal sources and to the conduct and attitudes of those who make the legal sources, interpret them, use them, and treat them as authoritative.") (footnote omitted).

73. *See, e.g.*, Gerald J. Postema, "Law's Autonomy and Public Practical Reason," in Robert P. George, ed., *The Autonomy of Law: Essays on Legal Positivism* (Oxford University Press, 1996), 83; Frederick Schauer and Virginia Wise, *Legal Positivism as Legal Information*, 82 Cornell L. Rev. 1080, 1082, 1093–99 (1997). Although positivism's commitment to the sources thesis occasionally leads some to conclude that only positivists recognize the unique role of legal sources for legal reasoning, in fact that view is widely shared among legal theorists. *See* above at 146n100.

74. *See* Frederick Schauer, "Positivism Before Hart," in Michael Freeman and Patricia Mindus, eds., *The Legacy of John Austin's Jurisprudence* (Springer, 2013).

75. Schauer, "Positivism Before Hart," in Freeman and Mindus, *John Austin's Jurisprudence*, 276.

76. Schauer, "Positivism Before Hart," in Freeman and Mindus, *John Austin's Jurisprudence*, 279. Schauer says that decisional positivism "seeks to create institutions relying on relatively precise rules, minimizing adjudicative discretion, limiting the law-making power of judges and other law-application officials, restricting legal decision-makers to a limited set of easily identifiable sources, and in general fostering predictability and limiting judicial authority." *Id.* Schauer's characterization is correct with respect to the positivists before Hart (Bentham and Austin) whom he studies in his essay. And perhaps as a means of differentiating positivists from others who hold superficially similar views, this is fair enough. Nevertheless, I believe conceptual positivism and decisional positivism together create intellectual space for a necessary but nonexclusive place for legal sources in legal reasoning that need not limit common law judges quite as stringently as Bentham or Austin supposed. In Schauer's terms, this represents decisional positivism's "non-normative aspect" in relation to "just how heavily legal decisions are constrained by the texts of formal legal sources and just how much the array of those sources is a limited subset of the full array of social sources" available to a judge or legal decision maker. *Id.* at 280. Moreover, as I have mentioned, in its recognition of a unique status for legal sources in legal reasoning, decisional

positivism, standing alone, does not necessarily distinguish positivism from other theories of law. *See* above at 146n100 and below at 162–63n103.

77. Schauer, "Positivism Before Hart," in Freeman and Mindus, *John Austin's Jurisprudence*, 277.

78. *See* Hart, *Positivism and the Separation of Law and Morals*, 597–98.

79. Joshua Cohen, *Philosophy, Politics, Democracy: Selected Essays* (Harvard University Press, 2009), 358, 359.

80. Rawls, *Political Liberalism*, 94.

81. Cohen, *Philosophy, Politics, Democracy*, 349.

82. Cohen, *Philosophy, Politics, Democracy*, 350.

83. Cohen, *Philosophy, Politics, Democracy*, 350–51.

84. Tellingly, for purposes of my concerns with his approach and my argument in this book, Cohen equates the political conception of truth with "the political conception of objectivity." *See* Cohen, *Philosophy, Politics, Democracy*, 349 n. 3.

85. Cohen, *Philosophy, Politics, Democracy*, 366–67 (emphasis in original) (footnote omitted).

86. For a discussion that suggests Hobbes' own view was more complex (or conflicted) than Cohen indicates, *see* Jeremy Waldron, "Legal Judgment and Moral Reservation," in Agustín José Menéndez and John Erik Fossum, eds., *Law and Democracy in Neil MacCormick's Legal and Political Theory: The Post-Sovereign Constellation* (Springer, 2011), 114–15.

87. *See, e.g.*, Hart, *The Concept of Law*, 253–54 ("I still think legal theory should avoid commitment to controversial philosophical theories of the general status of moral judgments and should leave open, as I do in this book (p. 168), the general question of whether they have . . . 'objective standing.'"); Hart, *Positivism and the Separation of Law and Morals*, 624–25 ("Emphasis on the distinction between law as it is and law as it ought to be may be taken to depend upon and to entail what are called 'subjectivist' or 'relativist' or 'noncognitive' theories concerning the very nature of moral judgments, moral distinctions, or 'values.' . . . I think (though I cannot prove) that insistence upon the distinction between law as it is and law as it ought to be has been, under the general head of 'positivism,' confused with a moral theory according to which statements of what is the case ('statements of fact') belong to a category or type radically different from statements of what ought to be ('value statements.')").

88. *See* Brian Bix, *On the Dividing Line Between Natural Law Theory and Legal Positivism*, 75 Notre Dame L. Rev. 1613, 1617–18 (2000).

89. *See, e.g.*, Joseph Raz, *The Authority of Law*, 39–40 ("A jurisprudential theory is acceptable only if its tests for identifying the content of the law and determining its existence depend exclusively on facts of human behaviour capable of being described in value-neutral terms, and applied without resort to moral argument.").

90. *See* above at 158–59n70. *See also* Coleman, "Authority and Reason," in George, *The Autonomy of Law*, 291 ("That some communities—including perhaps our own—incorporate moral principles into law does not violate the separability thesis. The separability thesis is not the claim that law and morality are necessarily separated; rather, it is the claim that they are not necessarily connected.").

91. *See, e.g.*, Hart, *The Concept of Law*, 205–12; Hart, *Positivism and the Separation of Law and Morals*, 617–21.

92. *See* Hart, *The Concept of Law*, 94.

93. Hart, *The Concept of Law*, 95.

94. *See* Benjamin C. Zipursky, "The Model of Social Facts," in Jules Coleman, ed., *Hart's Postscript: Essays on the Postscript to* The Concept of Law (Oxford University Press, 2001), 260 ("[I]n a legal community, officials accept certain propositions about validity, and . . . it is by virtue of their doing so that those propositions are in force in that legal community."). *Cf.* John Chipman Gray, *The Nature and Sources of the Law* (Ashgate, 1997), 54 ("[Judges] seek the rules which they follow not in their own whims, but they derive them from sources often of the most general and permanent character, to which they are directed, by the organized body to which they belong, to apply themselves."); Roscoe Pound, "What Is the Common Law?," in Roscoe Pound, ed., *The Future of the Common Law* (Peter Smith, 1965), 7–8.

95. *See* Zipursky, "The Model of Social Facts," in Coleman, *Hart's Postscript*, 232–33 ("What, then, can we say about Hart's frequent and pivotally important statements that rules of recognition are social rules? . . . [F]or a rule of recognition of a legal system (considered as an abstract union of primary and secondary rules) to be the rule of recognition *of a community* is for there to be a certain kind of social practice among the legal officials in that community of accepting that rule of recognition.") (emphasis in original).

96. Hart, *The Concept of Law*, 258.

97. *See* Hart, *The Concept of Law*, 105 ("[W]hen we consider how the judge's own statement that a particular rule is valid functions in a judicial decision . . . he plainly is not concerned to predict his own or others' official action. His statement that a rule is valid is an internal statement recognizing that the rule satisfies the tests for identifying what is to count as law in his court, and constitutes not a prophecy of but part of the *reason* for his decision.") (emphasis in original).

98. *See* Cristóbal Orrego, "Hart's Last Legal Positivism: Morality Might Be Objective, Legality Certainly Is Not," in Kenneth Einar Himma, ed., *Law, Morality, and Legal Positivism* (Franz Steiner Verlag, 2004), 75.

99. *See, e.g.*, Raz, *The Authority of Law*, 47–48 ("The sources of law are those facts by virtue of which it is valid and which identify its content."); Coleman, "Authority and Reason," in George, *The Autonomy of Law*, 288 ("In developing incorporationism [inclusive positivism] I have focused almost exclusively on its conceptions of legality and validity and on the role the rule of recognition plays in determining both."). I should also mention a further disagreement among inclusive positivists. Coleman argues that the "epistemic function" of the rule of recognition permits a distinction between the identification and the validation of the law. *See id.* at 291–93. It is unclear whether Hart would accept Coleman's bifurcation of the epistemic function of the rule of recognition. Hart did not seem to differentiate validation from identification in his writings on the rule of recognition. But for my purposes here, I only want to emphasize that in his discussions of the rule of recognition and its function in legal reasoning, Hart repeatedly refers to the validity and validation of legal rules, rather than to their truth, even where he discusses the possibility that a rule of recognition may incorporate "moral criteria for the identification of the law." *See* Hart, *The Concept of Law*, 100–110, 207–12, 247, 250–59, 269.

100. *See, e.g.*, Brian Zamulinski, *Rehabilitating the Declaratory Theory of the Common*

Law, 2 J. L. & Cts. 171, 181 (2014) ("[J]udge-made law qua moral facts neither has nor needs a rule of recognition. . . . The law that can be discovered constrains the law that can be made because enacting a seriously immoral statute would imply the repeal of the law qua moral facts. . . . Since the law qua moral facts cannot be repealed, if an immoral statute were valid, the law would contradict itself. But the law as a whole must be consistent. Since consistency cannot be maintained unless immoral statutes give way, they must give way."). Although Zamulinski goes on to classify (and dismiss) Hart's inclusive positivism as an alternative to his own view (*see id.*), he then seems to embrace just that position (through judicial decisions rather than constitutional provisions) in his rejection of natural law theory. *See id.* at 182 ("The declaratory theorist's claim is not that there is a conceptual connection between law and morality of the sort that natural law theorists propose but that moral facts can literally be substantive law in systems that include judge-made law. The invalidity of immoral statutes in such a system does not depend on a definition of law but on the fact that moral facts *have been incorporated as* substantive law.") (emphasis supplied). *See also id.* at 185 ("In light of the declaratory theory, the common law qua system of 'judge-made law' is a rational, self-correcting project that identifies a subset of moral facts as substantive law, where the substantive law is a set of publicly enforced standards.").

101. *See, e.g.*, Raz, *Ethics in the Public Domain*, 332–33, 334 ("[I]t follows from the sources thesis—as we have just seen—that there is much more to legal reasoning than applying the law, and the rest, which I will call as I did all along reasoning according to law, is—arguably—applying moral considerations. . . . I have divided reasoning into reasoning about the law and reasoning according to law. The first is governed by the sources thesis, the second I believe to be quite commonly straightforward moral reasoning. . . . Observation of judicial practice, at least in the countries that I am familiar with, does more than confirm this argument. It provides strong grounds for the additional contention that it is sound moral practice, which is followed in many legal systems, to require the courts to engage in moral reasoning.").

102. *See* Raz, *The Authority of Law*, 114, 199–200; Hart, *The Concept of Law*, 185, 203–5. The pervasive misperception of positivism in this aspect is sometimes astonishing. *See, e.g.*, Stephen Macedo, *Morality and the Constitution: Toward a Synthesis for "Earthbound" Interpreters*, 61 U. Cin. L. Rev. 29, 36–37 (1992) ("Positivism's virtues are that it allows us to purchase clarity and predictability, but it does this at the price of sacrificing those aspirations that might also be pursued through the institutions of law: political aspirations toward principled debate and criticism, which might be thought to contribute to the moral improvement of the polity."). Without putting too fine a point on it, this is effectively the opposite of Hart's and Raz's view. Along with the sources already cited in this note and the previous one, *see* Joseph Raz, *Dworkin: A New Link in the Chain*, 74 Calif. L. Rev. 1103, 1110, 1115 (1986); Joseph Raz, "Legal Principles and the Limits of Law," in Marshall Cohen, ed., *Ronald Dworkin and Contemporary Jurisprudence* (Rowman & Allanheld, 1983), 85.

103. *See* above at 146n100. *See generally* Robert P. George, *Natural Law*, 52 Am. J. Juris. 55, 72 (2007) ("Natural law theorists through the ages have taken note of the distinction between the systemic validity of a proposition of law—the property of belonging to a legal system—and the law's moral validity and bindingness as a matter of conscience. They have had no difficulty accepting the central thesis of what we today

call legal positivism, viz. that the existence and content of the positive law depends on social facts and not on its moral merits.").

104. *See* Leslie Green, *Positivism and the Inseparability of Law and Morals*, 83 N.Y.U. L. Rev. 1035, 1040–41 (2008).

105. *See* Neil MacCormick, "*The Concept of Law* and The Concept of Law," in Robert P. George, ed., *The Autonomy of Law: Essays on Legal Positivism* (Oxford University Press, 1996), 169 ("[O]ne vital point of legal institutions is exactly that they exist (*inter alia*) to settle authoritatively for practical purposes what cannot be settled morally.").

106. *See* Neil MacCormick, *Legal Reasoning and Legal Theory* (Oxford University Press, 1978), 86 ("[A]ppreciation of the necessary universality of justifying reasons for the decision of particular cases can enable us . . . [to see that] the constraints of formal justice obligate a court to attend to the need for generic rulings on points of law, and their acceptability as generic rulings, as essential to the justification of particular decisions."). *See also id.* at 84, 98–99, 214–15.

107. *See, e.g.*, Jerome Frank, *Courts on Trial: Myth and Reality in American Justice* (Princeton University Press, 1949), 155.

108. Warren, *Modes of Objectivity*, 82–83.

109. *See* David Lyons, *Moral Aspects of Legal Theory: Essays on Law, Justice, and Political Responsibility* (Cambridge University Press, 1993), 35 ("Let us assume that officials should, to do justice, be impartial . . . it does not follow that an official who fails to follow the law acts unjustly. Let us agree that an *application* of the law which is *not* impartial is *un*just; it does not follow that all *deviations* by officials from the law are unjust. . . . An official might deliberately refuse to follow the law; this is not the same as applying it in, for example, a biased or prejudiced manner. This distinction is important, for the official may refuse to follow the law on principled grounds, precisely in order to prevent an injustice of which he would be the instrument.") (emphasis in original). This point also relates to issues of individual and institutional judicial independence, which I discuss further in chapter 5.

110. *See* Neil MacCormick, *Rhetoric and the Rule of Law: A Theory of Legal Reasoning* (Oxford University Press, 2005), 89–90, 94–95, 239–47, 252–53. *See also* Richard H. S. Tur, *Defeasibilism*, 21 Oxford J. Leg. Stud. 355 (2001); Jordi Ferrer Beltran and Giovanni Battista Ratti, eds., *The Logic of Legal Requirements: Essays on Defeasibility* (Oxford University Press, 2012); Luis Duarte d'Almeida, *Allowing for Exceptions: A Theory of Defences and Defeasibility in Law* (Oxford University Press, 2015).

111. For more on this point, *see* Lyons, *Moral Aspects of Legal Theory*, 112–13 ("Moral judgments, as opposed to mere visceral reactions that can be expressed in words, presuppose some general standards. . . . It is important to appreciate that no part of the constraint of moral consistency or such presuppositions of its applicability as we have considered makes use of the notion of a uniquely true, correct, or sound moral judgment. This minimal constraint concerns merely how one's judgments, both specific and general, hang together. And yet this constraint has some determinate implications. It says, in effect, that one must apply the same standards to all cases that one is not honestly prepared to distinguish on principled grounds. That does not tell us what cases to distinguish or more generally what principles to apply. But it does tell us to be faithful to our own deepest values, whatever they may be, and to judge specific matters accordingly.").

112. Richard A. Posner, *The Federal Courts: Challenge and Reform* (2nd ed.) (Harvard University Press, 1996), 312. *See also* Martha C. Nussbaum, *Poets as Judges: Judicial Rhetoric and the Literary Imagination,* 62 U. Chi. L. Rev. 1477, 1483 (1995) ("Judges need criteria that are not arbitrary or capricious. . . . The reasons should meet a standard of public articulability and principled consistency."). The concept of principled consistency is sometimes associated with Herbert Wechsler's famous article on neutral principles. *See* Herbert Wechsler, *Toward Neutral Principles of Constitutional Law,* 73 Harv. L. Rev. 1, 19, 31–35 (1959). I prefer Nussbaum's conception of principled consistency to Wechsler's. While Wechsler seems to have viewed neutrality as an abstract value of detachment and formally consistent reasoning and results, Nussbaum's view of principled judicial decision making better reflects the view I intend to defend here: "[T]he real-life judge must also have other abilities and knowledge, and is constrained in many ways by her institutional role and by the demands of statute and precedent, which already establish what she may and may not consider salient. The literary aspects of judging can readily be incorporated into an understanding of judicial reasoning that derives from the common-law tradition. . . . [T]hat tradition does not permit a judge to exercise untethered sympathy or 'fancy.' . . . [The common law judge] is committed to neutrality, properly understood. . . . [S]he does not think of this sort of neutrality as requiring a lofty distance from the social realities of the cases before her. Indeed, she examines those realities searchingly, with imaginative concreteness and the emotional responses proper to [her role]." Nussbaum, *Poets as Judges,* 1482. *See also* MacCormick, *Legal Reasoning and Legal Theory,* 75–76 ("The court which today decides a specific case between individual parties ought to take account of its duty, at least its prima-facie duty, to decide the case consistently with prior decisions on the same or similar points. At the least, formal justice requires that it shall not save for strong reasons decide this case in a manner unlike the manner of its prior decisions in like cases. . . . That I must treat like cases alike implies that I must decide today's case on grounds which I am willing to adopt for the decision of future similar cases, just as much as it implies that I must today have regard to my earlier decisions in past similar cases. *Both* implications are implications of adherence to the principle of formal justice. . . . [T]here can genuinely be a conflict between the formal justice of following the precedent and the perceived substantive justice of today's case. . . . I must thereby commit myself to settling grounds for decision for today's and future similar cases. . . . [T]here will be [conflict] in the future if today I articulate grounds of decision which turn out to embody some substantive injustice or to be on other grounds inexpedient or undesirable. That is certainly a strong reason for being careful about how I decide today's case.").

113. *See generally* Fiss, *The Law as It Could Be,* 154, 155 ("[T]he meaning of a text does not reside in the text, as an object might reside in physical space or as an element might be said to be present in a chemical compound, ready to be extracted if only one knows the correct process. It recognizes a role for the subjective. Indeed, interpretation is defined as the process by which the meaning of a text is understood and expressed, and the acts of understanding and expression necessarily entail strong personal elements. At the same time, the freedom of those who interpret is not absolute. Interpreters are not free to assign any meaning they wish to the text. They are disciplined by a set of rules that specify the relevance and weight to be assigned to the

material . . . as well as by those that define basic concepts and that establish the procedural circumstances under which the interpretation must occur. . . . Rules are not rules unless they are authoritative, and only a community can confer that authority. Accordingly, the disciplining rules governing an interpretive activity must be seen as defining or demarcating an interpretive community consisting of those who recognize the rules as authoritative. This means, above all, that the objective quality of interpretation is bounded, limited, or relative. . . . Bounded objectivity is the only kind of objectivity to which the law—or any interpretive activity—ever aspires and the only one we care about."). Fiss seems to assume a "rules as rails" conception of the function and meaning of legal rules. *See* McDowell, *Mind, Value, and Reality*, 203–9. Even if that is his view, which is not entirely clear, nothing in the quoted passage (or its application to my argument) necessitates that position.

114. Barbara Herrnstein Smith, *Belief and Resistance: Dynamics of Contemporary Intellectual Controversy* (Harvard University Press, 1997), 16.

115. Smith, *Belief and Resistance*, 16.

116. *See* Burns, *A Theory of the Trial*, 212 ("[R]eflective judgment achieves its impartiality not by achieving a Platonic point of view above the contending views nor by an empathic intuition of the feelings of others, but by 'enlarging' its understanding in a distinctive manner: 'The greater the reach—the larger the realm in which the enlightened individual is able to move from standpoint to standpoint—the more 'general' will be his thinking.'") (quoting Hannah Arendt, *Lectures on Kant's Political Philosophy*, ed. Ronald Beiner (University of Chicago Press, 1982), 44).

117. *See generally* Robert G. McCloskey, *The American Supreme Court* (5th ed.) (University of Chicago Press, 2010), 17 ("[S]ince the constitutional questions that do successfully claim the attention of the Court are often those least answerable by rules of thumb, the predilections, the 'values' of the judges, must play a part in supplying answers to them."); Posner, *The Federal Courts*, 310 ("[M]any judicial decisions will be based, in part anyway, on value judgments rather than just on technical, professional judgments."); George Anastaplo, *The Amendments to the Constitution: A Commentary* (Johns Hopkins University Press, 1995), 91 ("[T]he Constitution, from the beginning, anticipated that American courts (whether National or State) would continue acting as courts in the common-law tradition had 'always' acted. A sense of fairness, consistent with precedents, general expectations, and the political, social, economic, and religious opinions and institutions of the Country, is relied upon in how the law is to be developed and applied."); Kent Greenawalt, *Policy, Rights, and Judicial Decision*, 11 Ga. L. Rev. 991, 1052–53 (1977).

118. *See, e.g.*, Richard A. Posner, *How Judges Think* (Harvard University Press, 2008), 120 ("Greater recognition of the role of the personal, the emotional, and the intuitive in judicial decisions would not weaken the force of these factors in judicial decision making, because there are no adequate alternatives and judges have to decide their cases with the tools at hand."); William J. Brennan, Jr., *Reason, Passion, And "The Progress Of The Law"*, 42 Record of the Ass'n of the Bar of the City of New York 948, 951, 952 (1987) ("It is my thesis that this interplay of forces, this internal dialogue of reason and passion, does not taint the judicial process, but is in fact central to its vitality. . . . Cardozo did not shrink from the implications of that admission. He rejected the prevailing myth that a judge's personal values were irrelevant to the decision pro-

cess, because a judge's role was presumably limited to application of existing law, a process governed by external, objective norms.").

119. *Cf.* David Bell, *The Art of Judgement*, 96 Mind 221, 224 (1987) (arguing that there are three requirements "that an acceptable doctrine of judgement might be expected to meet. . . . [T]hey concern the intersubjectivity, expressibility, and the truth of thoughts."). I prefer the term communicability rather than expressibility, because communicability better connotes the judgment's relationship to an audience to whom it is communicated (whereas expressibility might only suggest that the judgment be expressed and not necessarily communicated to another individual). *See* below at at 57, 63–66.

120. *Cf.* Lucia Corso, *Should Empathy Play Any Role in the Interpretation of Constitutional Rights?*, 27 Ratio Juris 94, 103 (2014) ("[A] constitutional judge . . . when required to express an opinion on the meaning of privacy or personal freedom . . . would not be able to decide the case without trying to understand what goes through the mind of the Latino suspect held in a police cell and confronted with white police officers, or how it feels for an adolescent to be strip-searched in front of her school mates, or what it means for a black man to be ejected from a railroad carriage because of the color of his skin.") (citations omitted).

121. *See* Herma Hill Kay, *Symposium: Celebration of the Tenth Anniversary of Justice Ruth Bader Ginsburg's Appointment to the Supreme Court of the United States*, 104 Colum. L. Rev. 1, 7 (2004).

122. Linda K. Kerber, *No Constitutional Right to Be Ladies: Women and the Obligations of Citizenship* (Hill & Wang, 1998), 202. Griswold would later identify Ginsburg and Thurgood Marshall as the leading public issue advocates before the Court. *See* Daniel Wathen and Barbara Riegelhaupt, *The Speeches of Frank M. Coffin: A Sideline to Judging*, 63 Me. L. Rev. 467, 492 (2011).

123. *See* Ruth Bader Ginsburg, *The Changing Complexion of Harvard Law School*, 27 Harv. Women's L.J. 303, 304 (2004).

124. *See* Diana Klebanow and Franklin L. Jonas, *People's Lawyers: Crusaders for Justice in American History* (Routledge, 2002), 358.

125. Ginsburg was recommended to Frankfurter by one of her professors at Harvard, Albert Sacks. Justice Frankfurter indicated that he "just wasn't ready to hire a woman." Neil A. Lewis, "Rejected as a Clerk, Chosen as a Justice: Ruth Joan Bader Ginsburg," N.Y. Times, June 15, 1993, at A1.

126. Michael J. Gerhardt, *Constitutional Humility*, 76 U. Cin. L. Rev. 23, 45 (2007).

127. *See* Ari L. Goldman, "Gerald Gunther, Legal Scholar, Dies at 75," N.Y. Times, Aug. 1, 2002, at B9 ("Professor Gunther, who was then on the Columbia faculty, 'got me my clerkship by pressuring every judge in the Southern District,' Justice Ginsburg said. She said that Professor Gunther had to promise that 'if I didn't work out, he would find a male lawyer to replace me.'").

128. *See* Malvina Halberstam, *Ruth Bader Ginsburg: The First Jewish Woman on the United States Supreme Court*, 19 Cardozo L. Rev. 1441, 1443 n. 4 (1998).

129. *See* Klebanow and Jonas, *People's Lawyers*, 362.

130. *See* Kenneth M. Davidson, Ruth Bader Ginsburg, and Herma Hill Kay, *Sex-Based Discrimination* (West Publishing Co., 1974).

131. *See* Katherine Franke, *Introduction: Symposium Honoring the Advocacy, Scholarship, and Jurisprudence of Justice Ruth Ginsburg*, 25 Colum. J. Gender & L. 1, 4 (2013).

132. *See* Kay, *Celebration of the Tenth Anniversary of Justice Ruth Bader Ginsburg's Appointment*, 19. The cases Ginsburg argued are *Frontiero v. Richardson*, 411 U.S. 677 (1973); *Kahn v. Shevin*, 416 U.S. 351 (1974); *Weinberger v. Wiesenfeld*, 420 U.S. 636 (1975); *Edwards v. Healy*, 421 U.S. 772 (1975); *Califano v. Goldfarb*, 430 U.S. 199 (1977); *Duren v. Missouri*, 439 U.S. 357 (1979).

133. *See, e.g.*, Reply Brief for Appellant, *Reed v. Reed*, 404 U.S. 71 (1971), 5, 20.

134. *See, e.g.*, Brief for Appellant, *Reed v. Reed*, 404 U.S. 71 (1971), 11–20.

135. *See* Maxwell L. Stearns, *Constitutional Process: A Social Choice Analysis of Supreme Court Decision Making* (University of Michigan Press, 2000), 189–90. In the details of the arguments, however, Ginsburg did not always contend that race and gender are identical for all constitutional purposes. *See* Serena Mayeri, *The Strange Career of Jane Crow: Sex Segregation and the Transformation of Anti-Discrimination Discourse*, 18 Yale J.L. & Human. 187, 259–62 (2006).

136. 518 U.S. 515 (1996).

137. *See, e.g.*, Mark Tushnet, *A Court Divided: The Rehnquist Court and the Future of Constitutional Law* (W. W. Norton, 2005), 120–29; Burt Neuborne, *A Symposium on the Legacy of Justice William J. Brennan, Jr.: Introduction of Justice Ruth Bader Ginsburg*, 95 Calif. L. Rev. 2213, 2214 (2007); Kathleen Peratis, *Rhetoric of Justice Ruth Bader Ginsburg: Brief Comparison of the Language of the Advocate with the Language of the Justice*, 25 Colum. J. Gender & L. 35, 38–40 (2013).

138. *See* Rosemary C. Salomone, *Same, Different, Equal: Rethinking Single-Sex Schooling* (Yale University Press, 2003), 165 (quoting Ginsburg's comment that writing the *VMI* judgment "was winning the *Vorchheimer* case twenty years later."). For more on *Vorchheimer*, *see* Mayeri, *The Strange Career of Jane Crow*, 256–64.

139. Nomination of Ruth Bader Ginsburg to be Associate Justice of the Supreme Court of the United States: Hearings Before the Senate Comm. on the Judiciary, 103rd Cong. (1993) [Ginsburg Hearings], 139. Transcript available at http://www.loc.gov/law/find/nominations/ginsburg/hearing.pdf.

140. Ginsburg Hearings, 124.

141. 42 U.S.C. § 1973b(b).

142. 509 U.S. 630 (1993).

143. Ginsburg Hearings, 252.

144. 133 S.Ct. 2612 (2013).

145. *See Shelby County*, 133 S.Ct. at 2631.

146. *Shelby County*, 133 S.Ct. at 2625. *See also id.* at 2621 ("[t]hings have changed in the South") (citation omitted), 2626 ("Those extraordinary and unprecedented features were reauthorized—as if nothing had changed."), 2629 ("Congress . . . reenacted a formula based on 40-year-old facts having no logical relation to the present day."), 2631 ("Our country has changed."), 2631 ("[O]ur Nation has changed.") (Thomas, J., concurring).

147. *Shelby County*, 133 S.Ct. at 2634 (Ginsburg, J., dissenting).

148. *See Shelby County*, 133 S.Ct. at 2633–41.

149. *Shelby County*, 133 S.Ct. at 2642 (Ginsburg, J., dissenting) (emphasis supplied).

150. 515 U.S. 900 (1995).

151. *Miller*, 515 U.S. at 919, 920.

152. *See Miller*, 515 U.S. at 921–22.

153. *Miller*, 515 U.S. at 919.

154. *See* Lewis, "Rejected as a Clerk, Chosen as a Justice," at A1.

155. *Miller*, 515 U.S. at 935 (Ginsburg, J., dissenting).

156. *Miller*, 515 U.S. at 944 (Ginsburg, J., dissenting).

157. *Miller*, 515 U.S. at 944 (Ginsburg, J., dissenting). *See also id.* at 947 ("In adopting districting plans, however, States do not treat people as individuals. . . . Rather, legislators classify voters in groups—by economic, geographical, political, or social characteristics. . . . That ethnicity defines some of these groups is a political reality.").

158. *See Miller*, 515 U.S. at 948–49.

159. 134 S.Ct. 2751 (2014).

160. 42 U.S.C. § 2000bb et seq.

161. *See Hobby Lobby*, 134 S.Ct. at 2775.

162. *See* 26 U.S.C. § 5000A(f)(2), § 4980H(a), § 4980H(c)(2), 42 U.S.C. § 300gg-13(a)(4).

163. *Hobby Lobby*, 134 S.Ct. at 2785 (Kennedy, J., concurring).

164. *Hobby Lobby*, 134 S.Ct. at 2796 n.17 (Ginsburg, J., dissenting). *See also id.* at 2797 n. 19 ("The Court does not even begin to explain how one might go about ascertaining the religious scruples of a corporation where shares are sold to the public. No need to speculate on that, the Court says, for 'it seems unlikely' that large corporations 'will often assert RFRA claims.' Perhaps so, but as Hobby Lobby's case demonstrates, such claims are indeed pursued by large corporations, employing thousands of persons of different faiths.") (internal citation omitted).

165. *Hobby Lobby*, 134 S.Ct. at 2797–98 (Ginsburg, J., dissenting) (quoting 42 U.S.C. §2000bb-1(a)).

166. *See Hobby Lobby*, 134 S.Ct. at 2798 ("The Court barely pauses to inquire whether any burden imposed by the contraceptive coverage requirement is substantial.") (Ginsburg, J., dissenting).

167. *Hobby Lobby*, 134 S.Ct. at 2790 (Ginsburg, J., dissenting).

168. Ginsburg reiterated this basis for her dissent in a later interview about the case: "Contraceptive protection is something that every woman must have access to to control her own destiny. I certainly respect the belief of the Hobby Lobby owners. On the other hand, they have no constitutional right to foist that belief on the hundreds and hundreds of women who work for them who don't share that belief. I had never seen the free exercise of religion clause interpreted in such a way." *See* below at n171.

169. *Hobby Lobby*, 134 S.Ct. at 2799 (Ginsburg, J., dissenting) (citations omitted).

170. *See* Guy Gugliotta and Eleanor Randolph, "A Mentor, Role Model and Heroine of Feminist Lawyers," Wash. Post, June 15, 1993, at A14 ("[T]o be a woman, a Jew and mother to boot, that combination was a bit much. Probably motherhood was the major impediment.").

171. Ruth Bader Ginsburg, Associate Justice of the Supreme Court of the United States, interview by Katie Couric, Washington, DC (July 31, 2014). The full interview is available here: http://news.yahoo.com/video/exclusive-ruth-bader-ginsburg-hobby-091819044.html.

172. Interview by Katie Couric with Ruth Bader Ginsburg.

173. *See* Sandra Day O'Connor, *Justice O'Connor Reflects on Arizona's Judiciary*, 43 Ariz. L. Rev. 1, 1 (2001) ("[I] grew up on a cattle ranch in Greenlee County, miles from any town.").

174. *See* Clarence Thomas, *My Grandfather's Son* (Harper Collins, 2007), chs. 1–2.

175. *See Mississippi Univ. for Women v. Hogan*, 458 U.S. 718 (1982). Ginsburg stated that Justice O'Connor's opinion in *Hogan* "was the closest guide" for the judgment in *VMI*, which O'Connor joined. *See United States v. Virginia*, 518 U.S. at 523–24.

176. *United States v. Morrison*, 529 U.S. 598, 601–2 (2000).

177. *Morrison*, 529 U.S. at 617. *Morrison* was a 5-4 ruling in which O'Connor joined the majority and Ginsburg was among the dissenting justices.

178. 538 U.S. 343 (2003). The Virginia statute at issue in *Black* made it a felony for someone to burn a cross "with the intent of intimidating any person or group of persons" and indicated that "[a]ny such burning of a cross shall be prima facie evidence of an intent to intimidate a person or group of persons." *Id.* at 348 (quoting Va. Code Ann. § 18.2–423 (1996)).

179. Transcript of Oral Argument at 22-24, *Virginia v. Black*, 538 U.S. 343 (2003). The transcript is available here: www.supremecourt.gov/oral_arguments/argument_transcripts/01-1107.pdf.

180. As one commentator put it, Justice Thomas's remarks "changed the tenor of the debate, if not the minds of his colleagues, about the role of the law and the definition of justice." Dahlia Lithwick, "Personal Truths and Legal Fictions," N.Y. Times, Dec. 17, 2002, at A35.

181. Surprisingly, given the precedent of *R.A.V. v. City of St. Paul*, 505 U.S. 377 (1992) and other cases, the Court ruled that "The First Amendment permits Virginia to outlaw cross burnings done with the intent to intimidate because burning a cross is a particularly virulent form of intimidation." *Black*, 538 U.S. at 363. *See also id.* at 353 (referring to the Klan's "reign of terror" in the South), 356 ("The burning cross became a symbol of the Klan itself."), 357 ("[T]he burning of a cross is a 'symbol of hate.'") (quoting *Capitol Square Review and Advisory Bd. v. Pinette*, 515 U.S. 753, 771 (1995)) (Thomas, J., concurring). Although the Court went on to conclude that the prima facie evidence provision of the statute was unconstitutional because it "does not distinguish between a cross burning done with the purpose of creating anger or resentment and a cross burning done with the purpose of threatening or intimidating a victim," *Black*, 538 U.S. at 366, the Court's ruling that some cross burning was not protected expression under the First Amendment and could be criminalized is itself a notable development.

182. Thomas's dissent continued along the same lines as his questioning at the argument. He concluded that cross burning is conduct, not speech, and that the prima facie provision creates a justifiable inference of intention rather than an irrebuttable presumption. *See id.* at 394–95, 396–98.

183. *See* Lithwick, "Personal Truths and Legal Fictions," at A35 ("This court has always protected such symbolic expression, with prior cases deeming laws singling out cross- and flag-burning unconstitutional. But with his personal narrative, Justice Thomas changed the terms of the legal debate. After he spoke, members of the court took turns characterizing burning crosses as uniquely threatening symbolic speech . . . and as therefore undeserving of First Amendment protection."); Linda Greenhouse, "An Intense Attack by Justice Thomas on Cross-Burning," N.Y. Times, Dec. 12, 2002, at Al ("The case . . . raised tricky questions of First Amendment doctrine, and it was not clear how the court was inclined to decide it—until Justice Clarence Thomas spoke."). Although Lithwick and Greenhouse seem to disagree about how difficult a case *Black*

was for the Court to decide, they agree entirely on the influence of Thomas's comments upon the other members of the Court.

184. Like Justice Ginsburg, despite graduating with honors from Stanford Law School, Justice O'Connor received no offers of employment. *See* O'Connor, *Justice O'Connor Reflects on Arizona's Judiciary*, 1 ("When I graduated from law school in 1952, I received no offer of employment as a lawyer. There was one half-hearted offer of a job as a legal secretary. In time, I persuaded the District Attorney of San Mateo County to give me a job as a deputy. My career as a lawyer was launched. John and I were married, and within a year he was drafted, then accepted in the Judge Advocate General's Corps, and assigned to a post in Germany. I gave up my hard-won job and followed John to Germany, where I obtained a job as a lawyer in the Quartermaster Market Center in Frankfurt am Main. On John's discharge from the Army in 1957, we came to Phoenix. . . . Once again, I failed to find a law firm that would consider hiring a woman."). *See also* Martin D. Ginsburg, *Some Reflections on Imperfection*, 39 Ariz. St. L.J. 949, 951 (2007) ("Prior to 1981 Sandra Day O'Connor and Ruth Bader Ginsburg had not met, they were from very different places and backgrounds, but they did have something formatively important in common. While each had gone to a great university and to great law schools—Stanford, Cornell, Harvard, Columbia—and each had graduated at the top of her class, in the 1950s no law firm would hire either of them.").

185. *See* Arthur S. Miller and Ronald F. Howell, *The Myth of Neutrality in Constitutional Adjudication*, 27 U. Chi. L. Rev. 661, 664 (1960) ("Neutrality, if it means anything, can only refer to the thought processes of identifiable human beings. . . . The choices that are made by judges in constitutional cases always involve value consequences, thus making value choice unavoidable. The principles which judges employ in projecting their choices to the future, or in explaining them, must also refer to such value alternatives.").

186. *Cf.* Ruth Bader Ginsburg, *A Tribute to Justice Sandra Day O'Connor*, 119 Harv. L. Rev. 1239, 1239 (2006) ("The first woman to serve on the Supreme Court brought to the Conference table experience others did not possess: the experience of growing up female in the 1930s, 40s, and 50s, of raising a family, of doing all manner of legal work—government service, private practice, successive successful candidacies for legislative and judicial office, leadership of her state's Senate, state court judicial service, first on a trial court, then on an appellate bench.").

187. *See* P. S. Atiyah and R. S. Summers, *Form and Substance in Anglo-American Law: A Comparative Study of Legal Reasoning, Legal Theory, and Legal Institutions* (Oxford University Press, 1987), 21–28; Patterson, *Normativity and Objectivity in Law*, 355 ("The forms of argument make it possible for us to engage in the myriad activities we call 'law' (e.g., arguing, asserting, deciding). The forms are the very thing that give law its normativity, for they enable us to show how assertions are correct and incorrect, true and false. The forms are the grammar of law."). On Patterson's account, there are (at least) four traditional forms of argument at common law: textual, historical, doctrinal, and prudential. *See id.* at 352–53.

188. *Cf.* Philip Soper, "Law's Normative Claims," in Robert P. George, ed., *The Autonomy of Law: Essays on Legal Positivism* (Oxford University Press, 1996), 222 ("[T]he law's claim to justice typically comprises two major subsidiary claims: first, claims about the content of the law; and second, claims about the procedures by which the

content is determined and the law enforced. Claims about content are made whenever the substantive purposes of legal rules are essential to the normative defence of the rule: the law's posture in such cases is that it has made its best judgment about the underlying substantive purposes and reached a conclusion that reflects the law's view about how the issue should be resolved. . . . Procedural claims are the state's fall-back response to the possibility that content claims might be wrong. Procedural claims—that the state has proceeded in a morally defensible fashion . . . are an inescapable part of the claim to justice.").

189. As I hope is apparent at this point, my discussion of the formal aspects of legal judgment and their relation to the systemic value of formal justice in the common law tradition should not be misunderstood as an endorsement of formalism. The difference between formal reasoning and formalistic reasoning is easy to miss. As Patrick Atiyah explained, "[W]e ought to distinguish between formal reasoning and formalistic reasoning. . . . Where reasons of substance ought to be considered by the decision-maker, and he refuses to consider them, any formal reasons he gives for his decision will be out of place and unjustifiable, and hence can fairly be called formalistic. . . . But the fact that formalistic reasons are always bad does not justify us in jumping to the conclusion that all formal reasoning is bad. Indeed, it is quite apparent that the law uses, and, I will argue, correctly uses, formal reasons in all sorts of situations." P. S. Atiyah, "Form and Substance in Legal Reasoning" in Neil MacCormick and Peter Birks, eds., *The Legal Mind: Essays for Tony Honoré* (Oxford University Press, 1986), 21. Formalism amounts to the claim that the only legitimate basis for judicial decision making involves the enforcement of existing legal norms (or the notion that every legal case can be decided solely by reference to existing legal norms). *Cf.* Atiyah and Summers, *Form and Substance in Anglo-American Law*, 28–31; Lyons, *Moral Aspects of Legal Theory*, 42–44, 52–57. I argue instead that judicial decisions must be expressed within recognized forms of legal judgment with regard to authoritative sources and modes of argument. But within this formal structure, the common law also always preserves space for individual judicial evaluation, assessment, and (on occasion) alteration of existing law. Judges are the institutional actors who must determine the substantive value of legal standards that precede and are produced by the judicial process.

190. *See below* at 71–72, 73–75. *See also* MacCormick, *Rhetoric and the Rule of Law*, 144, 147–48 ("For J the judge in the case to be justified in deciding for C or D, in such a dispute, J must surely be willing to make a ruling on the law upholding not merely *ad hoc* and *ad hominem* C's claim so advanced or D's defence so presented. J must be willing to do so on terms that hold good for any persons who satisfy the same qualifications and engage in the same acts in the same circumstances.").

191. *See* MacCormick, *Rhetoric and the Rule of Law*, 77 ("[T]he argumentation at this level cannot be properly conceived of in simply bivalent true-or-false terms. We enter here the realms of the better-or-worse, the arguable, the preferable, the more or less persuasive.").

192. *See* Steven L. Winter, *A Clearing in the Forest: Law, Life, and Mind* (University of Chicago Press, 2001), 317 ("If there is one thing that practicing lawyers certainly know, it is that the life of the law is not logic but *persuasion* . . . . The law that emerges from this process is a social product—that is, the product of an interaction between particular, situated historical actors. It is not—and, as Robert Cover points out, can

never be—the work of a single 'heroic' judge trying to advance some particular political or social agenda. It follows that any theory of law that takes seriously the insight that law is not a 'thing' but an activity that judges do, must take into account the role of persuasion in the decisionmaking process.") (emphasis in original) (footnotes omitted). *See also* Dworkin, *Law's Empire,* 254; Charles E. Wyzanski, Jr., *A Trial Judge's Freedom and Responsibility,* 65 Harv. L. Rev. 1281, 1302–4 (1952).

193. *See* Ronald Kahn, *The Commerce Clause and Executive Power: Exploring Nascent Individual Rights in* National Federation of Independent Business v. Sebelius, 73 Md. L. Rev. 133, 176–77 (2013) ("[T]he development of constitutional law is a process involving both the comparison of principles and the social and economic constructions Justices articulate in support of these principles. These comparisons require that Justices apply the principles they advocate to the lived lives of individuals, as described in precedent and as applied in cases before the Supreme Court.").

194. *See* Kahn, *The Commerce Clause and Executive Power,* 177. Kahn carefully examines Chief Justice John Roberts's majority opinion and Ginsburg's dissent in *Nat'l Fed'n of Indep. Bus. v. Sebelius,* 132 S. Ct. 2566 (2012), and concludes that Roberts's attempt to establish a doctrinal distinction for Commerce Clause purposes between inaction and action, drawn in part from an implicit liberty interest in choosing whether and how to engage in commerce, is unlikely to endure because the "inaction-action" distinction is inconsistent with the reality of the choice at issue and with the principle derived from the pertinent precedents. *See id.* at 173–76.

195. *See, e.g.,* MacCormick, *Rhetoric and the Rule of Law,* 77 ("Every statement of law, both in judicial justification and in doctrinal commentaries, rests at least on an implicit, and often on an explicit and articulated, interpretative argument. Such arguments presuppose, and often articulate value systems and value judgements."). *See also* Julie Dickson, *Evaluation and Legal Theory* (Hart Publishing, 2001), 32. As Dickson explains, no legal theory can avoid being evaluative (and, for this reason, Dickson resists attempts to characterize different legal theories as descriptive or normative, or as "value-free" or "morally evaluative"). Dickson's point holds in relation to judging, as well. Common law judging can never be value-free. Judging requires evaluation, directly or indirectly, although that evaluation need not necessarily be moral in nature. *Cf. id.* at 37–57, 65–67.

196. *See* Tara Smith, *Originalism, Vintage or Nouveau: "He Said, She Said" Law,* 82 Fordham L. Rev. 619, 624, 625 (2013) ("The problem is, the law *is* political. . . . To make laws is to take a stand on the proper relationship between governors and the governed, a stand on the kinds of restrictions that it is legitimate to forcibly impose on people. In this specific philosophical sense, then, law is political, and judicial rulings about the meanings of laws must be informed by these premises.") (emphasis in original).

197. *Cf.* Irving R. Kaufman, *The Anatomy of Decisionmaking,* 53 Fordham L. Rev. 1, 15 (1984) ("[T]he 'personal element—that individual sense of justice—is not only inextinguishable, but essential for the orderly development of the law.' . . . Our gravest error may be in repressing our individual values in the hopes of achieving a pure legal result.") (citation omitted).

198. *See* Gardner, *Law as a Leap of Faith,* 257–58; Dworkin, *Law's Empire,* 89–90; Raz, *Authority of Law,* 196 ("These explanations of the piecemeal progress of the com-

mon law are not meant to deny that over the years the common law may undergo radical transformation. Nor do they diminish the important contributions of single judgments by great judges to such developments. The very knowledge that one's pronouncements from the Bench can later by revised and moderated, while acting to restrain many judges from departing too far from existing doctrine, does on occasion encourage bold spirits to experiment."); Wyzanski, *A Trial Judge's Freedom and Responsibility*, 1303 ("Novel remedies begin as permissible exercises of discretion by the court of first instance. They win approval and imitation by similarly circumstanced courts. And in the end what was discretionary has become mandatory. Here is the common law at work—a progressive contribution by the judges, trial as well as appellate.").

199. *See* MacCormick, *Rhetoric and the Rule of Law*, 78 ("[C]onsiderations in favour of universalism . . . in no way entail a denial that particular reasons must always exist for particular decisions, justified ones anyway. Nor do they imply that inattention to the full particular detail of a case would be compatible with just or satisfactory decision-making."); Raz, *Ethics in the Public Domain*, 234–35 ("The sources thesis leads to the conclusion that courts often exercise discretion and participate in the law-making process. . . . Saying this does not mean, however, that courts in exercising their discretion either do or should act on the basis of their personal views on how the world should be ideally run. That would be sheer folly. Naturally judges act on their personal views, otherwise they would be insincere. . . . But judges are not allowed to forget that they are not dictators who can fashion the world to their own blueprint of the ideal society.").

200. *See* above at 163n110. *See also* Graham Mayeda, *Uncommonly Common: The Nature of Common Law Judgment*, 19 Can. J.L. & Juris. 107, 124 (2006).

201. MacCormick, *Rhetoric and the Rule of Law*, 146, 147, 149 (emphasis in original).

202. *See* Brian Z. Tamanaha, *Law as a Means to an End: Threat to the Rule of Law* (Cambridge University Press, 2006), 234–37.

203. Unlike Tamanaha, I argue that a reorientation away from objectivity and toward intersubjectivity will more helpfully respond to these and other challenges to subjectivity in judging. In relation to the argument in the text, however, this broader divergence in our approaches is immaterial.

204. Tamanaha, *Law as a Means to an End*, 239–40.

205. *See, e.g.*, Richard A. Posner, *The Problematics of Moral and Legal Theory* (Harvard University Press, 1999), 148–49 ("[T]his is just to say that personal values and political preferences are apt to play an important role in courts that have broad discretion, and hence that we want a diverse bench and also that we want our judicial candidates carefully screened not only for temperament and character and intelligence and knowledge of the law but also for their experiences and values."). Restrictions of space prevent me from discussing various issues concerning political influences on judicial selection, means of assessing merit and ideology in judicial selection, and the relative values of judicial nomination and judicial election as methods of judicial selection. As Judge Posner suggests, the best way to account for the interaction between judicial values and decisions is not to deny or decry the importance of personal values in judgments, but instead to ensure that our processes of judicial selection are sufficiently attentive and sensitive to this interaction.

206. *See* Eisenberg, *Nature of the Common Law*, 12–13.

207. Jeffrey A. Segal, Harold J. Spaeth, and Sara C. Benesh, *The Supreme Court in the American Legal System* (Cambridge University Press, 2005), 16–17, 22. To support the contemporary relevance of the "mouthpiece" conception of judging, the authors cite a Supreme Court opinion from 1936. *See id.* at 16 n. 17 (citing *United States v. Butler*, 297 U.S. 1, 62 (1936)). The authors do not mention that the approach to judicial decision making described in *Butler* has been criticized consistently since it appeared. *See, e.g.*, Alexander M. Bickel, *The Least Dangerous Branch: The Supreme Court at the Bar of Politics* (2nd ed.) (Yale University Press, 1986), 90; 3 Arthur M. Schlesinger, Jr., *The Age of Roosevelt: The Politics of Upheaval, 1935–1936* (Houghton Mifflin, 1960), 458; Vincent M. Barnett, Jr., *Constitutional Interpretation and Judicial Self-Restraint*, 39 Mich. L. Rev. 213, 217 (1940).

208. Lawrence Baum, *Judges and Their Audiences: A Perspective on Judicial Behavior* (Princeton University Press, 2006), 8.

209. Baum, *Judges and Their Audiences*, 7.

210. Baum, *Judges and Their Audiences*, 6. According to Baum, the "strategic conception of judicial behavior is now the closest thing to a conventional wisdom about judicial behavior." *Id.* at 7 (citation omitted).

211. *See* Theodore W. Ruger, *Justice Harry Blackmun and the Phenomenon of Judicial Preference Change*, 70 Mo. L. Rev. 1209, 1217–18 (2005) ("Empirical literature on judicial preference change is sparse, due to the fact that prevailing models of political science research on the Supreme Court assume that judicial preferences are generally fixed over time. As several leading empirical scholars recently stated in summarizing their field, 'the "stability assumption" is sufficiently widespread that almost all tests of preference-based theories of judicial decision making treat it as a given.' For modeling purposes, the studies treat the different Justices as having heterogeneous preferences, but generally consider each Justice's own voting behavior as fixed longitudinally through time. A stark example of this assumption is the prominent role that Segal/Cover scores play in attitudinal political science literature on the Court. Segal/Cover scores distill the assessments of expert commentary on the Justices' views prior to their confirmation by the Senate into numerical scores along a single linear scale ranging from –1 to 1.").

Chapter 3

1. Hannah Arendt, *The Life of the Mind: Thinking* (Harcourt Brace Jovanovich, 1978), 215.

2. All of my own citations to Kant's third *Critique* are to Immanuel Kant, *The Critique of Judgement*, trans. James Creed Meredith (Oxford University Press, 1928). When I refer to this edition of Kant's third *Critique*, I will spell the title as Meredith did. When I refer to the third *Critique* more generally, I will use the conventional US spelling. I would also mention, if for no reason other than its historical serendipity in relation to this chapter's subject, that Meredith was a respected judge who served on the Supreme Court of Ireland.

3. For reasons of scope and space, I also do not attempt to place Kant's aesthetic theory in its broader historical context (or in relation to other important theorists

such as Lord Shaftesbury, Joseph Addison, David Hume, Edmund Burke, or Friedrich Schiller), nor do I address larger questions of aesthetics to which Kant's answers are contested, such as: (1) the relationship of art to utility, (2) whether aesthetic responses are best conceived as natural or ideal, (3) whether artistic taste is innate or cultivated, and (4) the extent to which beauty (and the capacity to appreciate beauty) signifies or symbolizes morality.

4. Kant was born in Königsberg in 1724 and his major work of aesthetic theory, the *Critique of Judgment*, was first published in 1790. *See* Paul Guyer, "Introduction," in Paul Guyer, ed., *The Cambridge Companion to Kant and Modern Philosophy* (Cambridge University Press, 2006), 3–4. Henry II is often credited with establishing the common law system in England in the middle of the twelfth century. *See* R. C. van Caenegem, *The Birth of the English Common Law* (2nd ed.) (Cambridge University Press, 1988), 40–41. Obviously, the historical development of the common law system is a much larger topic than I can address here, and important aspects of that system (reliance on precedent, judicial independence, etc.) evolved over time.

5. Michael Denneny, "The Privilege of Ourselves: Hannah Arendt on Judgment," in Melvyn A. Hill, ed., *Hannah Arendt: The Recovery of the Public World* (St. Martin's Press, 1979), 263. Hannah Arendt famously argued that Kant's third *Critique* was central to an understanding of his broader political theory. *See, e.g.*, Hannah Arendt, *Lectures on Kant's Political Philosophy*, ed. Ronald Beiner (University of Chicago Press, 1982), 4, 61–63; Hannah Arendt, *Between Past and Future: Eight Exercises in Political Thought* (Penguin Books, 2006), 216–19, 237–38. In addition to what she saw as its inherent philosophical interest and its inescapably political nature, Arendt's observations on the nature of judgment in Kant's third *Critique* are helpful to my argument, as well. Although I do not systematically address Arendt here, her reading of Kant has surely influenced my understanding and I cite her in relation to specific points of contact throughout this chapter. I should also mention that Arendt's reading of Kant is itself the subject of scholarly debate. *See, e.g.*, Ronald Beiner, *Philosophy in a Time of Lost Spirit: Essays on Contemporary Theory* (University of Toronto Press, 1997), 184.

6. A notable exception is Linda Ross Meyer. *See* Linda Ross Meyer, *The Justice of Mercy* (University of Michigan Press, 2010), chap. 1; Linda Meyer, *Between Reason and Power: Experiencing Legal Truth*, 67 U. Cin. L. Rev. 727 (1999). I cannot entirely (or adequately) address the breadth of Meyer's work here. Her analysis is enlightening and is in many ways consistent with and supportive of my argument. My one reservation about her view, however, is that Meyer presents the goal of aesthetic and legal judgment as truth rather than validity. For reasons I will explain, this seems a problematic and ultimately misleading characterization of Kant's project in the third *Critique* and of the common law's conception of judging. For example, Meyer writes, "If the question is really one of truth and not of power, then we must explain how truth can be both shareable and yet subject to dispute. . . . Kant seems to find a basis for the unity of human experience that does *not* rely on subjective experiences of the effect of particular objects on particular people, the contingent agreement of inter-subjectivity, nor on universal principles of reason that we would share with all other reasonable beings." Meyer, *Between Reason and Power*, 748, 749 (emphasis supplied). Framing the inquiry in terms of truth or power leads Meyer to find her cognitive bridge in the form(s) of rhetoric. I am sympathetic to this effort, and it is shared by others as a way

through these problems in the understanding of law. *See* above at 170n187. I agree that understanding the nature of legal reasoning helps us to unravel certain perceived problems about the realities of legal indeterminacy. Meyer's account, however, misstates Kantian aesthetic judgment, because Kant's theory does not, as Meyer claims, seek to avoid the subjective experiences of particular people or the central role of intersubjective agreement in the formulation of judgments of taste. Indeed, these are indispensable to Kantian aesthetic theory. In my view, reorienting our focus from truth to validity helps us to appreciate the authentic operation of subjective experience and intersubjective agreement in Kantian aesthetic judgment and in common law legal judgment.

7. I am using the term "taste" here to describe a faculty or judgment in Kant's terms, which are entirely different from the use of the term in the previous chapter.

8. *See* above at 149–50n15.

9. *See* Graham Mayeda, *Uncommonly Common: The Nature of Common Law Judgment*, 19 Can. J.L. & Juris. 107 (2006).

10. I do not organize this chapter in accordance with Kant's four "moments" of a judgment of taste (*viz.*, disinterestedness, universality, purposiveness, and necessity), although I will discuss disinterestedness, universality, and necessity at some length. My principal reasons for eschewing the moments as an organizational structure are: (1) that approaching Kant's work in this way would necessitate familiarity with Kant's *Critique of Pure Reason*, and (2) the moments do not seem the most effective means of applying Kant's aesthetic theory to the common law. On the relationship between the four moments in the first and third *Critiques*, *see* Christian Helmut Wenzel, *An Introduction to Kant's Aesthetics: Core Concepts and Problems* (Blackwell, 2005), 10–18; Béatrice Longuenesse, "Kant's Leading Thread in the Analytic of the Beautiful," in Rebecca Kukla, ed., *Aesthetics and Cognition in Kant's Critical Philosophy* (Cambridge University Press, 2006), 195–97. Although it would take me too far from the focus of this book to address this in detail, I should mention that scholars disagree as to the equivalence between Kant's analytic method and structure in the first *Critique* and the third *Critique*. Some (Paul Guyer and Salim Kemal, for example) argue that Kant did not intend for the logical functions of cognitive judgment in the first *Critique* to be read as tracking the four moments of aesthetic judgment in the *Critique of Judgment*. *See, e.g.*, Paul Guyer, *Kant and the Claims of Taste* (2nd ed.) (Cambridge University Press, 1997), 114–16; Salim Kemal, *Kant and Fine Art: An Essay on Kant and the Philosophy of Fine Art and Culture* (Oxford University Press, 1986), 150–51. Others (such as Henry Allison) contend that Kant meant for the moments of aesthetic judgment to be understood as mirroring the table of logical functions of cognitive judgment in the *Critique of Pure Reason*. *See* Henry E. Allison, *Kant's Theory of Taste: A Reading of the* Critique of Aesthetic Judgment (Cambridge University Press, 2001), 72–84. For a comprehensive examination of judgment in Kantian thought, which explores the relationship between the first and third *Critiques*, *see* Béatrice Longuenesse, *Kant and the Capacity to Judge: Sensibility and Discursivity in the Transcendental Analytic of the* Critique of Pure Reason (Princeton University Press, 1998).

11. *See* Charles Martindale, *Latin Poetry and the Judgement of Taste: An Essay in Aesthetics* (Oxford University Press, 2005), 39 ("Kant maintains that there are no rules for beauty or concepts under which objects can be subsumed as beautiful (if there were,

the judgement of taste would be logical, not aesthetic)."). *See also id.* at 23, 29–30. I am grateful to Meghan Reedy for introducing me to Martindale's work.

12. Stephan Körner, *Kant* (Yale University Press, 1955), 175. In fact, the German term Kant used, *urteilskraft*, is more accurately translated into English as the "power of judging" or the "power of judgment," and many scholars now translate the title of the third *Critique* this way. For more on analysis of the third *Critique* beyond its applicability to aesthetics, *see* David Bell, *The Art of Judgement*, 96 Mind 221, 231–32 (1987).

13. Lewis White Beck, *Essays on Kant and Hume* (Yale University Press, 1978), 55 (quoting Meredith, "Introduction," in Kant, *Critique of Judgement*, 31). The footnote to this passage in Professor Beck's book indicates that it appears on page 91 of the Meredith introduction to the third *Critique*. This is an error.

14. Paul Guyer views this considered aesthetic judgment as the result of "a double process of reflection both producing pleasure and evaluating it." Guyer, *Kant and the Claims of Taste*, 133. There is some dispute about whether these stages of apprehension of a work of art are successive or simultaneous. *See e.g.*, Craig Burgess, *Kant's Key to the Critique of Taste*, 39 Phil. Q. 484, 485, 491 (1989). Burgess's essay is an effort to expose an error in Guyer's work. According to Burgess, Guyer "assumes that the two types of reflection comprising aesthetic experience are successive" whereas Burgess argues that they occur simultaneously. For ease of expression, I will sometimes describe the process of aesthetic judgment as though it occurs sequentially. But this should not be read as an endorsement of Guyer's view on this subject. For my purposes, the important point here is that Burgess and Guyer agree that the feeling of pleasure engendered by contemplating a beautiful object is a consequence of (not a precursor to) the judgment that the object is beautiful.

15. *See* Kant, *Critique of Judgement*, § 9, at 57 ("Hence it is the universal capacity for being communicated incident to the mental state in the given representation which, as the subjective condition of the judgement of taste, must be fundamental, with the pleasure in the object *as its consequent*.") (emphasis supplied). *See also id.* at 58–59 ("[T]his purely subjective (aesthetic) estimating of the object, or of the representation through which it is given, is antecedent to the pleasure in it.").

16. *See* Eva Schaper, "Taste, Sublimity, and Genius: The Aesthetics of Nature and Art," in Guyer, *The Cambridge Companion to Kant*, 375 ("[N]ot only I, but every subject of experience standing in the same relation to the object would feel the same, and, further, have the same justification for having such a feeling in virtue of sharing the same structure of mentality. . . . We rely on our innermost feelings of pleasure alone when estimating the beautiful—an aesthetic judgment 'is one whose determining ground *cannot be other than subjective*' (§1, 5:203)—and yet we claim for the deliverances of taste a suprapersonal import. We believe it to be binding for all subjects and not merely for the one on whose experience it is based.") (quoting Kant, *Critique of Judgment*) (emphasis in original).

17. *See* Donald W. Crawford, *Reason-Giving in Kant's Aesthetics*, 28 J. of Aesthetics and Art Criticism 505, 506–7 (1970) ("The pure judgment of taste is based on a feeling of pleasure, but this feeling is occasioned not by mere sensation but by the contemplation of, or reflection upon, the form of that being considered—by a consideration of whether it is suitable for cognition in general. . . . Although the pleasure resulting from the awareness of this purposiveness of form is subjective, the awareness itself must be

intersubjective as a necessary condition for communication . . . and hence there is a basis for the universal validity of judgments of taste.").

18. *See* Kemal, *Kant and Fine Art*, 157–58, 166. Kemal also mentions a third characteristic, necessity, which is the claim that other future judges of an object should concur with my judgment of it. I discuss this in detail below at 67–69.

19. *See* Paul Guyer and Henry Allison, "Dialogue: Paul Guyer and Henry Allison on Allison's *Kant's Theory of Taste*," in Rebecca Kukla, *Aesthetics and Cognition in Kant's Critical Philosophy* (Cambridge University Press, 2006), 129 ("[F]eeling for Kant plays an essential judgmental role. Indeed, this is the only way in which I can understand the Kantian conception of an 'aesthetic power of judgment.' Thus, in the very first section of the third *Critique*, Kant states explicitly that the feeling of pleasure or displeasure 'grounds an entirely special faculty for discriminating and judging'. In short, . . . Kant is committed to the view that in a judgment of taste one judges *through one's feeling*.") (quoting Kant, *Critique of Judgment*, § 1) (emphasis in original).

20. I do not address the question whether the capacity to make aesthetic judgments is an innate human trait or a cultivated and refined faculty. For my purposes, whichever answer one gives to this question, Kantian aesthetic theory requires that this capacity is shared by other potential judges of the artistic object to whom the judgment of taste is communicated. Kant sometimes refers to this shared capacity as a "common sense (*sensus communis*)." *See* Kant, *Critique of Judgement*, § 20, at 82. For the different uses Kant makes of this term, *see* Kemal, *Kant and Fine Art*, 181–86, 196–214, esp. at 184 ("the common sense is both the feeling shared *and* the ability to judge that the feeling *is* shared.") (emphasis in original).

21. *See* above at 8–9 and below at 78.

22. *See* Maxwell L. Stearns, *Standing Back From the Forest: Justiciability and Social Choice*, 83 Calif. L. Rev. 1309, 1376 (1995).

23. *See Bell v. Thompson*, 545 U.S. 794, 830 (2005) (Breyer, J., dissenting).

24. *See* below at 186n68, 187n77. *See also* Douglas E. Edlin, *Judges and Unjust Laws: Common Law Constitutionalism and the Foundations of Judicial Review* (University of Michigan Press, 2008), 114–19.

25. The concept of freedom (of the individual as a self-legislating and autonomous agent) is central to much of Kant's work in the three *Critiques*. *See, e.g.*, Guyer, *Cambridge Companion to Kant*, 20–21. Although I cannot possibly engage with the entire scope of Kantian freedom and autonomy in relation to aesthetic judgment or to the common law, I do want to emphasize one aspect in particular. Kant understood freedom—or more precisely autonomy—to require that individuals may formulate their judgments in the absence of external pressures and through the exercise of their own reason. This conception of freedom fittingly describes the position and action of common law judges. *Cf.* Susan Meld Shell, *Kant and the Limits of Autonomy* (Harvard University Press, 2009), 110–12. The common law expects judges to bring their own reason and experience to the judgments they make, and the common law tradition protects judges from external pressures in the course of reaching their decisions.

26. *See* below at 91–92.

27. *See* Neil MacCormick, *Rhetoric and the Rule of Law: A Theory of Legal Reasoning* (Oxford University Press, 2005), 277 ("[T]here is no point in offering an argument unless it tries to show something, to show at least why some opinion or opinions are le-

gally better or sounder than others. . . . No one has a judgement other than his or her own to apply to these questions and the result reached can only be a matter of that person's judgement. . . . That judgement, however, is one about the possible grounds of rightness."). MacCormick indicates that this form of argumentation implies a belief in "objective interpersonal criteria of legal soundness." *Id.* While I believe the word "objective" is problematic in this context, I agree entirely with MacCormick's view of the personal and interpersonal nature and evaluation of legal judgments.

28. *See* above at 138n52.

29. *See* below at 209n13, 211n26, and 220–21n98.

30. *See* below at 95–101.

31. *See, e.g.*, Louis L. Jaffe, *English and American Judges as Lawmakers* (Oxford University Press, 1969), 21 ("A judiciary which is gagged or has the sense of being gagged in one area may well be gagged in all. The judge should have a sense of moral freedom, a sense of independence in the service of justice. We cannot look to him to resist abuse of power if he is made to feel impotent.").

32. Jeremy Waldron, *Kant's Legal Positivism*, 109 Harv. L. Rev. 1535, 1560 (1996).

33. *See* above at 46–47.

34. *See* below at 91–95, 102–4.

35. *Cf.* Arendt, *Between Past and Future*, 217 ("The power of judgment rests on a potential agreement with others . . . even if I am quite alone in making up my mind, in an anticipated communication with others with whom I know I must finally come to some agreement. From this potential agreement judgment derives its specific validity. . . . [J]udgment must liberate itself . . . from the idiosyncrasies which naturally determine the outlook of each individual in his privacy . . . but which are not fit to enter the market place, and lack all validity in the public realm.").

36. For more on this point in relation to an aesthetic community, *see* Kemal, *Kant and Fine Art*, 159 ("[W]e need criteria by which the success of our actual judgements is assured. And Kant proposes that we assess whether particular justifications are successful, and our preferred subjective responses universalizable, by considering whether others can gain our experience. As to justify an aesthetic judgement is to enable another subject to gain the same experience, a successful judgement must also be one that is communicated. Here, we rely on . . . a regulative ideal of satisfactory communication, and by means of this ideal seek to ensure the *success* of our actual particular aesthetic judgements.") (emphasis in original). The concept of universalizability is another important link between Kantian aesthetic judgment and common law legal judgment. *See* Neil MacCormick, *Legal Reasoning and Legal Theory* (Oxford University Press, 1978), 84, 86, 98–99, 214–15; MacCormick, *Rhetoric and the Rule of Law*, 99, 146, 147, 149–51. And universalizability also famously serves as a foundation for Kantian moral theory through the categorical imperative. *See* Immanuel Kant, *Groundwork of the Metaphysics of Morals* (Mary Gregor, trans.) (Cambridge University Press, 1998), 4:421, at 31 ("There is, therefore, only a single categorical imperative and it is this: act only in accordance with that maxim through which you can at the same time will that it become a universal law.") (italics deleted). (Of course, Kant actually offered more than one formulation of the categorical imperative.) For more on the forms and processes of communication in relation to a legal community, *see* Philip Bobbitt, *Constitutional Fate: Theory of the Constitution* (Oxford University Press, 1982),

chaps. 1–7 (discussing a typology of constitutional arguments); Dennis Patterson, *Law and Truth* (Oxford University Press, 1996), 51 ("Assertions in law are claims the truth of which are vindicated by intersubjective (not mind-independent) justificatory criteria. . . . The forms of argument are the grammar of legal justification—the way lawyers show that propositions of law are true or false. Apart from these forms of argument, there is no legal truth."). To some (myself included), it seems problematic that Patterson describes the goal of his book as determining claims of "truth" in law. *See, e.g.*, Andrew Halpin, *Reasoning with Law* (Hart Publishing, 2001), 140–41 ("Patterson does not demonstrate that from forms of argument that are successful we derive conclusions in terms of *truth*. Indeed his emphasis in *Law and Truth* on the roles of persuasion and commendation in legal argument would suggest otherwise.") (emphasis in original). While I share this concern about Patterson's way of stating the goal of his project, his references to the forms of legal argument and to the necessity of intersubjective evaluation as predicates for legal judgment broadly support the argument made here.

37. Körner, *Kant*, 183.

38. Körner, *Kant*, 183 (emphasis in original). For Kant's own articulation of this point, *see Critique of Judgement*, § 7, at 52 ("With the agreeable, therefore, the axiom holds good: *Every one has his own taste* (that of sense). The beautiful stands on quite a different footing. It would, on the contrary, be ridiculous if any one who plumed himself on his taste were to think of justifying himself by saying: This object . . . is beautiful *for me*. For if it merely pleases *him*, he must not call it *beautiful* . . . . [W]hen he puts a thing on a pedestal and calls it beautiful, he demands the same delight from others. He judges not merely for himself, but for all men, and then he speaks of beauty as if it were a property of things. Thus he says the *thing* is beautiful . . . he *demands* this agreement of them [other judging subjects]. He blames them if they judge differently, and denies them taste.") (emphasis in original). *See also id.*, § 9, at 59 ("In a judgement of taste the pleasure felt by us is exacted from every one else as necessary, just *as if*, when we call something beautiful, beauty was to be regarded as a quality of the object forming part of its inherent determination according to concepts; although beauty is for itself, apart from any reference to the feeling of the Subject, nothing.") (emphasis supplied).

39. *See* Longuenesse, "Kant's Leading Thread in the Analytic of the Beautiful," in Kukla, *Aesthetics and Cognition in Kant's Critical Philosophy*, 201.

40. Kant, *Critique of Judgement*, § 8, at 55.

41. Kant, *Critique of Judgement*, § 8, at 54–55.

42. Kant, *Critique of Judgement*, § 8, at 55. *See also id.*, § 6, at 51 ("Accordingly he [the judge] will speak of the beautiful *as if* beauty were a quality of the object and the judgement logical (forming a cognition of the Object by concepts of it); although it is only aesthetic, and contains merely a reference of the representation of the object to the Subject.") (emphasis added).

43. *Cf.* Kemal, *Kant and Fine Art*, 317 n. 5. It is, of course, more complicated than this. According to Kant, cognitive judgments are objective in the full sense that they may be determined to be true or false, and they are also intersubjective in the sense that they may be communicated and they carry a claim to assent by other judging subjects. Aesthetic judgments share intersubjectivity with cognitive judgments (in terms of their communicability and claim to universality) but they are not—and this

is the point I wish to emphasize—objective (*i.e.*, they depend for their validity on subjects' shared responses and capacities of response rather than on empirical claims and falsifiability). For an excellent discussion of the nuanced comparisons and contrasts between cognitive and aesthetic judgments, *see* Kemal, *Kant and Fine Art*, 161–70.

44. *See* Linda Meyer, *"Nothing We Say Matters":* Teague *and New Rules*, 61 U. Chi. L. Rev. 423, 470–71 (1994) ("Because language grows from context, it makes sense for the judgment to be taken in context, rather than the judge's reasoning or enunciated rule, to be authoritative. . . . [A]fter reading many cases, the sense of the right result in the case under decision is clearer than the 'principle' that would capture the continuity. Having looked at a series of examples, one intuitively knows 'how to go on in the same way' without necessarily being able to state the rule. In short, the common law assumes that our ability to sense the continuation of a pattern in a particular context will be keener than our ability to explicate a rule.").

45. Stephen R. Perry, *The Varieties of Legal Positivism*, 9 Can. J.L. & Juris. 361, 369–70 (1996). *See also* John Chipman Gray, *The Nature and Sources of the Law* (Ashgate, 1997), 147 ("[I]t is not true that we can trace historically the development of theological, philosophical, or scientific truths in the utterances of successive thinkers; what we can trace is the development of human knowledge and belief of those truths; but the truths themselves are entirely independent of human knowledge and belief. . . . So the laws of light do not depend upon the ideas of Sir Isaac Newton or any other physicist with regard to them. 'We do not infer that philosophers make the laws of nature; how then can we infer that judges make the law of the land?' is what Professor Hammond says. . . . Because the laws of nature are independent of human opinion, while the Law of the land is human opinion."); Joel B. Grossman, *Lawyers and Judges: The ABA and the Politics of Judicial Selection* (John Wiley & Sons, 1965), 214 ("The products of scientific decision are open to verification by accepted methods. Its premises are acknowledged, and its results are empirical. But the judicial decision is the product of a greater array of forces, its premises are often inarticulate, and its results are not similarly verifiable."); Kent Greenawalt, *Law and Objectivity* (Oxford University Press, 1992), 208 ("Standards of legal correctness must be accessible to human beings; they cannot rest on some truth that is wholly undiscoverable by human beings. . . . The answer to a legal question must *in some sense* be provided by the law.") (emphasis in original); Ronald Dworkin, *Justice in Robes* (Harvard University Press, 2006), 152 ("Some of our concepts are governed . . . by an entirely different set of background assumptions: that the correct attribution of the concept is fixed by a certain kind of fact about the objects in question. . . . What philosophers call 'natural kinds' provide clear examples. . . . Are the political concepts of democracy, liberty, equality, and the rest like that? Do these concepts describe, if not natural kinds, at least political kinds that like natural kinds can be thought to have a basic ingrained physical structure or essence? Or at least some structure that is open to discovery by some wholly scientific, descriptive, non-normative process? Can philosophers hope to discover what equality or legality really is by something like DNA or chemical analysis? No. That is nonsense."). *Cf.* George Steiner, *Real Presences* (University of Chicago Press, 1989), 75 ("Two indispensable criteria must be satisfied by theory: verification or falsifiability by means of experiment and predictive application. There are in art and poetics no crucial experiments, no litmus-paper tests. There can be no verifiable or falsifiable deduc-

tions entailing predictable consequences in the very concrete sense in which a scientific theory carries predictive force.").

46. *See* above at 9–14.

47. *See* Beck, *Essays on Kant and Hume*, 168, 170 ("[U]nless there is some standard for assessing a judgment, that is to say, unless the judgment first is 'necessary' in contrast to 'arbitrary,' the judgment cannot be said to be right *or* wrong . . . *Error in taste* arises from sinning against the conditions of aesthetic validity . . .") (emphasis in original).

48. *See, e.g.*, Kemal, *Kant and Fine Art*, 168; Guyer, *Kant and the Claims of Taste*, 8.

49. Beck, *Essays on Kant and Hume*, 169.

50. For example, imagine a case in which the law dictates that the plaintiff should prevail and a judge decides in the plaintiff's favor not on the basis of the evidence or the law but instead out of a fondness for the plaintiff's necktie.

51. *See* Guyer, *Kant and the Claims of Taste*, 131–33. For more on this point, *see* Kemal, *Kant and Fine Art*, 163, 164, 165 ("[C]oncepts are used to make objective judgements—which can be true or false, depending on whether they correspond to the way the world is. As the truth of a judgement depends on its agreement with an object, in an important sense agreement with other subjects does not provide objective judgements with any greater validity. . . . Validity does not depend on the existence of other individuals, but has consequences for their judgements on the same objects in that it compels their agreement. . . . In all these features, aesthetic judgements differ significantly from cognitive ones. And accounts of Kant's aesthetic theory are likely to be mistaken where they try to apply the epistemological model of the First *Critique* too quickly to the Third *Critique* . . . . [W]e must treat the subjectivity, autonomy, basis in feeling, and intersubjectivity of actual aesthetic judgements as recommendations and require a distinctive necessity of them—one gained through cultural development."). Just to follow up on a point raised above in note 10, even those scholars who believe the structure of aesthetic judgment in the third *Critique* should be read as tracking the logical functions of cognitive judgment in the first *Critique* agree that the distinction between objectivity and intersubjectivity holds in relation to Kant's approach and argument in the *Critique of Pure Reason* and in the *Critique of Judgment*. *See* Allison, *Kant's Theory of Taste*, 77 ("[A]n aesthetic judgment is a *judgment*, and therefore necessarily has a scope. But, once again, since it is an *aesthetic* judgment, its scope or quantity cannot be understood according to the model of the logical quantity of a cognitive judgment about objects ("All S are P"), but must rather concern the sphere of judging subjects to whom the feeling is applicable. In short, as Kant argues . . . the universality of a judgment of taste, as an aesthetic judgment, can only be a subjective universality. Furthermore, even though the judgment of taste has a subjective basis and cannot be quantified over objects, it expresses an evaluation of an object or its representation. . . . [T]he relation here differs markedly from its logical counterpart, since it holds between the feeling of the judging subject and the object judged.") (emphasis in original). And for their part, scholars who argue for the differentiation of cognitive and aesthetic judgments also concede that these judgments should be recognized as, in certain respects, "complementary to each other in culture." Kemal, *Kant and Fine Art*, 151; *see also id.* at 268.

52. Guyer, *Kant and the Claims of Taste*, 132 (quoting Kant, *Critique of Judgment*, §

8) (brackets and emphasis in original). *See also* Longuenesse, *Kant and the Capacity to Judge*, 168–69 n. 4 ("[A]ccording to Kant, . . . for them [aesthetic judgments] we claim *subjective*, although we make no claim to *objective*[,] universality and necessity.") (emphasis in original).

53. *See* Kant, *Critique of Judgement*, § 9, at 59 ("[W]hen we call something beautiful, beauty was to be regarded as a quality of the object forming part of its inherent determination according to concepts; although beauty is for itself, apart from any reference to the feeling of the Subject, nothing."). This indicates that Kant did not mean to describe or ascribe beauty as an objective quality in any "mind-independent" sense, which means that beauty is not something that exists in an object irrespective of our perception and evaluation of that object (in the way that, for example, an object's chemical composition does). For more on the relationship of objectivity to mind-independence, *see* Matthew H. Kramer, *Objectivity and the Rule of Law* (Cambridge University Press, 2007), 3–14. In the previous chapter, I explained some other distinctions between objectivity and intersubjectivity that touch on this discussion. *See* above at 26–30.

54. *See* Ted Cohen and Paul Guyer, "Introduction," in Ted Cohen and Paul Guyer, eds., *Essays in Kant's Aesthetics* (University of Chicago Press, 1982), 12 ("The statement '*x* is beautiful' is deceptive, then, insofar as it may seem to signal an underlying logical (objective) judgment, but Kant's deep and radical idea is that there is no deception whatever in *using* the statement, for using it is the only way to say what one wants to say about it. The form of words may seem to be appropriate only if one purports to say something 'objectively' true about *x*, something which has a genuine contradictory, but it is in fact justified whenever one refuses the disagreement of others who judge about *x* . . . . Kant is the first to formulate the point precisely, in this way: one says '*x* is beautiful' instead of '*x* pleases me' or 'I like *x*' just when one wants to make a judgment with more than personal import.") (emphasis in original).

55. *See, e.g.*, Kant, *Critique of Judgement*, § 6, at 16–17. And, of course, Kant called the first book of the third *Critique* the "Analytic of the Beautiful."

56. Here I may be extrapolating from Kant's theory in a way that diverges from his own view. It is not clear that Kant himself would have seen artistic objects as succeeding when conveying a sense of something other than beauty. In addition, Kant seemed to see a tripartite spectrum of aesthetic responses to an object: beautiful (producing pleasure), ordinary (producing indifference), and ugly (producing displeasure). *See* Paul Guyer, *Values of Beauty: Historical Essays in Aesthetics* (Cambridge University Press, 2005), 143–44.

57. *Cf. Dillon v. United States*, 184 F.3d 556, 566 (6th Cir. 1999) ("[W]e are not at liberty to act as free-wheeling chancellors of old, riding roughshod over rules that in our opinion are inequitable. The rule of law requires that such a change come from either Congress or the Supreme Court, which I in fact would urge be done. In the meantime, I agree with the wisdom of President Ulysses S. Grant's statement that 'the best way to get rid of a bad law is to enforce it.'") (Gilman, J., dissenting). President Grant's precise statement, to which Judge Gilman refers, is from his first inaugural address: "I know no method to secure the repeal of bad or obnoxious laws so effective as their stringent execution" (March 4, 1869).

58. *See generally* T. R. S. Allan, *Constitutional Justice: A Liberal Theory of the Rule of*

Law (Oxford University Press, 2001), 249–50; George Anastaplo, *The Constitution of 1787: A Commentary* (Johns Hopkins University Press, 1989), 3, 135; Philip Soper, *A Theory of Law* (Harvard University Press, 1984), 55, 64; Judith N. Shklar, *Legalism: Law, Morals, and Political Trials* (Harvard University Press, 1964), 117; Matthew D. Adler, *Judicial Restraint in the Administrative State: Beyond the Countermajoritarian Difficulty*, 145 U. Pa. L. Rev. 759, 784–85 (1997).

59. A complicating factor here is that aesthetic judgments are evaluations of artistic objects, but legal judgments are not solely evaluations of existing legal sources. A legal judgment (in the form of a judicial decision) is itself also an independent source of law.

60. Guyer, *Kant and the Claims of Taste*, 62.

61. *See* MacCormick, *Rhetoric and the Rule of Law*, 277 ("The kind of reasoning which goes forward in legal decision-making, legal argumentation, and indeed in legal thought in all its forms and levels . . . proceeds under a pretension to correctness, an implicit claim to being correct.") (citing Robert Alexy, *A Theory of Legal Argumentation: The Theory of Rational Discourse as Theory of Legal Justification* (Oxford University Press, 1989), 104–8, 214–20); Gerald J. Postema, "Objectivity Fit for Law," in Brian Leiter, ed., *Objectivity in Law and Morals* (Cambridge University Press, 2001), 105, 107 ("Ordinarily, to say that a judgment is objective . . . is to say something about the relationship between the judging subject, the judgment, and its subject matter, and, in view of that relationship, to vouch for the credibility, if not necessarily the truth, of the judgment. . . . Correctness or validity of a judgment implies that it is *worthy* of acceptance or endorsement.") (emphasis in original). Postema also very helpfully summarizes Kant's view of intersubjective validity via communication and mutual agreement across the different realms of theoretical and practical reason as "probative of truth" even though the respective bases for assessing a judgment's objectivity will vary depending upon the availability of a preexisting or autonomously produced object of the judgment. *See id.* at 110–11.

62. On the provision of supportive reasons in Kantian aesthetic judgment, *see* Crawford, *Reason-Giving in Kant's Aesthetics*, 508, 509. On the provision of supportive reasons in the common law tradition, *see* above at 153n34, 161n97, 164n112.

63. Kemal, *Kant and Fine Art*, 87, 88.

64. Barbara Herrnstein Smith's excellent discussion of "the unquiet judge" relates well to the discussion in the text. *See* Barbara Herrnstein Smith, *Belief and Resistance: Dynamics of Contemporary Intellectual Controversy* (Harvard University Press, 1997), chap. 1. Very briefly stated, Smith argues that the absence of a commitment to objectivist thought does not in any way disable normative claims, convictions, and justifications. Objectivists, Smith says, frequently assume that nonobjectivists cannot make normative judgments of value (because they have no external basis on which to ground their conclusions). Nonobjectivists are urged to (and often do) retreat to postures of quietism—the abstention from making value judgments—as a result of their rejection of objectivism. Smith's point, which supports and reinforces my argument, is that a rejection of objective truth as the goal for judgment does not entail an incapacity to judge or to justify one's judgments. *See id.* at 2–3. Once we reject the false dichotomy between "objective reasons" and "subjective preferences," we can see that "judgments that do not claim objective status . . . [can] reflect not merely the[ ] indi-

vidual or partisan preferences [of judges] but the interests and values of larger relevant groups, including, sometimes, the entire relevant community." *Id.* at 3, 4. There is a valuable parallel here between Smith's and Kant's accounts of the subjective and the intersubjective in the process of judging. Moreover, applying this analysis to judgments of law, Smith argues that judges can and should acknowledge that their values and experiences inform their judgments, while at the same time attempting to justify their judgments by reference to the "extensive and effective explanatory and justifactory [*sic*] resources at their disposal. Contrary to the common charge or fear, then, neither the authority nor the persuasiveness of a non-objectivist judge's rulings would be hobbled by the fact that, in justifying them, she did not invoke any 'objective grounds' but only indicated . . . how she weighed and weighted such matters in the light of historical evidence and judicial precedent (as she interprets them), broader communal interests and communal goals, and her own general values, beliefs, and prior experiences." *Id.* at 16–17.

65. Andrew Bowie, *Aesthetics and Subjectivity: From Kant to Nietzsche* (2nd ed.) (Manchester University Press, 2003), 36.

66. *See* above at 37–48. *See also* Martin Shapiro, *Judges as Liars*, 17 Harv. J. L. & Pub. Pol'y 155 (1994).

67. *See* Steven L. Winter, *A Clearing in the Forest: Law, Life, and Mind* (University of Chicago Press, 2001), 318 ("[T]he central concern of the conventional view is to avoid subjectivity in legal decisionmaking. It requires reason to do so because it does not recognize any other kind of constraint. On this model, persuasion represents the antithesis of reason—and, thus, is understood to exacerbate the danger of subjectivity—because it appeals to extrarational considerations. . . . [However,] if persuasion works only to the extent that the decisionmaker already shares the values being appealed to, then it is hard to see in what sense the resulting process could be said to be 'subjective.' Quite the contrary. Persuasion is, by definition, an *intersubjective* process—not only in the trivial sense that it takes at least two people to occasion persuasion, but also in the more important sense that persuasion can proceed only on the basis of shared values and perspectives.") (emphasis in original). It is not entirely clear whether Winter seeks to devalue the subjective aspect of the decisional process or to challenge conventional views of what subjectivity means. And there is a question begged here about the extent and kinds of values and perspectives that must be shared for the process of persuasion to proceed. In fairness to Winter, though, I should mention that his larger project aims to reinterpret the "subject-object" dichotomy itself as a means of reframing our understanding of human cognition and law as a process and a product of human imagination (as he uses that term). For reasons of space and focus, I cannot address Winter's more expansive project here. For now, it is enough to observe that, *pace* Winter, the Kantian and common law traditions are concerned more with explaining the complementary and reflexive dynamics of subjectivity and intersubjectivity in the process of judgment, rather than challenging or redefining the subjective aspect of the process. With these qualifications in mind, Winter's insightful comments concerning the threat subjectivity allegedly poses for legal judgment and the intrinsic importance of intersubjectivity for the process of persuasion help to illuminate the discussion in the text.

68. To be sure, errors and disagreements occur with respect to empirical cognitive

judgments, as well. But the point is that the means of testing cognitive judgments and the conclusions reached as a result of a realized error differ importantly (at least so far as Kant is concerned) from the means of testing aesthetic judgments and the conclusions reached as a result. *See* Kemal, *Kant and Fine Art*, 317 n. 5. In the legal context, dissenting opinions are the most familiar (and perhaps the most important) institutional demonstration of the value of disagreement. *See, e.g.*, William J. Brennan, Jr., *In Defense of Dissents*, 37 Hastings L.J. 427, 430–35 (1986). *See also Employers' Liability Cases* [*Howard v. Illinois Central R.R. Co.*], 207 U.S. 463, 505 (1908) (Moody, J., dissenting); *Briscoe v. Bank of Kentucky*, 36 U.S. (11 Pet.) 257, 329 (1837) (Story, J., dissenting).

69. *See* Kant, *Critique of Judgement*, § 8, at 56 ("The judgement of taste itself does not *postulate* the agreement of every one (for it is only competent for a logically universal judgement to do this, in that it is able to bring forward reasons); it only *imputes* this agreement to every one, as an instance of the rule in respect of which it looks for confirmation, not from concepts, but from the concurrence of others.") (emphasis in original). *See also* Kemal, *Kant and Fine Art*, 172–73 ("Kant goes on to link the possibility of error in actual judgements with the need for communication. At best, in aesthetic judgements we can only *impute* agreement to everyone. . . . For the only way to confirm an aesthetic judgement is to bring another subject to gain the pleasure felt by the judging subject. That is, given that a putative judgement may be mistaken . . . the only way he can support his claim for the rightness of his own judgement is by enabling another subject to make the same judgement . . . it goes to confirm that our own reflection and pleasure are universalizable and that our actual judgement is not mistaken. . . . Though we may not recognize our mistakes through our own reflection, we could do so when our judgement is unable to gain concurrence.") (emphasis in original).

70. Guyer, *Kant and the Claims of Taste*, 1 (quoting Kant, *Critique of Judgment*, § 8).

71. *See* below at 67–70.

72. For more on the form of Kantian aesthetic judgments, *see* Donald W. Crawford, *Kant's Aesthetic Theory* (University of Wisconsin Press, 1974), 92, 96–100 (noting the distinction in Kant's theory between the form of aesthetic judgment and the content of specific judgments). For more on the form and structure of common law legal judgments, *see* above at 48–50.

73. Patterson, *Law and Truth*, 19–20, 146–50; MacCormick, *Legal Reasoning and Legal Theory*, 55–57, 64–65, 121–23, 186–88, 250–51.

74. *See* Patterson, *Law and Truth*, 97–98. A useful link to Kant on this point is his treatment of aesthetic judgments as "recommendations." *See* Kemal, *Kant and Fine Art*, 170, 180, 181.

75. Of course, there are questions of vertical and horizontal *stare decisis* that complicate matters here. In the interests of clarity and space, I cannot pursue these questions at length. Nevertheless, in an effort to forestall certain possible objections, I would argue that judges do not often make decisions they know are wrong. To the extent that *stare decisis* sometimes requires judges to reach decisions with which they disagree, the common law permits (and might even require) them to say so. In addition, if a judge's reasoning in criticizing existing precedent (even if the judge felt compelled to follow it in her ruling) is persuasive, future judges may well choose to follow the reasoning of their predecessor rather than their predecessor's ruling in future

cases. So the individual judge's claim to the correctness of her reasoning and her preferred judgment remains (even when that judge was obliged to decide otherwise due to institutional constraints).

76. For more on the importance of legal reasoning for the justification of legal judgments, and the distinctions between legal judgments and logical conclusions, *see* MacCormick, *Rhetoric and the Rule of Law*, 39–40, 67–72, 98–99, 144, 147–48.

77. *See, e.g.*, Ronald Dworkin, *Law's Empire* (Harvard University Press, 1986), 229 (when a judge communicates his judgment, "future judges confront a new tradition that includes what he has done"); Charles E. Wyzanski, Jr., *A Trial Judge's Freedom and Responsibility*, 65 Harv. L. Rev. 1281, 1303 (1952).

78. *See* Kant, *Critique of Judgement*, § 9, at 57, 58 ("Were the pleasure in a given object to be the antecedent, and were the universal communicability of this pleasure to be all that the judgement of taste is meant to allow to the representation of the object, such a sequence would be self-contradictory. For a pleasure of this kind would be nothing but the feeling of mere agreeableness to the senses, and so, from its very nature, would possess no more than private validity. . . . [T]he subjective universal communicability of the mode of representation in a judgement of taste is to subsist apart from the presupposition of any definite concept . . . [I]t must be just as valid for every one, and consequently as universally communicable . . ."). This section of the third *Critique* is notoriously opaque. Whatever else it means, however, Kant differentiated purely private reactions from intersubjectively valid judgments in virtue of a specific process of cognition and communication.

79. *See, e.g.*, Kant, *Critique of Judgement*, § 9, at 57 ("[I]t is the universal capacity for being communicated incident to the mental state in the given representation which, as the subjective condition of the judgement of taste, must be fundamental."). *See also* Allison, *Kant's Theory of Taste*, 80 ("[T]he subjective universality (or universal communicability) of one's feeling is part of what one *means* in judging an object beautiful.") (emphasis in original).

80. *See* Melissa Zinkin, "Intensive Magnitudes and the Normativity of Taste," in Rebecca Kukla, ed., *Aesthetics and Cognition in Kant's Critical Philosophy* (Cambridge University Press, 2006), 159 ("When I claim that something is beautiful, I do not merely demand that someone else agrees with me, in the sense of adding her judgment to mine and saying she thinks so too. . . . I do not think that my judgment could count as a judgment of taste unless I believe everyone *ought* to agree with me.") (emphasis supplied).

81. *See* Longuenesse, "Kant's Leading Thread in the Analytic of the Beautiful," in Kukla, *Aesthetics and Cognition in Kant's Critical Philosophy*, 200.

82. *See* John Reid, *Doe Did Not Sit—The Creation of Opinions by an Artist*, 63 Colum. L. Rev. 59 (1963).

83. *See* above at 13–14, 24–25, 36–37. *See also Grutter v. Bollinger*, 288 F.3d 732, 752–53 (6th Cir. 2002) (*en banc*) (Moore, J., concurring); Thomas E. Baker, *Rationing Justice on Appeal: The Problems of the U.S. Courts of Appeals* (West Publishing Co., 1994), 119–20; Karl Llewellyn, *The Common Law Tradition: Deciding Appeals* (Little, Brown, 1960), 26; Frederick Schauer, *Giving Reasons*, 47 Stan. L. Rev. 633 (1995); Martha J. Dragich, *Will the Federal Courts of Appeals Perish If They Publish? Or Does the Declining Use of Opinions to Explain and Justify Judicial Decisions Pose a Greater Threat?*, 44 Am. U. L. Rev. 757, 765–84

(1995); Owen M. Fiss, *The Forms of Justice*, 93 Harv. L. Rev. 1, 13 (1979), reprinted in Owen Fiss, *The Law as It Could Be* (New York University Press, 2003), 11; Max Radin, *The Requirement of Written Opinions*, 18 Calif. L. Rev. 486, 489 (1930); Roscoe Pound, *The Theory of Judicial Decision*, 36 Harv. L. Rev. 940, 940–43, 952–59 (1923).

84. *See* Bell, *The Art of Judgement*, 225 (explaining that a judgment must be "taken to be true" by the judge offering it). The key here is that a judge must in good faith believe his judgment to be the proper legal conclusion, but this is different from the judgment's being "true" in an objective sense.

85. *Cf.* Longuenesse, "Kant's Leading Thread in the Analytic of the Beautiful," in Kukla, *Aesthetics and Cognition in Kant's Critical Philosophy*, 214.

86. On the confluence of legal and moral obligation with respect to a judge's duty to articulate and develop the law, *see, e.g.*, MacCormick, *Legal Reasoning and Legal Theory*, 33 ("That 'must' is not the 'must' of causal necessity or of logical necessity. It is the 'must' of obligation. The judge has a *duty* to give that judgment. It is merely banal to observe that his having a duty so to give judgment does not mean or entail that he does or that he will give, or that he has given, such a judgment. . . . The judge's issuing an order is an act which he performs or does not perform, and in so acting he either fulfils or does not fulfil his duty.") (emphasis in original); Greenawalt, *Law and Objectivity*, 22–25, 89; Kent Greenawalt, *Conflicts of Law and Morality* (Oxford University Press, 1987), 32 ("A duty attaches to a particular position or to one's status as a human being; one speaks of the duties of judges and parents and of people generally. In this usage, one can speak of moral obligations and duties, but one can also speak of obligations and duties that are other than moral. These nonmoral duties, or obligations, may carry moral weight—'it is morally right that judges perform their legal duties'—but moral argument is needed to link the nonmoral duty to what one morally ought to do.").

87. Kemal, *Kant and Fine Art*, 206, 207 (footnotes omitted).

88. *See* Crawford, *Kant's Aesthetic Theory*, 162 ("[I]n Kant's aesthetic theory the activity of judging the beautiful is intimately connected with the appreciator's experience of the beautiful. . . . Verdictive judgments of taste are, for Kant, the natural culmination of the process of experiencing beauty, at least in the social context in which we wish to communicate our knowledge and feelings to others. Kant explains the existence of the institution for making judgments of taste in terms of our innate desire to obtain and share knowledge, our desire to reach and communicate that which lies beyond the realm of our sense experience. . . . Thus, although the verdictive judgment is a social act, it is the making public of a product of a natural human activity—exercising our reflective power of judgment in order to apprehend a unity (purposiveness) in a manifold of intuition.").

89. *See* Paul Guyer, "Pleasure and Society in Kant's Theory of Taste," in Cohen and Guyer, eds., *Essays in Kant's Aesthetics*, 52 ("Kant does not always or even usually say that in solitude there is no *pleasure* in the beautiful; most frequently he does say merely that there is no *taste* in solitude. . . . But if the judgment on the communicability of a felt pleasure is properly distinguished from the reflection leading to that pleasure, the claim that there is no *taste* in solitude need not mean that no one in solitude can take pleasure in beauty, but implies only that the solitary cannot be imagined to make judgments of taste about his pleasures. . . . [I]n fact it may be only in society that an

individual can learn to make that judgment about his own feelings requisite to *call* an object which pleases him 'beautiful.'") (emphasis in original). I discuss certain senses in which a judgment of taste necessitates a conception of the self as a part of a larger community in the next section.

90. *See* Zinkin, "Intensive Magnitudes and the Normativity of Taste," in Kukla, *Aesthetics and Cognition in Kant's Critical Philosophy*, 149–50.

91. *See* Kemal, *Kant and Fine Art*, 185–86.

92. *See* Crawford, *Kant's Aesthetic Theory*, 162–63.

93. *See* Harold J. Berman, *Law and Language: Effective Symbols of Community* (Cambridge University Press, 2013), 38 ("It should be stressed that language presupposes a transfer of meanings not only *from* speaker to listener (or writer to reader) but *between* them; for some response from the listener (or reader) is presupposed in every utterance. Such reciprocal interaction is not only a purpose of language but also what language *is* operationally: speech does inevitably effectuate an exchange. . . . We need a new verb, 'speak-listen,' to express the reciprocal character of language in action. . . . [L]anguage is thus understood in the first instance as a process of creating relationships among those who jointly engage in it.") (emphasis in original); Marianne Constable, *Our Word Is Our Bond: How Legal Speech Acts* (Stanford University Press, 2014), 80–81 ("[A] legal speech act is not, strictly speaking, *caused* by its speaking subject. . . . Joint speaking and hearing do not cause, but together *are*, what the (singular) social act *is* . . . . Even the most conventional or performative utterances of law involve a hearing 'you' and a speaking 'I' who understand one another's language and how to speak with one another. In dialogue, persons take turns being 'you' and 'I,' initiating new states of affairs and opening up and closing down possibilities of response, without determining them. . . . [T]he utterances of I-who-speak are designed to recall to you-who-hear who 'we'—who share practices of speech and hearing, or of language and of law—are.") (emphasis in original).

94. It may well be that communication requires a community at all times. By limiting my statement to Kant and the common law, I do not mean to contest the "private language argument." *See* Ludwig Wittgenstein, *Philosophical Investigations*, ed. P. M. S. Hacker and Joachim Schulte (4th ed.) (Wiley-Blackwell, 2009), paras. 243–326. I limit my statement to Kant and the common law because of the focus of this chapter and this book.

95. *See, e.g.*, Kant, *Critique of Judgement*, § 6, at 51 ("[T]he judgement of taste . . . must involve a claim to validity for all men."); § 7, at 52 ("[W]hen he puts a thing on a pedestal and calls it beautiful, he demands the same delight from others. He judges not merely for himself, but for all men . . . he *demands* this agreement of them. He blames them if they judge differently, and denies them taste. . . . [A]esthetic judgement [is] capable of making a rightful claim upon the assent of all men.") (emphasis in original); § 8, at 56 ("[When] we call the object beautiful, we believe ourselves to be speaking with a universal voice, and lay claim to the concurrence of every one."); § 9, at 59 ("In a judgement of taste the pleasure felt by us is exacted from every one else as necessary.").

96. *See* above at 172–73n198, 187n77.

97. *See* Heidi Li Feldman, *Objectivity in Legal Judgment*, 92 Mich. L. Rev. 1187, 1223–24, 1227–28 (1994). As Feldman emphasizes, important as convergence or

consensus is in determining a judgment's intersubjective validity, we must always understand the evaluative process as involving the judge and the community together. *See id.* at 1229 ("If the judgment applies a blend concept—which, as such, has a social nature—the judgment will be interpersonally valid in a strong sense. That is, it will be interpersonally reason-giving, and those who have converged upon it will regard it as reason-giving for one another, as well as for themselves. Convergence simply suggests—rather than vouchsafes—objectivity. . . . [C]onvergence upon a blend judgment signals objectivity only when genuinely shared goals, values, and interests inform the *dialogical* method by which the judgment was reached, and when that method is genuinely *dialogical*.") (emphasis supplied).

98. *See* above at 142n69, 170–71nn187–189 and accompanying text.

99. *See* above at 153n34, 161n97, 164n112 and accompanying text.

100. *See* above at 155–56n49, 163n106, 179–80n36, 187n76, and accompanying text.

101. *See* above at 171–72nn191–192, 185n67.

102. Scholars disagree about whether the community of subjects to whom a judgment is communicated—"those with the capacity to judge"—includes everyone with this potential as a rational agent or only those with an already refined faculty of taste. *See, e.g.*, Anthony Savile, *Aesthetic Reconstructions: The Seminal Writings of Lessing, Kant, and Schiller* (Blackwell, 1987), 153–59. Analogizing to the common law, people also disagree about whether the audience for a legal judgment is the public itself or the legal community. *See generally* Lawrence Baum, *Judges and Their Audiences: A Perspective on Judicial Behavior* (Princeton University Press, 2006) (considering differently configured potential audiences for judicial decisions and arguing that the way we define the audience affects the way we perceive the judge's actions). I tend to think it is most accurate to think here in terms of a broadly described legal community, but for purposes of my argument either the more expansive or the more restrictive conception of the community is acceptable, and I will refer to both groups as the potential audience for legal judgments in the discussion that follows.

103. Kant distinguishes between the act of judging and the product of judging. *See, e.g.*, Ralf Meerbote, "Reflection on Beauty," in Cohen and Guyer, eds., *Essays in Kant's Aesthetics*, 61. In a manner consistent with the argument of this chapter, the formulation of the judgment and the independent existence of the judgment are related in terms of the common law, too. In other words, the reasoning that supports a judge's decision and the rule of law contained within the decision are intimately connected, but still distinct, in the process of legal reasoning and evaluation of the judge's ruling as a judgment about the law, and as an ongoing source of legal authority.

104. *See* Gerald J. Postema, "*A Similibus ad Similia*: Analogical Thinking in Law," in Douglas E. Edlin, ed., *Common Law Theory* (Cambridge University Press, 2007), 119–20 ("[T]he reasoning process by which judgments are formed is necessarily normative. . . . The root thought here is the Kantian idea that judging is an activity for which judgers are, and take themselves to be, responsible. . . . In making judgments, judgers vouch for the correctness of their judgments. Of course, the correctness of their judgments cannot be constituted by their commitment to them; for then no distinction between their seeming to be correct and their being so could be made, and without that no mistakes would be possible, and without the possibility of mistake, the normative idea of correct-

ness loses its content. . . . Thus, judgments stand in need of reasons and are capable of functioning as reasons for other judgments, and judgers are regarded and regard themselves as beings capable of giving, requesting, and being challenged to give reasons.").

105. *See* Meerbote, "Reflection on Beauty," in Cohen and Guyer, *Essays in Kant's Aesthetics*, 75 (A judge "would be right to expect and to demand that his declaration be concurred in by other human beings. 'To concur' here means not that some other person would merely *accept* his judgment—there is for Kant no such thing as aesthetic belief based on testimony or even authority—but rather that any other human being, were he to apprehend the same object in a fashion identical in all nonaesthetic respects . . . *should* likewise declare the object to be beautiful. Any undesirable arbitrariness is ruled out, according to this analysis, by the requirement of such qualitative identity of pleasurable responses of all human beings under the stated conditions, and hence the analysis guarantees the possibility of the *correctness* of the judgment by means of this very requirement.") (emphasis in original).

106. Arendt, *Lectures on Kant's Political Philosophy*, 72. *See also id.* at 67 ("I judge as a member of this community and not as a member of a supersensible world.").

107. Kemal, *Kant and Fine Art*, 151. *Cf.* Constable, *Our Word Is Our Bond*, 78 ("Assessing the 'fact' and 'value' of an act such as Cardozo's [or any judge's] holding is as much about verifying the particular conditions surrounding Cardozo's announcement as it is about the correspondence of the state of affairs named in the holding to post-1928 New York law. Being able to judge such conditions and states is a matter of language and of time. . . . Claiming that Cardozo's act of holding happened and that the holding is New York State law requires knowledge of speech and of the world that is shared among those who speak the same tongue. Such speaking . . . involves dialogue with others over time."); Dennis Patterson, *Normativity and Objectivity in Law*, 43 Wm. & Mary L. Rev. 325, 348 (2001) ("The normativity of rule-following—the ground of correctness and incorrectness—is not to be found in the agreement of others *as such*. Agreement is a necessary feature of the normativity of our practices, but the 'agreement' must be regularity in reaction to use. In short, when we say there must be 'agreement in actions' what we are really saying is that there must be harmony in application, over time. This harmony in reaction and application is constitutive of legal practice and, thus, is the basis of our legal judgments.") (emphasis in original).

108. Graham Mayeda emphasizes that the distinctive role of the courts in protecting individual rights requires that the relevant community to whom a legal judgment is communicated must include those who are sometimes excluded from the majoritarian political community. *See* Mayeda, *Uncommonly Common*, 122.

109. *See* above at 62.

110. *Cf.* Arendt, *Between Past and Future*, 214–15 (discussing the intrinsically public nature of art and politics).

111. As Arendt put it, a judgment "cannot function in strict isolation or solitude; it needs the presence of others . . . whose perspectives it must take into consideration, and without whom it never has the opportunity to operate at all. . . . [J]udgment, to be valid, depends on the presence of others. . . . [Kant] was highly conscious of the public quality of beauty." Arendt, *Between Past and Future*, 217, 218.

112. Kemal, *Kant and Fine Art*, 88. *See also* Terry Eagleton, *The Ideology of the Aesthetic* (Blackwell, 1990), 75 ("When, for Kant, we find ourselves concurring spontaneously

in an aesthetic judgment . . . we exercise a precious form of intersubjectivity, establishing ourselves as a community of feeling subjects linked by a quick sense of our shared capacities.").

113. *See generally* J. R. Lucas, "On Processes for Resolving Disputes," in Robert S. Summers, *Essays in Legal Philosophy* (Blackwell, 1970), 177–78 ("I go further, and make it part of the *definition* of a community that disputes between its members are never settled by force, but by some method common to all its members. It is in virtue of this that we can talk of a community's being a single entity. The members of a community are not always of one mind, necessarily not always of one mind. What is common to them is not their views on all questions, but a way, a *method*, of settling, or at least of *deciding*, those *disputes* that cannot be resolved by argument alone. A community, therefore, is defined as a body of individuals who have a common method of deciding disputes.") (emphasis in original).

114. *See* above at 171–72nn191–192, 185n67.

115. Guyer, *Kant and the Claims of Taste*, 8.

116. Guyer, *Kant and the Claims of Taste*, 242.

117. Guyer and Allison, "Dialogue," in Kukla, *Aesthetics and Cognition in Kant's Critical Philosophy*, 132. While Guyer and Allison agree that Kant's theory incorporates a justificatory dynamic into aesthetic judgment, they disagree about the proper characterization of the ultimate goal of aesthetic judgment (as an "expectation" of agreement or as a "demand" of agreement). I do not address this further disagreement here.

118. *See* Meyer, *"Nothing We Say Matters,"* 471 ("Although law is dependent upon these situational intuitions, we should not skeptically conclude that it is therefore subjective or 'result-oriented' in a narrow, selfish way. We share these intuitions with others within our practice. From this standpoint, law is no more subjective than language, whose structure itself requires that law be tied to context. And language works pretty well: most of the time, we understand each other.") (footnotes omitted). *Cf.* Robert P. Burns, *A Theory of the Trial* (Princeton University Press, 1999), 206 ("The power of language to invoke dimensions of situations beyond the simple referents of its statements is thus a pervasive aspect of ordinary conversation. Indeed, these unspoken dimensions are the meanings that, in a strong sense, actually 'constitute' the community's identity.").

119. *See* John Bell, "The Acceptability of Legal Arguments," in Neil MacCormick and Peter Birks, eds., *The Legal Mind: Essays for Tony Honoré* (Oxford University Press, 1986), 54 ("The notion of the legal audience has two aspects. The first, emphasized here, is its epistemological character: legal reasoning is only possible as justifications directed to a particular legal audience. The audience provides a focus for argument, a way of making it accessible to all, and thus of making the claim to universality which is characteristic of justification. However, it also has a technical character. In the real world of practical discourse, the criteria for whether a legal argument is acceptable may well be the reactions of the actual legal community."). *See also* above at 140n57.

120. *See* Postema, *"A Similibus ad Similia,"* in Edlin, *Common Law Theory*, 125 ("[A]lthough it is only individuals who participate in analogical reasoning, these individuals proceed as members of a group, participants in a social practice: and even when the reasoning is carried on, as it were, in their own heads, it is an interior version

of an essentially exterior, interpersonal, public enterprise. They deliberate . . . not for their own part only, but as members of a larger whole.").

121. *See* Meyer, *"Nothing We Say Matters,"* 473 ("Although knowledge of legal distinctions requires special legal knowledge and experience, common law reasoning presupposes that the 'importance' of facts is already available to the judge, just as the 'importance' of facts in everyday description is already available to the competent user of a natural language. The judge is not just reading prior statements of other judges; she is supposed to know already what sorts of facts might be important in particular contexts.").

122. *Cf.* H. Jefferson Powell, *Constitutional Conscience: The Moral Dimension of Judicial Decision* (University of Chicago Press, 2008), 71–72 ("Persuasion in a constitutional-law argument, furthermore, depends on the extent to which the interpreter seems, *to the reader* (or hearer), to grasp the point of the constitutional enterprise. . . . [The interpreter] assume[s] that the Constitution is, or gives rise to, law in a technical sense, the sort of human practice in which there is a role for technical expertise, learning, and skill which are not common among any citizen body as a whole. But his own practice, while technically skilled, [i]s aimed at allowing those lacking the relevant professional training . . . to understand and indeed *to judge his professional judgment.*") (emphasis supplied).

123. *Cf.* Alan Brudner, *Constitutional Goods* (Oxford University Press, 2004), 366; Owen Fiss, *The Law as It Could Be* (New York University Press, 2003), 8–11; Joseph Raz, "On the Authority and Interpretation of Constitutions," in Larry Alexander, ed., *Constitutionalism: Philosophical Foundations* (Cambridge University Press, 1998), 174–75 ("[T]he reference to the 'self-legitimating' character of the 'constitution' is not to the formal legal existence of the constitution but to the constitution as it exists in the practices and traditions of the country concerned."); Robin L. West, *Are There Nothing But Texts in This Class? Interpreting the Interpretive Turns in Legal Thought*, 76 Chi.-Kent L. Rev. 1125, 1131 (2000) ("To truly understand a text is to interpret it, and to interpret it, just is to do so by using, not setting aside, the prejudices and traditions that constitute both the reader (or hearer) and the reader's (or hearer's) community—it is precisely those prejudices and traditions that facilitate the reader's conversational capacity. So to understand the Due Process Clause or the First Amendment in anything but a hermeneutical, participatory fashion is . . . impossible for us human creatures."); Walter F. Murphy, *Civil Law, Common Law, and Constitutional Democracy*, 52 La. L. Rev. 91, 130 (1991) ("To maximize the constitutive enterprise's chances of success, founders must take their own past into account. Men and women who would create a new constitution cannot . . . simply transpose a constitutional text from one state to another, no matter how successfully that document has operated in its original context. A nation has its own history and sets of collective, if typically fuzzy, inaccurate, and conflicting memories of that history. Founders cannot erase and replace these myths. It is highly probable that if a people are to accept a constitution as legitimate, it must reflect some of their history, perhaps even retain some familiar institutions, processes, and proximate ends.").

124. *See, e.g.*, Stanley Ingber, *Judging without Judgment: Constitutional Irrelevancies and the Demise of Dialogue*, 46 Rutgers L. Rev. 1473, 1478–79 (1994) ("Unsurprisingly,

therefore, our Constitution's most significant clauses, such as the Due Process and Equal Protection Clauses, are indeterminate. . . . This indeterminacy becomes the very mechanism by which judgment informs constitutional deliberation. . . . Judgment, rather than deductive prowess, is required precisely in those situations posing genuine dilemmas, forcing us to choose between or otherwise accommodate conflicting interests and obligations. Resolution of these dilemmas necessitates the development of a value hierarchy not itself provided by the constitutional text. Thus, the choices compelled by constitutional deliberation are themselves 'constitutive' in nature. They delineate our 'moral identity' as they constitute us as this sort of community rather than that sort—as a community that, at least in some contexts, values this more than that.") (footnotes deleted).

125. I exclude from this discussion "sham" or "fictive" constitutions. *See* Beau Breslin, *From Words to Worlds: Exploring Constitutional Functionality* (Johns Hopkins University Press, 2009), 26–27.

126. The famous phrase and image of imagined communities comes from Benedict Anderson, *Imagined Communities: Reflections on the Origin and Spread of Nationalism* (rev. ed.) (Verso, 1991).

127. Paul Campos, *Three Mistakes About Interpretation*, 92 Mich. L. Rev. 388, 391–92 (1993).

128. *See* above at 58–59, 181–82n45.

129. *See* above at 29–30, 184–85n64.

130. *See* above at 143n78, 143–44n80, 144n82.

131. *See* above at 14, 140n57, 142n69, 164–65n113.

132. Kirk Pillow, "Understanding Aestheticized," in Rebecca Kukla, ed., *Aesthetics and Cognition in Kant's Critical Philosophy* (Cambridge University Press, 2006), 263–64 (emphasis in original) (citation omitted).

133. Kant, *Critique of Judgement*, § 2, at 42. *See also id.*, § 6, at 50–51.

134. Kant, *Critique of Judgement*, § 2, at 43. *See also id.* at § 5, at 48, 49 ("[T]he judgement of taste is simply *contemplative*, i.e. it is a judgement which is indifferent as to the existence of an object. . . . [T]aste in the beautiful may be said to be the one and only disinterested and *free* delight.") (emphasis in original).

135. Kant, *Critique of Judgement*, § 2, at 43.

136. *See* Kant, *Critique of Judgement*, § 6, at 50 ("This definition of the beautiful is deducible from the foregoing definition of it as an object of delight apart from any interest.").

137. *See* Allison, *Kant's Theory of Taste*, 94–95 ("The short answer is that one cannot be indifferent, but that, appearances to the contrary, the disinterestedness thesis does not really require that one be. . . . This explication indicates that the disinterestedness thesis concerns the quality of the liking (or disliking) *by means of which* an object is deemed beautiful (or nonbeautiful). In other words, it is the determination of aesthetic value that must be independent of interest, because any such dependence would make this determination subserve some other value, thereby undermining both the autonomy and the purity of taste.") (emphasis in original).

138. Pillow, "Understanding Aestheticized," in Kukla, *Aesthetics and Cognition in Kant's Critical Philosophy*, 262–63. *See also* Paul Guyer, *Disinterestedness and Desire in Kant's Aesthetics*, 36 J. Aesthetics & Art Criticism 449, 450 (1978) ("Kant's explanation

of aesthetic response does imply that we cannot take a *certain form* of interest in beautiful objects, but this does not mean that we must look beyond the phenomenon of aesthetic response itself to explain our desires with respect to natural and artistic beauty.") (emphasis in original).

139. *See* Kant, *Critique of Judgement*, § 6, at 50–51 ("For where any one is conscious that his delight in an object is with him independent of interest, it is inevitable that he should look on the object as one containing a ground of delight for all men. For, since the delight is not based on any inclination of the Subject (or on any other deliberate interest), but the Subject feels himself completely *free* in respect of the liking which he accords to the object, he can find as reason for his delight no personal conditions to which his own subjective self might alone be party. Hence he must regard it as resting on what he may also presuppose in every other person. . . . The result is that the judgement of taste, with its attendant consciousness of detachment from all interest, must involve a claim to validity for all men.") (emphasis in original). *See also* Allison, *Kant's Theory of Taste*, 81.

140. *Cf.* Richard A. Posner, *The Federal Courts: Challenge and Reform* (Harvard University Press, 1996), 349 ("It is easy to confuse impartiality with indifference, a tendency fostered by the modern usage of the word 'disinterest' (which formerly meant impartiality—and still does to purists) as a synonym for lack of interest.").

141. The Oxford English Dictionary defines "uninterested" as "unconcerned, indifferent." I should mention, in connection with Judge Posner's observation in the previous note, that this is the second definition offered by the OED. The first definition is "impartial, disinterested." In this respect, I am an unrepentant "purist" where the different shades of meaning between these two terms are concerned.

142. *See* above at 22. The Oxford English Dictionary defines "disinterested" as "not influenced by one's own advantage; impartial, free from personal interest." Again, this is the second listed definition. The first definition treats disinterested and uninterested as synonymous. For more on this point, *see* Martindale, *Latin Poetry and the Judgement of Taste*, 22.

143. *See* Kant, *Critique of Judgement*, § 2 n. 1, at 43 ("A judgement upon an object of our delight may be wholly *disinterested* but withal very *interesting*.") (emphasis in original). I need to be careful about a point of translation here. In English, uninterested can be defined as indifferent. In German, the term *gleichgültig* might be translated as indifferent or uninterested, and the term *uninteressierte* might be translated as disinterested or uninterested. Kant used both of these terms in his writing of the third *Critique*. I am not arguing that Kant did or would accept the distinction that I discuss in the text and I am not quibbling over varying translations of *gleichgültig* or *uninteressierte*. I simply wish to identify the different German terms and to explain that I use the English terms uninterested and disinterested to underscore the terminological distinction in English and to challenge the assumption people often make about common law judges (that they should be both disinterested *and* uninterested). *Cf.* Paul Guyer, *Kant and the Experience of Freedom: Essays on Aesthetics and Morality* (Cambridge University Press, 1993), chaps. 2–3; Meerbote, "Reflection on Beauty," in Cohen and Guyer, *Essays in Kant's Aesthetics*, 70–71.

144. Kant, *Critique of Judgement*, § 13, at 64 ("Every interest vitiates the judgement of taste and robs it of its impartiality."). Arendt stressed impartiality as the "the most

important condition for all judgments," and she connected it directly to disinterest. Arendt, *Lectures on Kant's Political Philosophy*, 68.

145. *See* Mayeda, *Uncommonly Common*, 121 ("To make Arendt's theory an acceptable theory of *legal* judgment, we must thus adapt it by deriving the normativity of impartiality, not from disinterest, but from the function of the judge as a person involved in an actual dispute. . . . We see this in the fact that the presence of the judge affects the nature of the arguments given in court. She is intimately involved in settling the dispute. Only certain types of claims are admissible before her.") (emphasis in original). *See also* above at __. Mayeda argues that this understanding requires discarding the Kantian notion of disinterestedness. I believe it requires understanding the Kantian notion more precisely. In this context, however, this is a relatively minor point. I agree generally with Mayeda's view here.

146. Arendt's comments on Kantian aesthetic judgment apply quite closely to this aspect of my argument. *See* Arendt, *Lectures on Kant's Political Philosophy*, 42 ("You see that *impartiality* is obtained by taking the viewpoints of others into account; impartiality is not the result of some higher standpoint that would then actually settle the dispute by being altogether above the melée.") (emphasis in original). *Cf. Caperton v. A.T. Massey Coal Co.*, 556 U.S. 868, 882–83 (2009) ("Following accepted principles of our legal tradition respecting the proper performance of judicial functions, judges often inquire into their subjective motives and purposes in the ordinary course of deciding a case. This does not mean the inquiry is a simple one. 'The work of deciding cases goes on every day in hundreds of courts throughout the land. Any judge, one might suppose, would find it easy to describe the process which he had followed a thousand times and more. Nothing could be farther from the truth.' The judge inquires into reasons that seem to be leading to a particular result. Precedent and *stare decisis* and the text and purpose of the law and the Constitution; logic and scholarship and experience and common sense; and fairness and *disinterest* and neutrality are among the factors at work.") (quoting Benjamin N. Cardozo, *The Nature of the Judicial Process* (Yale University Press, 1921), 9) (emphasis supplied).

147. *See* above at 54.

148. Whether Kant understood the formulation of an aesthetic judgment to occur in separable stages is not a point that I pursue here. I describe the process in this manner for the sake of clarity and ease of exposition.

149. *See* Kant, *Critique of Judgement*, § 6, at 50–51 ("This definition of the beautiful is deducible from the foregoing definition of it as an object of delight apart from any interest. For where any one is conscious that his delight in an object is with him independent of interest, it is inevitable that he should look on the object as one containing a ground of delight for all men. . . . [S]ince the delight is not based on any inclination of the Subject . . . the Subject feels himself completely *free* in respect of the liking which he accords to the object. . . . Hence he must regard it as resting on what he may also presuppose in every other person; and therefore he must believe that he has reason for demanding a similar delight from every one.") (emphasis in original).

150. *See* Kemal, *Kant and Fine Art*, 158 ("The Analytic of the Beautiful sets out our expectations of judgements of taste. . . . We learn that judgements must be disinterested and formal in order to ensure that they are singular but subjectively universal and necessary. . . . What makes the universality of aesthetic judgements subjective is

that it attaches to a mere feeling, and the feeling is universal in that we expect it to carry more authority than an expression of merely personal preferences.").

151. *See* Crawford, *Reason-Giving in Kant's Aesthetics*, 507 ("Of course, showing that a judgment of taste is impure is not sufficient to show that it is false; it simply shows it is ill-founded. One can always be right for the wrong reasons.").

152. *See, e.g., Model Code of Judicial Conduct*, canon 1 ("A judge . . . shall avoid impropriety and the appearance of impropriety."); *Code of Conduct for United States Judges*, canon 2 ("A judge should avoid impropriety and the appearance of impropriety in all activities.").

153. *See, e.g.*, Crawford, *Kant's Aesthetic Theory*, 170 ("Analyzing aesthetic value in terms of pleasure allows it to remain at the level of being felt; by giving it a basis in purposiveness and form, Kant allows for the possibility of positive reasons. Thus, in Kant's aesthetic theory we see a necessary, intimate connection between experience and evaluation.").

Chapter 4

1. John Chipman Gray, *The Nature and Sources of the Law* (Ashgate, 1997), 151.

2. *See generally* A. V. Dicey, *Lectures on the Relation between Law and Public Opinion in England during the Nineteenth Century* (Macmillan, 1905), 486 ("Judge-made law is real law. . . . Whoever fairly considers how large are the masses of English law for which no other authority than judicial decisions or reported cases can be found, will easily acquiesce in the statement that law made by the judges is as truly law as are laws made by Parliament."); Brian Z. Tamanaha, *Beyond the Formalist-Realist Divide: The Role of Politics in Judging* (Princeton University Press, 2010), 14–26, 125–31.

3. *See, e.g.*, Orrin G. Hatch, *The Constitution as the Playbook for Judicial Selection*, 32 Harv. J. L. & Pub. Pol'y 1035, 1039 (2009) ("Judges do not have authority to make law, so they do not have authority to choose what the words of our laws say or what they mean. In other words, judges apply the law to decide cases, but they may not make the law they apply.").

4. An interesting and pointed exchange between Justices White and Scalia underscores the nature of the disagreement on this point (even among judges). *Compare James B. Beam Distilling Co. v. Georgia*, 501 U.S. 529, 549 (1991) ("I am not so naïve (nor do I think our forebears were) as to be unaware that judges in a real sense 'make' law. But they make it *as judges make it*, which is to say *as though* they were 'finding' it—discerning what the law *is*, rather than decreeing what it is today *changed to*, or what it will *tomorrow* be.") (Scalia, J., concurring) (emphasis in original) *with id.* at 546 ("[E]ven though the Justice [Scalia] is not naïve enough (nor does he think the Framers were naïve enough) to be unaware that judges in a real sense 'make' law, he suggests that judges (in an unreal sense, I suppose) should never concede that they do and must claim that they do no more than discover it, hence suggesting that there are citizens who are naïve enough to believe them.") (White, J., concurring). This exchange is also helpful in demonstrating that Justice Scalia does not deny the judicial lawmaking function either (however he believes judges should choose to characterize what they do). In fact, when he is off the bench, Justice Scalia's disagreement with Justice White on this point seems far less stark. *See* Antonin Scalia, *The Rule of Law as a Law of Rules*,

56 U. Chi. L. Rev. 1175, 1176–77 (1989) ("In a judicial system such as ours, in which judges are bound, not only by the text of code or Constitution, but also by the prior decisions of superior courts, and even by the prior decisions of their own court, courts have the capacity to 'make' law. Let us not quibble about the theoretical scope of a 'holding'; the modern reality, at least, is that when the Supreme Court of the federal system, or of one of the state systems, decides a case, not merely the outcome of that decision, but the mode of analysis that it applies will thereafter be followed by the lower courts within that system, and even by that supreme court itself. And by making the mode of analysis relatively principled or relatively fact-specific, the courts can either establish general rules or leave ample discretion for the future.").

5. Following up on the example with which I began this book, in response to questioning before the Senate Judiciary Committee, Justice Sotomayor asserted at her confirmation hearing that "judges must apply the law and not make the law." Nomination of Sonia Sotomayor to be an Associate Justice of the Supreme Court of the United States: Confirmation Hearing Before the S. Comm. on the Judiciary, 111th Cong. (2009), 70. In fairness, however, I should clarify that Justice Sotomayor's comment was made in the course of distinguishing between a judicial decision based upon what the law requires and what the judge's sympathies toward individual litigants might otherwise encourage her to do. Justice Sotomayor also went on to distinguish between the prejudices toward a litigant that would improperly bias a judge's decision in a particular case, and the life experiences and perspectives that influence a judge's outlook on any case she would decide. Responding to the question "is there any circumstance in which a judge should allow their prejudices to impact their decision making?" Justice Sotomayor responded, "Never their prejudices. . . . Life experiences have to influence you. . . . [T]here are situations in which some experiences are important in the process of judging because the law asks us to use those experiences." *Id.* at 70–71.

6. *See, e.g.*, Richard A. Posner, "What Am I, a Potted Plant? The Case Against Strict Constructionism," in David M. O'Brien, ed., *Judges on Judging: Views from the Bench* (4th ed.) (CQ Press, 2013), 227 ("Everyone professionally connected with law knows that . . . [judges] make law, only more cautiously, more slowly, and in more principled, less partisan, fashion than legislators."); H. L. A. Hart, *The Concept of Law* (3rd ed.) (Oxford University Press, 2012), 97 ("[I]f courts are empowered to make authoritative determinations of the fact that a rule has been broken, these cannot avoid being taken as authoritative determinations of what the rules are. So the rule which confers jurisdiction will also be a rule of recognition, identifying the primary rules through the judgments of the courts and these judgments will become a 'source' of law.").

7. "Tautologically true" is probably an overstatement. Raz, for example, embraces the notion that judges, when establishing legal norms, should act as legislators do. *See* Joseph Raz, *The Authority of Law: Essays on Law and Morality* (2nd ed.) (Oxford University Press, 2009), 197 ("[W]ithin the admitted boundaries of their law-making powers courts act and should act just as legislators do, namely, they should adopt those rules which they judge best."). There are a few problems here, though. First, as MacCormick explains, it is inaccurate to say that courts act as legislators do when they make law. *See* above at 48. The institutional position, obligations, and constraints under which judges act are entirely different from those of legislators, and these differences affect

the way judges articulate legal norms. Second, it is unclear that judges should act as legislators do, because judges and legislators do not serve the same constituencies in the same ways. Third, Raz's underlying assumption that legislators generally "adopt those rules which they judge best" seems problematic descriptively and normatively. Raz has the British Parliament in mind here, and perhaps this is a fairer functional description of Parliament than it is of, say, the United States Congress. But in any case, it does not seem an accurate description of legislators *tout court*. Moreover, it is not clear that legislators should (or do) usually adopt those rules which *they* judge best. It may very well be the case that legislators should (and often do) adopt those rules which they believe their constituents want them to adopt (even when these are not the rules the legislators themselves believe to be best). Raz's assumption about the legislative function recalls the classic dichotomy between the "delegate" and "trustee" conceptions of the legislative role, which traces back to Edmund Burke's "Speech to the Electors of Bristol" (3 November 1774) in 2 Edmund Burke, *The Works of the Right Honorable Edmund Burke* (Oxford University Press, 1906), 95 ("[I]t ought to be the happiness and glory of a representative to live in the strictest union, the closest correspondence, and the most unreserved communication with his constituents. Their wishes ought to have great weight with him; their opinions high respect; their business unremitted attention. . . . But his unbiased opinion, his mature judgment, his enlightened conscience, he ought not to sacrifice to you, to any man, or to any set of men living. . . . Your representative owes you, not his industry only, but his judgment; and he betrays, instead of serving you, if he sacrifices it to your opinion."). Burke, like Raz, favored the trustee conception of representation. (Burke, it also should be noted, was not re-elected.) Although I do not intend these comments to suggest my endorsement of either view of the legislative role in representative government (or, indeed, that these are the only two options), it does seem fair to say that no matter how one understands the legislative function, it should not be equated or conflated with the judicial function.

8. *See* above at 170–71nn187–188.

9. *See* 4 John Finnis, *Philosophy of Law: Collected Essays* (Oxford University Press, 2011), 399–400 ("[A]djudication is not the telling of some story which if accurate might be called history—or prescient prediction—and if inaccurate a myth or fairy tale. Adjudication is the effort to identify the rights of the contending parties *now* by identifying what were, in law, the rights and wrongs, or validity or invalidity, of their actions and transactions *when entered upon and done*. If those rested on a view of the law then widely settled, the judge may nonetheless have the duty now to take and act upon a contrary view of the law. . . . [A]n important element in judicial duty . . . [is] the duty of judges to differentiate their authority and responsibility, and thus their practical reasoning, from that of legislatures.") (emphasis in original).

10. Neil MacCormick, *Rhetoric and the Rule of Law: A Theory of Legal Reasoning* (Oxford University Press, 2005), 277 n. 33. *See also* Cécile Fabre, *A Philosophical Argument for a Bill of Rights*, 30 Brit. J. Pol. Sci. 77, 92 (2000) ("Judges, including constitutional judges, are subject to strict rules of reasoning and argument. Their decisions, which they must justify, are constrained by previous decisions, and in that sense they are under more constraints than the legislature.").

11. As I indicated above at note 7, I do not address whether this means the legisla-

tor should act as his constituents want him to act or on the legislator's own view of what is in the best interests of his constituents.

12. The classic example here is probably "logrolling," which is the practice of one legislator voting for a colleague's legislation in exchange for that other legislator's vote in the future. *See generally* James M. Buchanan and Gordon Tullock, *The Calculus of Consent: Logical Foundations of Constitutional Democracy* (University of Michigan Press, 1962), chaps. 10–12. *Cf.* Henry M. Hart, Jr. and Albert M. Sacks, *The Legal Process: Basic Problems in the Making and Application of Law* (Foundation Press, 1994), 1359 (listing reasons a legislator might not vote in favor of proposed legislation aside from the bill's merits).

13. *See* Melvin Aron Eisenberg, *Nature of the Common Law* (Harvard University Press, 1988), 9–10. Of course, where judges are publicly elected, views of their electoral accountability will differ.

14. *See* John Gardner, *Law as a Leap of Faith: Essays on Law in General* (Oxford University Press, 2012), 38–42.

15. *See generally* Gray, *The Nature and Sources of the Law*, 72 ("A judge of an organized body is a man appointed by that body to determine duties and the corresponding rights *upon the application of persons claiming those rights*. It is the fact that such application must be made to him, which distinguishes a judge. . . . The essence of a judge's office is that he shall be impartial, that he is to sit apart, is not to interfere voluntarily in affairs . . . but is to determine cases which are presented to him.") (emphasis in original); Charles L. Black, Jr., *The People and the Court: Judicial Review in a Democracy* (Macmillan, 1960), 167–69; Kent Greenawalt, *Law and Objectivity* (Oxford University Press, 1992), 54–58; Neil MacCormick, *Legal Reasoning and Legal Theory* (Oxford University Press, 1978), 32–33, 53–54. *See also Southern Pacific Co. v. Jensen*, 244 U.S. 205, 221 (1917) ("A common-law judge could not say, 'I think the doctrine of consideration a bit of historical nonsense and shall not enforce it in my court.'") (Holmes, J., dissenting);

16. *See* Ronald Dworkin, *Law's Empire* (Harvard University Press, 1986), 244 ("[J]udges are in a very different position from legislators. . . . Judges must . . . deploy arguments why the parties actually had the 'novel' legal rights and duties they enforce at the time the parties acted or at some other pertinent time in the past."); 401 ("[L]aw is a matter of rights tenable in court. This makes the content of law sensitive to different kinds of institutional constraints, special to judges, that are not necessarily constraints for other officials or institutions.").

17. *Cf. Pennsylvania v. Local Union 542*, 388 F. Supp. 155, 180 (E.D. Pa. 1974), *aff'd*, 478 F.2d 1398 (3d Cir. 1974), *cert. denied*, 421 U.S. 999 (1975) ("[T]he critical issue is, what conduct by black judges will assure their impartiality? Should they be robots? Should they demean their heritage by asking for less than first class citizenship for other blacks? Should they not tell the truth about past injustices? Of course, there is a dramatic difference between the role which legislators, politicians, and elected officials play in our society, one which is far closer to the cutting edge of policy development, and the role which could be tolerated or expected from a federal judge. I willingly accept those limitations; they are inherent in the judicial process. I am aware that Judge Higginbotham is not Senator Higginbotham, or Mayor Higginbotham, or Governor Higginbotham, but I also know that Judge Higginbotham should not have

to disparage blacks in order to placate whites who otherwise would be fearful of his impartiality."). I discuss the relationship between a judge's impartiality and judicial independence in the next chapter.

18. I am grateful to Tracy Lightcap for this point.

19. The ergodic/nonergodic distinction has been employed in various fields. One prominent example involves the dispute among economists concerning whether their field is properly understood as ergodic or nonergodic. *Compare* Paul Samuelson, "Classical and Neoclassical Monetary Theory," in Robert W. Clower, ed., *Monetary Theory: Selected Readings* (Penguin, 1969), 12, 170, 184–85 (arguing that economics is ergodic) *with* Paul Davidson, *The Keynes Solution: The Path to Global Economic Prosperity* (Palgrave Macmillan, 2009), 167 (noting that Keynes himself rejected the ergodic axiom in economics).

20. *See* above at 58–59, 181–82n45.

21. Gregory Shaffer and Tom Ginsburg, *The Empirical Turn in International Legal Scholarship*, 106 Am. J. Int'l L. 1, 45 (2012) (quoting Douglass C. North, *Understanding the Process of Economic Change* (rev. ed.) (Princeton University Press, 2005), 5).

22. *See* Douglass C. North, *Dealing with a Non-Ergodic World: Institutional Economics, Property Rights, and the Global Environment*, 10 Duke Envtl. L. & Pol'y F. 1, 2 (1999) ("Let me begin by asserting that the world we live in is not an ergodic world; it is a non-ergodic world. . . . That does not mean that there are not ergodic aspects of the world.").

23. *See* George R. Cooper and Clare D. McGillem, *Probabilistic Methods of Signal and System Analysis* (3rd ed.) (Oxford University Press, 1998), 197. *See also* above at 189n93.

24. *Cf.* Okezie Chukwumerije, *Rhetoric Versus Reality: The Link Between the Rule of Law and Economic Development*, 23 Emory Int'l L. Rev. 383, 431–32 (2009).

25. *See* John N. Drobak and Douglass C. North, *Understanding Judicial Decision-Making: The Importance of Constraints on Non-Rational Deliberations*, 26 Wash. U. J. L. & Pol'y 131, 138–39, 150–51 (2008).

26. I am modifying Douglass North's term "adaptive efficiency" to echo the point he makes, but with reference to a system that might be better thought of as capable of evolutionary change rather than efficient change. *Cf.* North, *Dealing with a Non-Ergodic World*, 12 ("I use the term 'adaptive efficiency' to describe how economies and societies work effectively, not at a moment in time, but through time. . . . Our institutions have been flexible, here and there. So, the United States has continued to have economic growth, despite the enormous amount of stresses, strains, and tensions that have evolved in our economy over time. Thus, adaptive efficiency is certainly a required characteristic of any institutions that we devise with regard to the global environment. We must think in terms of creating not only a structure that will improve the environment today but a structure with built-in flexibility so that it can adjust to the tensions, strains, and unanticipated circumstances of tomorrow.").

27. *See* MacCormick, *Rhetoric and the Rule of Law*, 150–51 ("[T]he very fact that justifications have to focus themselves on rulings about disputed points of law narrows the field of argumentation as between parties and of judicial deliberation on the questions they put in issue. . . . [This] restricts the range of legally justifiable resolutions that can conceivably be advanced."). *See also id.* at 147.

28. Such as the recognition of an independent negligence claim for an infant

harmed *in utero*. *See Woods v. Lancet*, 303 N.Y. 349, 354–55 (1951) ("Negligence law is common law, and the common law has been molded and changed and brought up-to-date in many another cases. Our court said, long ago, that it had not only the right, but the duty to re-examine a question where justice demands it. . . . Chancellor KENT, more than a century ago, had stated that upwards of a thousand cases could then be pointed out in the English and American reports 'which had been overruled, doubted or limited in their application', and that the great Chancellor had declared that decisions which seem contrary to reason 'ought to be examined without fear, and revised without reluctance, rather than to have the character of our law impaired, and the beauty and harmony of the system destroyed by the perpetuity of error.' And Justice SUTHERLAND, writing for the Supreme Court said that while legislative bodies have the power to change old rules of law, nevertheless, when they fail to act, it is the duty of the court to bring the law into accordance with present day standards of wisdom and justice rather than 'with some outworn and antiquated rule of the past.' . . . The sum of the argument against plaintiff here is that there is no New York decision in which such a claim has been enforced. Winfield's answer to that will serve: 'if that were a valid objection, the common law would now be what it was in the Plantagenet period.' . . . We act in the finest common-law tradition when we adapt and alter decisional law to produce common-sense justice. The same answer goes to the argument that the change we here propose should come from the Legislature, not the courts. Legislative action there could, of course, be, but we abdicate our own function, in a field peculiarly nonstatutory, when we refuse to reconsider an old and unsatisfactory court-made rule.") (citations omitted).

29. *Weintraub v. Krobatsch*, 64 N.J. 445, 447 (1974).

30. *Weintraub*, 64 N.J. at 447.

31. *Weintraub*, 64 N.J. at 448. A motion was also filed by the real estate broker for the amount of its commission. In the interest of clarity (and narrative drama), I do not discuss the broker's claims in the text.

32. *Weintraub*, 64 N.J. at 449 (quoting *Keen v. James*, 39 N.J. Eq. 527, 540–41 (E. & A. 1885)).

33. *Weintraub*, 64 N.J. at 450.

34. 311 Mass. 677 (1942).

35. *Swinton*, 311 Mass. at 679.

36. *See Swinton*, 311 Mass. at 678–79 ("The law has not yet, we believe, reached the point of imposing upon the frailties of human nature a standard so idealistic as this. That the particular case here stated by the plaintiff possesses a certain appeal to the moral sense is scarcely to be denied.").

37. William L. Prosser, *Law of Torts* (4th ed.) (West Publishing Co., 1971), 696.

38. *Weintraub*, 64 N.J. at 450 (citing *Kannavos v. Annino*, 356 Mass. 42 (1969)) (other citations omitted) (emphasis supplied).

39. *Weintraub*, 64 N.J. at 456. The New Jersey Supreme Court later extended the seller's duty to disclose material latent defects to off-site conditions that might reasonably affect a purchaser's interest in the subject property. *See Strawn v. Canuso*, 140 N.J. 43, 65 (1995).

40. *E.g., Holcomb v. Zinke*, 365 N.W.2d 507, 511–12 (N.D. 1985) ("our basic notions of fair dealing and fair play"); *Johnson v. Davis*, 480 So.2d 625, 627–29 (Fla.

1985) ("It would be contrary to all notions of fairness and justice for this Court to place its stamp of approval on an affirmative misrepresentation by a wrongdoer."); *Flakus v. Schug*, 213 Neb. 491, 494–95 (1983), overruled on other grounds, *Nielsen v. Adams*, 223 Neb. 262, 271–72 (1986); *Quashnock v. Frost*, 299 Pa. Super. 9, 19–24 (1982) ("our recent developments . . . would dictate a more modern and equitable approach than that of *caveat emptor* . . . justice, equity, and fair dealing require the vendor to speak"); *Thacker v. Tyree*, 171 W.Va. 110, 112 (1982); *Ollerman v. O'Rourke Company, Inc.*, 94 Wis.2d 17, 39–43 (1980); *Posner v. Davis*, 76 Ill. App. 3d 638, 643–44 (1979); *Miles v. Perpetual Savings & Loan Co.*, 58 Ohio St. 2d 97, 101 (1979). For examples of decisions in this vein that predate *Weintraub, see Obde v. Schlemeyer*, 56 Wash. 2d 449, 452–53 (1960) (noting that the claim for fraudulent concealment was distinct from a contractual claim in which the relief sought was rescission); *Lingsch v. Savage*, 213 Cal. App. 2d 729, 735–36 (1963).

41. *See, e.g, Blue v. R.L. Glosson Contracting, Inc.*, 173 Ga. App. 622, 623–24 (1985); *Watts Home, Inc. v. Alonzo*, 452 So.2d 1331, 1332–33 (Ala. Civ. App. 1984); *Schmeck v. Sea Oats Condominium Ass'n., Inc.*, 441 So.2d 1092, 1096–97 (Ct. App. Fla. 1983); *Cacace v. Morcaldi*, 37 Conn. Supp. 735, 740 (1981); *Altevogt v. Brinkoetter*, 85 Ill. 2d 44, 53 (1981); *Trahan v. Broussard*, 399 So. 2d 782, 784 (La. Ct. App. 1981); *Keel v. Titan Constr. Corp.*, 639 P.2d 1228, 1231 (Okla. 1981); *Wimmer v. Down East Prop., Inc.*, 406 A.2d 88, 92–93 (Me. 1979); *Norton v. Burleaud*, 115 N.H. 435, 436 (1975).

42. *See* Melvin A. Eisenberg, *Disclosure in Contract Law*, 91 Calif. L. Rev. 1645, 1674–80 (2003); Anthony T. Kronman, *Mistake, Disclosure, Information, and the Law of Contracts*, 7 J. Legal Stud. 1, 26 (1978). One lingering question in this area concerns a seller's ability to insulate himself from liability for nondisclosure through the inclusion of an "as is" clause in the contract. *See, e.g., Kaye v. Buehrle*, 8 Ohio App. 3d 381, 383 (1983). Some commentators believe that an "as is" clause should shield sellers from liability for nondisclosure (but not affirmative misrepresentations). *See* Florrie Young Roberts, *Disclosure Duties in Real Estate Sales and Attempts to Reallocate the Risk*, 34 Conn. L. Rev. 1, 39–45 (2001). Professor Roberts argues that "as is" clauses allow parties to bargain for and allocate risk in contracts and thereby enhance efficiency and certainty in real estate transactions. The problem with this view is that, purely in terms of efficiency and information access, sellers typically possess enhanced information about their property and preexisting incentives to acquire this information during their time of ownership. *See* Eisenberg, *Disclosure in Contract Law*, 1674–75, 1676–77. In effect, an "as is" clause simply reintroduces the discarded *caveat emptor* rule as a contractual provision, with the same asymmetries of access to information and the same inequities in enforcement and effect. *Cf. Ferguson v. Cussins*, 713 S.W.2d 5, 6 (Ct. App. Ky. 1986) ("The general rule is that real estate is sold in an 'as is' condition, and all prior statements and agreements, written and oral, are merged into the deed of conveyance, and the purchaser takes the property subject to the existing physical condition. The doctrine of *caveat emptor* obtains. There are certain exceptions to this rule, however, as where the defective condition is inherently nonobservable.") (citing *Borden v. Litchford*, 619 S.W.2d 715 (Ct. App. Ky. 1981)) (other citation omitted).

43. 42 U.S.C. §§ 2000a-2000e.

44. The 1964 Act describes public accommodations as: "Establishments affecting interstate commerce or supported in their activities by State action as places of public

accommodation; lodgings; facilities principally engaged in selling food for consumption on the premises; gasoline stations; places of exhibition or entertainment; other covered establishments. Each of the following establishments which serves the public is a place of public accommodation within the meaning of this title if its operations affect commerce, or if discrimination or segregation by it is supported by State action: (1) any inn, hotel, motel, or other establishment which provides lodging to transient guests, other than an establishment located within a building which contains not more than five rooms for rent or hire and which is actually occupied by the proprietor of such establishment as his residence; (2) any restaurant, cafeteria, lunchroom, lunch counter, soda fountain, or other facility principally engaged in selling food for consumption on the premises, including, but not limited to, any such facility located on the premises of any retail establishment; or any gasoline station; (3) any motion picture house, theater, concert hall, sports arena, stadium or other place of exhibition or entertainment." 42 U.S.C. § 2000a(b)(1)-(3) (internal citation omitted).

45. To distinguish (and avoid) the result of the *Civil Rights Cases*, 109 U.S. 3, 9–11, 17–18 (1883), which struck down similar provisions in the Civil Rights Act of 1875 due to the absence of any cognizable state action, the Supreme Court upheld the 1964 Act as an exercise of Congress's power to regulate interstate commerce. *See Heart of Atlanta Motel, Inc. v. United States*, 379 U.S. 241, 258–59 (1964); *Katzenbach v. McClung*, 379 U.S. 294, 300–305 (1964).

46. David B. Filvaroff and Raymond E. Wolfinger, "The Origin and Enactment of the Civil Rights Act of 1964," in Bernard Grofman, ed., *Legacies of the 1964 Civil Rights Act* (University Press of Virginia, 2000), 9. *See also* Michael W. McConnell, *Moderation and Coherence in American Democracy*, 99 Calif. L. Rev. 373, 380 (2011) ("[T]he Civil Rights Act of 1964 was probably the most important transformative legislation in our lifetimes.").

47. 54 Wash. 2d 440 (1959).

48. *Browning*, 54 Wash. 2d at 442–43.

49. Wash. Rev. Code § 9.91.010(2) (1953).

50. *Browning*, 54 Wash. 2d at 446.

51. *Browning*, 54 Wash. 2d at 446.

52. *Browning*, 54 Wash. 2d at 447 (quoting *Restatement of Torts* § 46 (1948)).

53. *Browning*, 54 Wash. 2d at 448 (quoting *Restatement of Torts* § 46 cmt. g).

54. *Browning*, 54 Wash. 2d at 449.

55. *Browning*, 54 Wash. 2d at 448–49.

56. *Browning*, 54 Wash. 2d at 448 (citation omitted).

57. Although the court ruled that a statutory violation was established on these grounds alone, the court also concluded that the amount of damages awarded could not similarly be assumed in the absence of a showing by the plaintiff that compensatory damages were warranted. *See Browning*, 54 Wash. 2d at 449–50. Put differently, the *Browning* court ruled that a claim for intentional infliction of emotional distress could be presumed by the fact of racial discrimination at a public accommodation, but the amount of damages awarded depended upon a specific demonstration of the severity of the distress suffered by the plaintiff. The Washington Supreme Court later ruled explicitly that there is no threshold of severity required for a plaintiff to establish a claim of intentional infliction of emotional distress. *See Nord v. Shoreline Savings Ass'n*, 116 Wash. 2d 477, 482–84 (1991).

58. *Browning*, 54 Wash. 2d at 456 (Mallery, J., dissenting) (citation omitted).

59. *Browning*, 54 Wash. 2d at 453, 454.

60. *See* above at 204n45.

61. *See* S. Rep. No. 88-872 at 53 (1964) (views of Sen. Strom Thurmond).

62. *Cf.* above at 26–27, 60–62.

63. *See Browning*, 54 Wash. 2d at 449 ("We can fully sympathize with the desire to punish the defendant for its discriminatory tactics, but punishment, under these circumstances, is the prerogative of the state.") (citations omitted). *Browning* reflects and reinforces the distinction between impartiality and objectivity and between values and biases, which I discussed in chapter 2.

64. *See Heart of Atlanta Motel*, 379 U.S. at 261.

65. *Cf. Heart of Atlanta Motel*, 379 U.S. at 258–59.

66. *See Heart of Atlanta Motel*, 379 U.S. at 259 n. 8 (citing Wash. Rev. Code § 9.91.010).

67. [1991] 1 All ER 759.

68. Sexual Offences (Amendment) Act 1976, § 1(1)(a) (internal numbering deleted) (emphasis supplied).

69. Matthew Hale, *The History of the Pleas of the Crown* (Nutt & Gosling, 1736), 629, quoted in *R. v. R.*, [1992] 1 AC 599, 615.

70. I say English law here to emphasize that Scotland had already revoked the marital exemption not long before *R. v. J.* was decided. *See S. v. HM Advocate*, [1989] SLT 469, 473. In the United States, limited exemptions from (or heightened requirements for) criminal liability for marital rape persisted in certain states into the twenty-first century. In Tennessee, for example, a defendant could not be convicted of spousal rape unless a deadly weapon was used, serious bodily injury was caused, or the spouses were living separately and one of them had filed for maintenance or divorce. *See* Tenn. Code Ann. § 39-13-507 (2003). This statutory provision was repealed by 2005 Tenn. Pub. Acts, ch. 456 (effective June 18, 2005).

71. *R. v. J.*, [1991] 1 All ER at 765.

72. *R. v. J.*, [1991] 1 All ER at 767–68 (Rougier, J.).

73. The Appellate Committee of the House of Lords was formally reconstituted and reconvened, beginning October 1, 2009, as the Supreme Court of the United Kingdom. *See* Constitutional Reform Act 2005, c. 4, § 23.

74. In fact, before the case reached the House of Lords, the Criminal Division of the Court of Appeal decided *R. v. R.* in a reported decision that presaged the House's judgment. Writing for the Court, Lord Lane concluded that the time had come to eliminate the marital rape exemption from English law: "It seems to us that where the common law rule no longer even remotely represents what is the true position of a wife in present-day society, the duty of the court is to take steps to alter the rule if it can legitimately do so in the light of any relevant parliamentary enactment. . . . [W]e do not consider that we are inhibited by the 1976 Act from declaring that the husband's immunity as expounded by Hale CJ no longer exists. We take the view that the time has now arrived when the law should declare that a rapist remains a rapist subject to the criminal law, irrespective of his relationship with his victim." *R. v. R.*, [1991] 2 All ER 257, 266 (CA).

75. *R. v. R.*, [1992] 1 AC 599, 616 (HL).

76. *See generally* A. V. Dicey, *Introduction to the Study of the Law of the Constitution*

(8th ed.) (Liberty Fund, 1982), 27 ("[T]he term 'sovereignty,' as long as it is accurately employed in the sense in which Austin sometimes uses it, is a merely legal conception, and means simply the power of law-making unrestricted by any legal limit. . . . [T]he sovereign power under the English constitution is clearly 'Parliament.' "); Vernon Bogdanor, *The New British Constitution* (Hart Publishing, 2009), 13 ("[T]he British Constitution could thus be summed up in just eight words: 'What the Queen in Parliament enacts is law.' . . . [T]he sovereignty of Parliament has been seen as the central principle of the British Constitution.").

77. Just eight years prior to *R. v. R.*, in 1984, the Criminal Law Revision Committee declined to recommend eliminating the marital exemption. *See* Criminal Law Revision Committee, *Fifteenth Report: Sexual Offences* (Cmnd 9688) (HMSO, 1984).

78. *R. v. R.*, [1992] 1 AC at 623 (quoting Lord Lane's judgment for the Court of Appeal in *R. v. R.*, [1991] 2 All ER 257 at 266).

79. Much more could be said about these issues. *See* Douglas E. Edlin, *Judges and Unjust Laws: Common Law Constitutionalism and the Foundations of Judicial Review* (University of Michigan Press, 2008), 53–78, 159–63, 169–87.

80. *Cf.* J. R. Spencer, "Criminal Law," in Louis Blom-Cooper, Brice Dickson and Gavin Drewry, *The Judicial House of Lords, 1876–2009* (Oxford University Press, 2009), 604 ("[I]n answer to those who have criticised the Law Lords for extending the criminal law when this ought to be left to Parliament, two points in my view can be made. The first is that the 'marital exemption' in rape was a rule which, at the end of the twentieth century, nobody defended on the merits. And the second is that the 'marital exemption' was an anomalous rule which conflicted with a broader and more important principle: that to be valid, a person's consent to acts done to his or her body must subsist at the time the act takes place.").

81. *See, e.g.*, *R. v. Clegg*, [1995] 1 AC 482, 500 ("Like Lord Simon, I am not averse to judges developing law, or indeed making new law, when they can see their way clearly, even where questions of social policy are involved. A good recent example would be the affirmation by this House of the decision of the Court of Appeal (Criminal Division) that a man can be guilty of raping his wife.") (Lord Lloyd) (citing *R. v. R.*). *Cf. DPP for Northern Ireland v. Lynch*, [1975] AC 653, 684–85 ("We are here in the domain of the common law; our task is to fit what we can see as principle and authority to the facts before us, and it is no obstacle that these facts are new. The judges have always assumed responsibility for deciding questions of principle relating to criminal liability and guilt.") (Lord Wilberforce).

82. *See, e.g.*, Criminal Justice and Public Order Act 1994, c. 33, § 142; *R. v. C.*, [2004] EWCA Crim 292, [2004] 3 All ER 1, [20]–[21].

83. *See, e.g.*, Editorial, The Independent, Oct. 24, 1991.

84. N. W. Barber, *Sovereignty Re-examined: The Courts, Parliament, and Statutes*, 20 Oxford J. Leg. Stud. 131, 146 (2000).

85. Barber, *Sovereignty Re-examined*, 147–48 (citing Marianne Giles, *Judicial Law-Making in the Criminal Courts: The Case of Marital Rape*, [1992] Crim. L. Rev. 407; J. L. Barton, *The Story of Marital Rape*, 108 Law Q. Rev. 260 (1992)).

86. *See* Andrew Ashworth, *Principles of Criminal Law* (5th ed.) (Oxford University Press, 2006), 65–66 ("Rectification of an anomaly (for example, the old rule that a

husband may [not] be convicted of the rape of his wife) may well lead to a new sphere of criminalization. . . . Thus the extension of the criminal law into areas such as . . . marital rape may be justified on the ground that the wrongs involved in such conduct are no less significant than those involved in many serious crimes already established. . . . One might well agree that we all prefer our behaviour to be subject to as few constraints as possible, but that preference must be placed in the context of our membership of a community.") (citing *R. v. R.*).

Chapter 5

1. Irving R. Kaufman, *Chilling Judicial Independence*, 88 Yale L.J. 681, 713 (1979).

2. "Structural" here refers to "the power of governmental bodies outside the judiciary to . . . modify judicial institutions. . . . Judicial independence is at risk . . . when the 'political branches' use or threaten to use their control over structure to shape adjudicative outcomes." Peter H. Russell, "Toward a General Theory of Judicial Independence," in Peter H. Russell and David M. O'Brien, eds., *Judicial Independence in the Age of Democracy: Critical Perspectives from around the World* (University Press of Virginia, 2001), 13–14. As I argue in this chapter, attempts to interfere with the judicial decision-making process as a way of influencing adjudicative outcomes are threats to the structural features of the institution that were meant to preserve the independence of the decision-making process.

3. An important form of legislative interference with judicial independence that I discuss elsewhere are ouster or jurisdiction-stripping clauses. *See* Douglas E. Edlin, *A Constitutional Right to Judicial Review: Access to Courts and Ouster Clauses in England and the United States*, 57 Am. J. Comp. L. 67 (2009).

4. Congressional efforts of this kind are nothing new. In *United States v. Klein*, the Supreme Court addressed federal legislation that would have prevented the Court from considering pardons issued by President Lincoln to those who aided the Confederacy when determining whether they were entitled to proceeds from the sale of their property. The Court ruled that Congress could not predetermine legislatively which evidence the Court could consider. *See United States v. Klein*, 80 U.S. (13 Wall.) 128, 147–48 (1872) ("In the case before us no new circumstances have been created by legislation. But the court is forbidden to give the effect to evidence which, in its own judgment, such evidence should have, and is directed to give it an effect precisely contrary. We must think that Congress has inadvertently passed the limit which separates the legislative from the judicial power. . . . Congress has already provided that the Supreme Court shall have jurisdiction of the judgments of the Court of Claims on appeal. Can it prescribe a rule in conformity with which the court must deny to itself the jurisdiction thus conferred, because and only because its decision, in accordance with settled law, must be adverse to the government and favorable to the suitor? This question seems to us to answer itself. The rule prescribed is also liable to just exception as impairing the effect of a pardon, and thus infringing the constitutional power of the Executive. It is the intention of the Constitution that each of the great co-ordinate departments of the government—the Legislative, the Executive, and the Judicial—shall be, in its sphere, independent of the others. To the executive alone is intrusted

the power of pardon; and it is granted without limit. . . . Now it is clear that the legislature cannot change the effect of such a pardon any more than the executive can change a law.") (Chase, C.J.).

5. *See, e.g., Plaut v. Spendthrift Farm, Inc.*, 514 U.S. 211, 219–26 (1995) (holding unconstitutional a provision of the Securities Exchange Act that would have forced courts to reopen final judgments); *Chicago & Southern Air Lines, Inc. v. Waterman Steamship Corp.*, 333 U.S. 103, 113 (1948) ("Judgments within the powers vested in courts by the Judiciary Article of the Constitution may not lawfully be revised, overturned or refused faith and credit by another Department of Government."); *Hayburn's Case*, 2 U.S. (2 Dall.) 409, 411, 413 (1792) (same).

6. *Plaut*, 514 U.S. at 218–19 (emphasis in original) (internal quotation marks deleted) (citations omitted).

7. I am wary of relying on dictionaries as authorities for this sort of point. But I will mention that the Oxford English Dictionary defines "adjudge" as "determine in one's own judgement." Oxford English Dictionary (5th ed.) (Oxford University Press, 2002), 27. This is not the only definition offered, of course.

8. *See generally* Shimon Shetreet and Sophie Turenne, *Judges on Trial: The Independence and Accountability of the English Judiciary* (2nd ed.) (Cambridge University Press, 2013), 4 ("Judicial independence must be secured both at the institutional level and at the individual level for judges to be protected from threats to their personal or professional security that may influence their official duties.").

9. Charles Gardner Geyh and Emily Field Van Tassel, *The Independence of the Judicial Branch in the New Republic*, 74 Chi.-Kent L. Rev. 31, 31 (1998). *See also* Thomas I. Vanaskie, *The Independence and Responsibility of the Federal Judiciary*, 46 Vill. L. Rev. 745, 758–59 (2001). Consistent with this book's argument, discussions of decisional independence are usually framed in terms of impartiality, not objectivity. In addition to the quotation from Geyh and Van Tassel, *see, e.g.*, William H. Pryor, Jr., *Not-So-Serious Threats to Judicial Independence*, 93 Va. L. Rev. 1759, 1765 (2007) ("decisional independence, that is, the ability of an individual judge to decide each case fairly and impartially based on the facts and law."); *An Independent Judiciary: Report of the ABA Commission on Separation of Powers and Judicial Independence* (Washington, D.C.: American Bar Association, 1997), 5.

10. The language of the US Constitution that is meant to ensure judicial independence through life tenure was drawn from the English statute that established judicial independence from parliamentary influence and interference. *Compare* US Const. art. III, § 1 ("The Judges . . . shall hold their Offices during good Behaviour") *with* Act of Settlement 1701, 12 & 13 Will. 3, c. 2, § 3 ("Judges Commissions be made *Quam diu se bene Gesserint*" [as long as he shall behave himself well]). *See* J. H. Baker, *An Introduction to English Legal History* (4th ed.) (Oxford University Press, 2007), 168 ("William III was advised to appoint all his judges during good behaviour, and from 1701 tenure during good behaviour was guaranteed by the Act of Settlement."); Robert Stevens, *The Act of Settlement and the Questionable History of Judicial Independence*, 1 Oxford U. Commonw. L. J. 253, 261 (2001) ("Historically, the Act of Settlement marks the crossroads of the English Constitution. The provisions of the Act . . . represented an inarticulate effort to have the kind of separation of powers spelled out with much greater clarity at the Constitutional Convention in Philadelphia 75 years later."). In *Federalist* 78, Hamilton

adverts to the reference of Article III to the Act of Settlement. *See* Alexander Hamilton, John Jay, and James Madison, *The Federalist* (Liberty Fund, 2001), 408 ("[T]here can be no room to doubt, that the convention acted wisely in copying from the models of those constitutions which have established *good behaviour* as the tenure of judicial offices. . . . The experience of Great Britain affords an illustrious comment on the excellence of the institution.") (emphasis in original).

11. John Ferejohn, *Independent Judges, Dependent Judiciary: Explaining Judicial Independence*, 72 S. Cal. L. Rev. 353, 370 (1999).

12. In Ferejohn's view, the relative security of institutional independence, which he calls the "dependent judiciary," derives mainly from the (contingent) confluence of political realities in which judicial opinion and majority opinion are unlikely to remain opposed for very long, and a political party is unlikely to remain in power over time with a sustained motivation to challenge judicial authority. *See* Ferejohn, *Independent Judges, Dependent Judiciary*, 381–82.

13. The language of Article III and its incorporation of the preexisting English statute and tradition may seem plain enough to have established this from the time of the Constitution's ratification. *See* above at 208n10. Whatever uncertainty may initially have existed concerning the power of Congress to constrain judicial independence through the power of impeachment, the failed attempt to remove Samuel Chase from the Supreme Court established the constitutional reality that judges may not be punished or penalized for their judicial decisions. *See generally* William S. Carpenter, *Judicial Tenure in the United States with Especial Reference to the Tenure of Federal Judges* (Yale University Press, 1918), 119–20, 121, 123 ("[T]he impeachment of Judge Pickering was only the initial step in a movement wherein the Republicans aimed to replace the Federalists upon the judiciary with their own partisans and to bring the judges within the control of the legislature. . . . [W]ith the assault upon Justice Chase it became apparent that the majority party in Congress had determined to carry out [Sen. William] Giles' plan to 'sweep the supreme judicial bench clean' through the process of impeachment. . . . He [Giles] treated with the utmost contempt the idea of an independent judiciary . . . [and asserted that] if the judges of the Supreme Court should dare, as they had done, to declare an act of Congress unconstitutional or to send a mandamus to the President, as they had done, it was the undoubted right of the House of Representatives to impeach them, and of the Senate to remove them for giving such opinions, however honest or sincere they may have been in entertaining them. . . . With the acquittal of Justice Chase the partisans of Jefferson were forced to abandon their attempt to bring about the removal of Federalist judges through the impeachment process.") (quoting 1 Charles Francis Adams, ed., *Memoirs of John Quincy Adams, 1795–1848* (J. B. Lippincott & Co., 1874), 322). At Chase's impeachment trial before the Senate, Chase's defenders argued specifically that "to permit the impeachment of a judge in these circumstances would prostrate the judiciary at the feet of the House and undermine its independence." Robert R. Bair and Robin D. Coblentz, *The Trials of Mr. Justice Samuel Chase*, 27 Md. L. Rev. 365, 382 (1967) (quoting the opening statement of Joseph Hopkinson).

14. *See* below at 96.

15. For a related example, *see* 28 U.S.C. § 2254(d)(1) ("An application for a writ of habeas corpus on behalf of a person in custody pursuant to the judgment of a State

court shall not be granted with respect to any claim that was adjudicated on the merits in State court proceedings unless the adjudication of the claim resulted in a decision that was contrary to, or involved an unreasonable application of, clearly established Federal law, as determined by the Supreme Court of the United States."). This legislation manifested Congress's effort to prevent lower federal courts from relying upon their own precedent as authoritative sources of legal doctrine when adjudicating petitions for *habeas corpus*. In his dissent from the Seventh Circuit's *en banc* opinion upholding the constitutionality of this provision, Judge Kenneth Ripple, joined by Judge Ilana Rovner, determined that Congress had impermissibly intruded into the process of judicial decision making. *See Lindh v. Murphy*, 96 F.3d 856, 886, 887, 890 (7th Cir. 1996), *rev'd on other grounds*, 521 U.S. 320 (1997) ("Under the new amendment, in ascertaining whether there has been a violation of the Constitution, the courts are restricted to the case law of the Supreme Court of the United States; they are not permitted to rely as well upon their own precedent. In short, Congress . . . has now specified that the judiciary is required to disregard the work product of one of its components, a source of law upon which the courts otherwise would rely in the adjudication of the case. . . . [T]here are limits on the power of Congress to dictate the process of decision-making within the judicial department with respect to the meaning of the Constitution. Although Congress has the authority to create and abolish the lower federal courts and to regulate their jurisdiction, it has no power to dictate how the content of the governing law will be determined within the judicial department. . . . [T]he Constitution assigns to each of the three coordinate branches their own responsibilities and vests in each their own powers . . . [and] if one branch, through its actions, 'unduly interferes' with the role of another, such actions are void. . . . The amended statute significantly 'interferes' with the judicial role and to a great extent prevents the judicial department from accomplishing its 'constitutionally assigned functions.' Simply put, the statute, as amended, deprives a federal court of the right to adjudicate the case. And a court that does not adjudicate advises: a role decidedly different than the one the Constitution envisions for courts and judges of the Third Article.") (Ripple, J., dissenting) (citations omitted).

16. Stephen B. Burbank, *The Courtroom as Classroom: Independence, Imagination and Ideology in the Work of Jack Weinstein*, 97 Colum. L. Rev. 1971, 1978 (1997). A couple of years later, Professor Burbank broadened his understanding of judicial independence to embrace courts *and* judges. *See* Stephen B. Burbank, *The Architecture of Judicial Independence*, 72 S. Cal. L. Rev. 315, 335, 336–37 (1999) ("The core of judicial independence, as defined above, consists of the freedom of courts to make decisions without control by the executive or legislative branches or by the people. . . . [T]he concept requires, close to the core, that those responsible for judicial decisions interpreting or making law themselves be impartial: free of interests, prejudices, or incentives that could materially affect the character or results of the judicial process. There are federal constitutional provisions that speak to this aspect of judicial independence, and to all judges."). As I will explain further, though, Burbank continues to believe that judicial independence is primarily about institutional independence.

17. *See, e.g.*, Charles Gardner Geyh, *Judicial Independence, Judicial Accountability, and the Role of Constitutional Norms in Congressional Regulation of the Courts*, 78 Ind. L. J. 153, 162 (2003) (Explaining that the historical reluctance of Congress to interfere

with the judiciary demonstrates "the need to talk about judicial independence in terms of the purposes it serves: to facilitate impartial decisionmaking and preserve the integrity of the judiciary as a separate branch of government. The term 'judicial,' when joined with 'independence,' can relate to judges individually, collectively, or as a branch. Thinking about judicial independence with reference to judges individually highlights the role independence plays in case decisionmaking."). *See also* above at 151–52n24.

18. US Const. art. III, § 1 (emphasis supplied).

19. Burbank, *The Architecture of Judicial Independence*, 341.

20. *See* William E. Nelson, Marbury v. Madison: *The Origins and Legacy of Judicial Review* (University Press of Kansas, 2000), 66–67; Jack N. Rakove, *Original Meanings: Politics and Ideas in the Making of the Constitution* (Knopf, 1996), 81-82, 175-77, 328, 345.

21. *See* Herbert Wechsler, *Toward Neutral Principles of Constitutional Law*, 73 Harv. L. Rev. 1, 3–4 (1959).

22. *See* Nelson, *The Origins and Legacy of Judicial Review*, 55–58; Forrest McDonald, *Novus Ordo Seclorum: The Intellectual Origins of the Constitution* (University Press of Kansas, 1985), 254, 276; Charles Grove Haines, *The American Doctrine of Judicial Supremacy* (2nd ed.) (University of California Press, 1932), 232–321; Edward S. Corwin, *The Supreme Court and Unconstitutional Acts of Congress*, 4 Mich. L. Rev. 616, 620, 624 (1906). *See also Eakin v. Raub*, 12 Serg. & Rawle 330, 344–58 (1825) (Gibson, J., dissenting).

23. *Northern Pipeline Construction Co. v. Marathon Pipe Line Co.*, 458 U.S. 50, 57, 58, 60 (1982) (citations omitted). *Cf.* A. L. Goodhart, *English Law and the Moral Law* (Stevens & Sons, 1953), 60 ("[I]f the judiciary were placed under the authority of either the legislative or the executive branches of the Government then the administration of the law might no longer have that impartiality which is essential if justice is to prevail.").

24. *Northern Pipeline*, 458 U.S. at 59 n. 10 (citation omitted) (emphasis supplied).

25. Quoted in Charles Lane, "Scalia Tells Congress To Mind Its Own Business," Wash. Post, May 19, 2006, at A19.

26. *See* Constitution Restoration Act of 2005, S. 520, 109th Cong. (2005); Constitution Restoration Act of 2004, S. 2082, 108th Cong. (2004). For some of Congress's other efforts in this regard, *see* American Justice for American Citizens Act, H.R. 4118, 108th Cong. § 3 (2004) ("Neither the Supreme Court of the United States nor any lower Federal court shall, in the purported exercise of judicial power to interpret and apply the Constitution of the United States, employ the constitution, laws, administrative rules, executive orders, directives, policies, or judicial decisions of any international organization or foreign state, except for the English constitutional and common law or other sources of law relied upon by the Framers of the Constitution of the United States."); The Reaffirmation of American Independence Resolution, H. Res. 568, 108th Cong. (2004).

27. Constitution Restoration Act, § 201.

28. Constitution Restoration Act, § 302.

29. Save Our State Amendment, H.R.J. Res. 1056, 52d Leg., Reg. Sess., Aplt. App. Vol. 1 at 168 (Okla. 2010).

30. *See Awad v. Ziriax*, 670 F.3d 1111, 1118 (10th Cir. 2012).

31. *See Awad*, 670 F.3d at 1128–1132.

32. For a small sample of the work on this question, *see* Daniel A. Farber, *The Supreme Court, the Law of Nations, and Citations of Foreign Law: The Lessons of History*, 95 Calif. L. Rev. 1335 (2007); Sarah H. Cleveland, *Our International Constitution*, 31 Yale J. Int'l Law 1 (2006); John O. McGinnis, *Foreign To Our Constitution*, 100 Nw. U. L. Rev. 303 (2006); Steven G. Calabresi and Stephanie Dotson Zimdahl, *The Supreme Court and Foreign Sources of Law: Two Hundred Years of Practice and the Juvenile Death Penalty Decision*, 47 Wm. & Mary L. Rev. 743 (2005); Ernest A. Young, *Foreign Law and the Denominator Problem*, 119 Harv. L. Rev. 148 (2005); Symposium, *The United States Constitution and International Law*, 98 Am. J. Int'l L. 42 (2004) (articles by T. Alexander Aleinikoff, Roger P. Alford, Harold Hongju Koh, Gerald L. Neuman, and Michael D. Ramsey). *See also Roper v. Simmons*, 543 U.S. 551, 575–578 (2005) (citing *Trop v. Dulles*, 356 U.S. 86, 102–103 (1958)) (other citations omitted); *Lawrence v. Texas*, 539 U.S. 558, 576–577 (2003); *Atkins v. Virginia*, 536 U.S. 304, 316 n. 21 (2002). In the context of my argument in this chapter (and this book as a whole), it is worth highlighting the Court's emphatic statement in *Atkins* that a judgment with respect to the constitutionality of executing mentally disabled individuals must ultimately rest on the justices' own determination: "[T]he objective evidence, though of great importance, did not 'wholly determine' the controversy, 'the Constitution contemplates that in the end *our own judgment* will be brought to bear on the question of the acceptability of the death penalty under the Eighth Amendment.' . . . Thus, in cases involving a consensus, our own judgment is 'brought to bear,' by asking whether there is reason to disagree with the judgment reached by the citizenry and its legislators." *Atkins*, 536 U.S. at 312–313 (emphasis supplied) (citation omitted). *See also Hayburn's Case*, 2 U.S. at 410 ("[W]e are under the indispensable necessity of acting according to the best dictates of *our own judgment*, after duly weighing every consideration that can occur to us.") (emphasis supplied).

33. For an exception, *see* Michael J. Gerhardt, *The Role of the Judge in the Twenty-First Century: What's Old Is New Again*, 86 B.U. L. Rev. 1267, 1284 (2006). *Cf.* Peter Rädler, "Independence and Impartiality of Judges," in David S. Weissbrodt and Rüdiger Wolfrum, eds., *The Right to a Fair Trial* (Springer, 1998), 735 ("Independence in a functional sense excludes the interference of non-judicial organs with the performance of judicial functions. In addition, maintaining the courts to work independently likewise protects the *personal* independence of the judges.") (emphasis in original).

34. *See, e.g., Roper*, 543 U.S. at 622–28; *Lawrence*, 539 U.S. at 598; *Atkins*, 536 U.S. at 347–48; *Thompson v. Oklahoma*, 487 U.S. 815, 868–69 n. 4 (1988). *See also* A Conversation on the Relevance of Foreign Law for American Constitutional Adjudication with U.S. Supreme Court Justices Antonin Scalia and Stephen Breyer, American University Washington College of Law (Jan. 13, 2005), transcript available at http://www.wcl.american.edu/secle/founders/2005/050113.cfm.

35. *See Statement of the Judges of the United States District Court for the Northern District of California*, 14 F.R.D. 335 (N.D. Cal. 1953). The judges unanimously agreed that the summoned judge should not testify about judicial proceedings, and he did not. *See id.* at 335–36 ("This separation of functions is founded on the historic concept that no

one of these branches may dominate or unlawfully interfere with the others. In recognition of the fundamental soundness of this principle, we are unwilling that a Judge of this Court appear before your Committee and testify with respect to any Judicial proceedings. The Constitution does not contemplate that such matters be reviewed by the Legislative Branch, but only by the appropriate appellate tribunals. The integrity of the Federal Courts, upon which liberty and life depend, requires that such Courts be maintained inviolate against the changing moods of public opinion."). Judge Louis Goodman did, however, appear before the Committee as requested. In the same year, the House of Representatives Judiciary Committee requested, and the House Committee on Un-American Activities subpoenaed, Justice Tom Clark to appear and testify concerning, among other things, his service as Attorney General and the work of the Department of Justice. In both instances, Justice Clark refused. *See* Letter from Associate Justice Tom C. Clark to Rep. Harold Velde, quoted in Roy E. Brownell II, *Vice Presidential Secrecy: A Study in Comparative Constitutional Privilege and Historical Development*, 84 St. John's L. Rev. 423, 488 (2010) ("I have your subpoena dated Nov. 10, 1953, calling upon me to appear before your committee. . . . As you know, the independence of the three branches of our Government is the cardinal principle on which our constitutional system is founded. This complete independence of the judiciary is necessary to the proper administration of justice. In order to discharge this high trust, judges must be kept free from the strife of public controversy. . . . For this reason, as much as I wish to cooperate with the legislative branch of the Government, I must forego an appearance before the committee.").

36. 18 U.S.C. §§ 3551-3673; 28 U.S.C. §§ 991-998. There are various state analogues to the federal sentencing reforms and guidelines, which I do not discuss here. England and Wales also instituted sentencing guidelines in a manner similar to the United States, with the establishment of a Sentencing Council and the statutory enactment of sentencing guidelines in the Coroners and Justice Act of 2009. *See* Coroners and Justice Act 2009, c. 25, Part 4.

37. 28 U.S.C. § 991. Congress also appended its own legislation to the Commission's Guidelines with respect to drug offenses, most notably in the form of widely disparate mandatory sentences for powder and crack cocaine. *See* 21 U.S.C. § 841.

38. *See, e.g.*, Kevin Clancy, John Bartolomeo, David Richardson, and Charles Wellford, *Sentence Decisionmaking: The Logic of Sentence Decisions and the Extent and Sources of Sentence Disparity*, 72 J. Crim. L. & Criminology 524 (1981); Shari Seidman Diamond and Hans Zeisel, *Sentencing Councils: A Study of Sentence Disparity and Its Reduction*, 43 U. Chi. L. Rev. 109 (1975); Marvin E. Frankel, *The Sentencing Morass and a Suggestion for Reform*, 3 Crim. L. Bull. 365 (1967).

39. *See United States v. Ming He*, 94 F.3d 782, 788–89 (2d Cir. 1996); *United States v. Roberts*, 726 F. Supp. 1359, 1363–66, 1372–73 (D.D.C. 1989) (Greene, J.). Judge Greene ruled that the SCA was unconstitutional for these and other reasons. *See id.* at 1374–75.

40. *See, e.g.*, Jon O. Newman, *The New Commission's Opportunity*, 8 Fed. Sent. Rep. 8 (1995); Donald P. Lay, *Rethinking the Guidelines: A Call for Cooperation*, 101 Yale L.J. 1755 (1992); Jack B. Weinstein, *A Trial Judge's Reflections on Departures from the Federal Sentencing Guidelines*, 5 Fed. Sent. Rep. 6 (1992). The Guidelines have also been extensively modified.

41. *See, e.g., United States v. Mendoza*, 2004 U.S. Dist. LEXIS 1449, at *17 (C.D.Cal. 2004) ("The Sentencing Guidelines, for the most part, have taken away from the Judiciary the ability to sentence the individual. The Sentencing Guidelines have mandated the Judiciary to sentence the crime, not the individual."). *Cf. Woodson v. North Carolina*, 428 U.S. 280, 304 (1976) ("A process that accords no significance to relevant facets of the character and record of the individual offender or the circumstances of the particular offense . . . treats all persons convicted of a designated offense not as uniquely individual human beings, but as members of a faceless, undifferentiated mass. . . . This Court has previously recognized that '[f]or the determination of sentences, justice generally requires consideration of more than the particular acts by which the crime was committed and that there be taken into account the circumstances of the offense together with the character and propensities of the offender.'") (citation omitted). With this overarching concern in mind, the SRA and the Guidelines permit judges to formulate sentences that depart upward or downward from the Guidelines on the basis of aggravating or mitigating factors, but even this discretionary authority is specified and limited by the Guidelines. *See Koon v. United States*, 518 U.S. 81, 92–96 (1996) (Breyer, J., concurring in part and dissenting in part).

42. *Mistretta v. United States*, 488 U.S. 361, 384–91 (1989).

43. *Mistretta*, 488 U.S. at 390.

44. *Mistretta*, 488 U.S. at 384–85.

45. *Mistretta*, 488 U.S. at 390 (citation omitted).

46. *Mistretta*, 488 U.S. at 390–91.

47. Similarly, the issue in *Mistretta* was not whether "Congress may delegate *to* the Judicial Branch nonadjudicatory functions that do *not* trench upon the prerogatives of another Branch and that are appropriate to the central mission *of the Judiciary*." *Mistretta*, 488 U.S. at 388 (emphasis supplied).

48. *See generally* Charles Fried, *Saying What the Law Is: The Constitution in the Supreme Court* (Harvard University Press, 2004), 74 ("Separation of powers, as it applies to the judiciary, thus means that Congress and the President may influence the judge only through the law. . . . It means that the ultimate adjudication of rights must be left to the courts. Undergirding this statement is the idea that if the judiciary's independence is to be an effective constitutional principle, then only the judiciary may do the judiciary's work."). *See also* above at 212nn32–33.

49. *Mistretta*, 488 U.S. at 413 (citing 18 U.S.C. § 3742).

50. *Mistretta*, 488 U.S. at 424–25 (citations omitted) (emphasis supplied).

51. *See generally* Daniel J. Freed, *Federal Sentencing in the Wake of Guidelines: Unacceptable Limits on the Discretion of Sentencers*, 101 Yale L.J. 1681, 1719–20 (1992).

52. *See* Kate Stith and José A. Cabranes, *Fear of Judging: Sentencing Guidelines in the Federal Courts* (University of Chicago Press, 1998), 196. The Ninth Circuit also held the SRA to be an unconstitutional violation of separation of powers doctrine. *See Gubiensio-Ortiz v. Kanahele*, 857 F.2d 1245, 1258–59 (9th Cir. 1988), *vacated, United States v. Chavez-Sanchez*, 488 U.S. 1036 (1989).

53. *See, e.g., United States v. Flores*, 336 F.3d 760, 768 (8th Cir. 2003) (Bright, J., concurring) ("It is not my position to criticize Congress. I simply point out that this enactment will exacerbate the problems with the Guidelines by making it even more difficult for district judges to do justice under the law as circumstances warrant. . . . I

want to conclude by making a plea to the district judges of this country who feel that they should have some say and some discretion in sentencing. Let your opinions disclose your views about the injustice of the sentencing decision or decisions you are obligated to impose by congressional mandate and/or the Sentencing Guidelines."); *United States v. Leviner*, 31 F. Supp. 2d 23, 25–26 (D.Mass. 1998) (Gertner, J.).

54. *See, e.g., United States v. Detwiler*, 338 F. Supp. 2d 1166, 1168 (D.Ore. 2004).

55. *See Detwiler*, 338 F. Supp. 2d at 1173.

56. *Detwiler*, 338 F. Supp. 2d at 1171. The Feeney Amendment was passed without notice, hearings, or substantive debate. *See id.* at 1170–72.

57. *See* Memorandum of Attorney General John Ashcroft to All Federal Prosecutors, "Department Policies and Procedures Concerning Sentencing Recommendations and Sentencing Appeals" (July 28, 2003), 4, A-1. The Memorandum is available here: http://www.washingtonpost.com/wpsrv/nation/shoulders/ashcroft080703.pdf.

58. *Mendoza*, 2004 U.S. Dist. LEXIS 1449, at *18, *19.

59. *Detwiler*, 338 F. Supp. 2d at 1173, 1174 (quoting *Mistretta*, 488 U.S. at 422–23 (Scalia, J., dissenting)).

60. *See Detwiler*, 338 F. Supp. 2d at 1174–75.

61. In addition to the cases already discussed, *see* Stith and Cabranes, *Fear of Judging*, chaps. 2–3; Ronald F. Wright, *Sentencers, Bureaucrats, and the Administrative Law Perspective on the Federal Sentencing Commission*, 79 Calif. L. Rev. 3, 24 (1991); Stephen L. Carter, *Constitutional Improprieties: Reflections on* Mistretta, Morrison, *and Administrative Government*, 57 U. Chi. L. Rev. 357, 357–64 (1990); Mark Nielsen, Mistretta v. United States *and the Eroding Separation of Powers*, 12 Harv. J. L. & Pub. Pol'y 1049, 1049-50 (1989).

62. *See United States v. Booker*, 543 U.S. 220, 245–46 (2005) ("We answer the question of remedy by finding the provision of the federal sentencing statute that makes the Guidelines mandatory, 18 U.S.C. § 3553(b)(1), incompatible with today's constitutional holding. We conclude that this provision must be severed and excised, as must one other statutory section, § 3742(e), which depends upon the Guidelines' mandatory nature. So modified, the federal sentencing statute, see Sentencing Reform Act of 1984 (Sentencing Act), makes the Guidelines effectively advisory. It requires a sentencing court to consider Guidelines ranges, but it permits the court to tailor the sentence in light of other statutory concerns as well.") (citations omitted). The Court also stated that the *Booker* decision did "not call into question any aspect of our decision in *Mistretta*," *Id.* at 242, because "the Act without its 'mandatory' provision and related language remains consistent with Congress' initial and basic sentencing intent." *Id.* at 264. As Justice Scalia observed in his dissent in *Booker*, this is a difficult position to maintain. *See id.* at 303–4.

63. *McBryde v. Committee to Review Circuit Council Conduct and Disability Orders*, 264 F.3d 52, 54 (D.C. Cir. 2001) (quoting the Judicial Council and Disability Act, 28 U.S.C. § 351(a) (1980)). This finding by the Committee describes the crossing of an imprecise but intuitive line. A judge may not be disciplined for displaying some impatience or irritation in his courtroom, unless that conduct reasonably seems to jeopardize his fairness and impartiality. *See, e.g., Liteky v. United States*, 510 U.S. 540, 555–56 (1994) ("[J]udicial remarks during the course of a trial that are critical or disapproving of, or even hostile to, counsel, the parties, or their cases, ordinarily do not support a

bias or partiality challenge. They *may* do so if they reveal an opinion that derives from an extrajudicial source; and they *will* do so if they reveal such a high degree of favoritism or antagonism as to make fair judgment impossible. . . . *Not* establishing bias or partiality, however, are expressions of impatience, dissatisfaction, annoyance, and even anger, that are within the bounds of what imperfect men and women, even after having been confirmed as federal judges, sometimes display.") (emphasis in original); *In re Hocking*, 451 Mich. 1, 16 (1996) ("[E]very angry retort or act of discourtesy during the course of a proceeding does not amount to judicial misconduct. . . . [A] judge is only subject to discipline when the comment amounts to 'conduct that is clearly prejudicial to the administration of justice.'") (citation omitted).

64. *See* 28 U.S.C. § 372(c)(6)(B).

65. *McBryde*, 264 F.3d at 54.

66. *See McBryde v. Committee to Review Circuit Council Conduct and Disability Orders*, 83 F. Supp. 2d 135, 171–78 (D.D.C. 1999).

67. *Cf. Chandler v. Judicial Council of the Tenth Circuit*, 398 U.S. 74, 136 (1970) ("An independent judiciary is one of this Nation's outstanding characteristics. Once a federal judge is confirmed by the Senate and takes his oath, he is independent of every other judge. He commonly works with other federal judges who are likewise sovereign. But neither one alone nor any number banded together can act as censor and place sanctions on him. Under the Constitution the only leverage that can be asserted against him is impeachment.") (Douglas, J., dissenting); *Hastings v. Judicial Conference of the United States*, 770 F.2d 1093, 1111 (D.C. Cir. 1985) ("Although I have no reason to doubt the integrity of members of the federal judiciary, I am willing to assume that there may be a few corrupt judges, who dishonor their title and role in our society. This does not change my view, however, that the Constitution specifies only one procedure for disciplining them—impeachment. . . . In my view, the Framers' choice here was to limit the accountability of individual judges for misconduct to impeachment in order to maximize judicial independence. . . . We must temper our eagerness to see that only honorable and dedicated women and men fill the judicial ranks with an awareness of the danger to the judiciary of impairing independence and inhibiting diversity of style and opinion among jurists.") (Edwards, J., concurring).

68. *McBryde*, 264 F.3d at 64.

69. *McBryde*, 264 F.3d at 64, 65.

70. US Const. art. II, § 4, quoted in *Chandler*, 398 U.S. at 136 (Douglas, J., dissenting). Judges may also be tried for alleged criminal activity before or after impeachment articles are brought. *See, e.g., United States v. Claiborne*, 727 F.2d 842, 845–47 (9th Cir. 1984) (*per curiam*).

71. *See McBryde*, 264 F.3d. at 65. *See also* American Bar Association Report of the Commission on Separation of Powers and Judicial Independence (1997), 58 ("Despite preliminary uneasiness among some judges that the Act threatened the judiciary's institutional independence, it is now generally agreed that the Act does no such thing."); Charles Gardner Geyh, *When Courts and Congress Collide: The Struggle for Control of America's Judicial System* (University of Michigan Press, 2006), 110 ("[T]he act is better understood as a congressional effort to promote judicial accountability by transferring disciplinary power to the courts, thereby enhancing the judiciary's independence as an institution and reducing the need for congressional intrusions via the

impeachment process."). For reasons I explain below, I believe it is better to analyze the Act in terms of a distinction between judicial decision making and judicial administration, rather than between inter- or intrabranch regulation of individual judicial action. So long as the Act does not allow interference (by Congress or other judges) with an individual judge's decisional autonomy, the risk of a statutory violation of the judge's constitutional independence under Article III is minimized. And the question still remains whether precluding a judge from hearing certain cases is interfering with his decision making or with the administration of his docket.

72. *Chandler*, 398 U.S. at 84.

73. *See In re Clay*, 35 F.3d 190, 192 (5th Cir. 1994) ("Courts and commentators focus on the importance of insulating judges from Congress and the Executive Branch. But as Chief Judge Kaufman noted, 'it is equally essential to protect the independence of the individual judge, even from incursions by other judges . . .' and giving one judge power over another chills judicial individualism. A judge must be free to decide a case according to the law as he sees it, without fear of personal repercussion or retaliation from any source.") (citation omitted).

74. Geyh, *When Courts and Congress Collide*, 9. *See also* ABA Report on Separation of Powers and Judicial Independence, iii ("Judicial independence includes the independence of an individual judge as well as that of the judiciary as a branch of government. Individual independence (otherwise known as decisional independence) is both substantive, in that it allows judges to perform the judicial function subject to no authority but the law, and personal, in the sense that it guarantees judges job tenure, adequate compensation and security. Branch independence (otherwise known as institutional independence) involves matters affecting the operation of the judiciary as a separate branch of government.").

75. *See* Fried, *Saying What the Law Is*, 72 ("The independence of the judiciary is the reciprocal of the separation of powers. . . . [J]udges must be allowed to do their work free from the interference—direction—of the executive or legislative branch. That work is the deciding of cases and controversies.").

76. H. Jefferson Powell, *The Three Independences*, 38 U. Rich. L. Rev. 603, 610, 611–12 (2004) (citations omitted).

77. Penny J. White, *An America without Judicial Independence*, 80 Judicature 174, 174–75 (1997). Justice (now Professor) White's description of judicial independence is especially noteworthy because she is the only member of the Supreme Court of Tennessee to lose a retention election, which resulted from her vote (with the majority) in *State v. Odom*, 928 S.W.2d 18 (Tenn. 1996). The *Odom* court upheld the conviction of the defendant for rape and murder, and upheld the Court of Criminal Appeals' decision to overturn the sentence of death for failing to meet the applicable statutory requirements. Justice White's retention election was held later that same year, and proponents of capital punishment characterized a vote against her retention as a vote to preserve capital punishment in Tennessee. *See* Paula Wade, *White's Defeat Poses Legal Dilemma: How Is a Replacement Justice Picked?*, Com. Appeal (Memphis, Tenn.), Aug. 3, 1996, at A1.

78. *See Yakus v. United States*, 321 U.S. 414, 467–68 (1944) ("[B]road as is Congress' power to confer or withhold jurisdiction, there has been none heretofore to confer it and at the same time deprive the parties affected of opportunity to call in question in

a criminal trial whether the law, be it statute or regulation, upon which the jurisdiction is exercised squares with the fundamental law. Nor has it been held that Congress can forbid a court invested with the judicial power under Article III to consider this question, when called upon to give effect to a statutory or other mandate. It is one thing for Congress to withhold jurisdiction. It is entirely another to confer it and direct that it be exercised in a manner inconsistent with constitutional requirements or, what in some instances may be the same thing, without regard to them. Once it is held that Congress can require the courts criminally to enforce unconstitutional laws or statutes, including regulations, or to do so without regard for their validity, the way will have been found to circumvent the supreme law and, what is more, to make the courts parties to doing so. This Congress cannot do. . . . [W]henever the judicial power is called into play, it is responsible directly to the fundamental law and no other authority can intervene to force or authorize the judicial body to disregard it. The problem therefore is not solely one of individual right or due process of law. It is equally one of the separation and independence of the powers of government and of the constitutional integrity of the judicial process.") (Rutledge, J., dissenting).

79. By focusing on the United States in the text, I do not mean to limit the scope of the discussion solely to that jurisdiction or to suggest that genuine judicial independence depends upon a US-style written constitution, judicial review, or separation of powers. *See, e.g.*, Beau Breslin, *From Words to Worlds: Exploring Constitutional Functionality* (Johns Hopkins University Press, 2009), 174–76. *See also* Edlin, *A Constitutional Right to Judicial Review*, 90–99.

80. The discussion in this section developed from *Institutional Identity and the Rule of Law:* Belmarsh, Boumediene, *and the Construction of Constitutional Meaning in England and the United States*, 41 Loy. L.A. L. Rev. 481 (2008).

81. *See A. v. Secretary of State for the Home Department*, [2004] UKHL 56, at [36], [81], [100]–[101], [144], [160], [164] (hereafter *Belmarsh*).

82. *See Belmarsh*, [2004] UKHL 56 at [43], [76]–[78], [83], [126], [132], [189]. In response to the House's declaration of incompatibility in *Belmarsh*, *id.* at [73], [139], [239], Parliament rescinded the challenged sections of the Anti-Terrorism Act through the Prevention of Terrorism Act of 2005. *See* Prevention of Terrorism Act 2005, § 16(2)(a) (repealing Anti-Terrorism, Crime and Security Act 2001, §§ 21–32).

83. *A. v. Secretary of State for the Home Department (No. 2)*, [2005] UKHL 71.

84. These decisions are often referred to as the *Belmarsh* cases in reference to the prison where the detainees are held. *See, e.g.*, Ruth Bader Ginsburg, *"A Decent Respect to the Opinions of Humankind": The Value of a Comparative Perspective in Constitutional Adjudication*, 1 F.I.U. L. Rev. 27, 41 (2006).

85. *See* Anti-Terrorism, Crime and Security Act 2001, § 23.

86. *Belmarsh II*, [2005] UKHL 71 at [1]. The United States courts that have addressed this point have tended to concentrate on the question of involvement of or authorization by United States officials. *See, e.g.*, *United States v. Yousef*, 327 F.3d 56, 138–39 (2d Cir. 2003) (citing *United States v. Toscanino*, 500 F.2d 267, 281 (2d Cir. 1974)) (other citations omitted); *United States v. Salameh*, 152 F.3d 88, 117 (2d Cir. 1998). However, the House was less concerned with the question of British involvement than with the impact of the tainted evidence upon the integrity of the judicial process itself. *See Belmarsh II*, [2005] UKHL 71 at [51]–[52] ("It trivialises the issue be-

fore the House to treat it as an argument about the law of evidence. The issue is one of constitutional principle, whether evidence obtained by torturing another human being may lawfully be admitted against a party to proceedings in a British court, irrespective of where, or by whom, or on whose authority the torture was inflicted. To that question I would give a very clear negative answer. I accept the broad thrust of the appellants' argument on the common law. The principles of the common law, standing alone, in my opinion compel the exclusion of third party torture evidence as unreliable, unfair, offensive to ordinary standards of humanity and decency and incompatible with the principles which should animate a tribunal seeking to administer justice.") (Lord Bingham). *See also id.* at [91].

87. *Belmarsh II*, [2005] UKHL 71 at [9].

88. *See Belmarsh II*, [2005] UKHL 71 at [11] ("[F]rom its very earliest days the common law of England set its face firmly against the use of torture. Its rejection of this practice was indeed hailed as a distinguishing feature of the common law. . . . In rejecting the use of torture, whether applied to potential defendants or potential witnesses, the common law was moved by the cruelty of the practice as applied to those not convicted of crime, by the inherent unreliability of confessions or evidence so procured and by the belief that it degraded all those who lent themselves to the practice.") (citing John Fortescue, *De Laudibus Legum Angliae*,ed. S. B. Chrimes (Cambridge University Press, 1942), 47–53; Thomas Smith, *De Republica Anglorum: A Discourse on the Commonwealth of England*, ed. L. Alston (Cambridge University Press, 1906), 104–7; Edward Coke, *Institutes of the Laws of England* (Flesher, Lee & Pakeman, 1644), Part III, 34–36; William Blackstone, *Commentaries on the Laws of England* (Oxford University Press, 1769), 320–21; 1 James Fitzjames Stephen, *A History of the Criminal Law of England* (Macmillan, 1883), 222) (other citations omitted). *See also id.* at [64]–[65].

89. *Belmarsh II*, [2005] UKHL 71 at [12] (quoting David Jardine, *A Reading on the Use of Torture in the Criminal Law of England Previously to the Commonwealth* (Baldwin & Cradock, 1837), 6, 12). *See also id.* at [81]–[83], [112], [129], [152].

90. *Belmarsh II*, [2005] UKHL 71 at [12], [13], [86].

91. The detainees also relied on provisions of EU and international law, which I will not discuss here. *See Belmarsh II*, [2005] UKHL 71 at [23]–[52]. And they extended their argument from torture to inhuman and degrading treatment. *See id.* at [53]. The more general argument made by the detainees in relation to evidence procured by torture would seem to obtain in the United States as well, probably in the form of a due process violation. For an argument to this effect, *see* Baher Azmy, *Constitutional Implications of the War on Terror:* Rasul v. Bush *and the Intra-Territorial Constitution*, 62 N.Y.U. Ann. Surv. Am. L. 369, 419–20, 429–31 (2007). *See also* John Duberstein, *Excluding Torture: A Comparison of the British and American Approaches to Evidence Obtained by Third Party Torture*, 32 N.C. J. Int'l L. & Com. Reg. 159, 180–91 (2006).

92. *See Belmarsh II*, [2005] UKHL 71 at [13]–[14] (citing Police and Criminal Evidence Act 1984, § 78; *Lam Chi-ming v. The Queen*, [1991] 2 AC 212, 220; *R. v. Harz*, [1967] 1 AC 760, 817; *Ibrahim v. The King*, [1914] AC 599, 609–10).

93. *Belmarsh II*, [2005] UKHL 71 at [15] (citing *Wong Kam-ming v. The Queen*, [1980] AC 247). I should mention that the House could not agree on whom the burden should rest. Lords Bingham, Nicholls, and Hoffmann concluded that the initial burden belongs to the individual to assert that evidence was obtained through tor-

ture, but at that point the burden should shift to the Secretary of State to demonstrate that evidence was not obtained through torture. And where the SIAC cannot definitively determine that the evidence was not obtained through torture, it should be excluded. *See Belmarsh II*, [2005] UKHL 71 at [56], [80], [98]. Lords Hope, Rodger, Carswell, and Brown agreed that the burden should not rest on the individual once the initial assertion of torture has been made, but Lords Hope, Rodger, Carswell, and Brown believed that the SIAC should determine whether the evidence was definitively acquired via torture, rather than establish that the evidence was *not* acquired via torture. *See Belmarsh II*, [2005] UKHL 71 at [116]–[126], [138]–[145], [156]–[158], [172]. The key here is that Lords Bingham, Nicholls, and Hoffmann would exclude evidence absent an affirmative showing that the evidence was not tainted, while Lords Hope, Rodger, Carswell, and Brown would accept evidence absent a demonstration that the evidence was tainted. A contrast here between the UK and US cases is that the House seemed willing to consider evidence of known practices regarding torture as probative of the likelihood that a particular individual was more likely to have been tortured. *See Belmarsh II*, [2005] UKHL 71 at [56]. A line of federal cases in the United States seems to establish a fairly broad prohibition against the introduction of evidence obtained through torture. *See, e.g, Filartiga v. Pena-Irala*, 630 F.2d 876, 883 (2d Cir. 1980) (quoting U.N. Declaration on the Protection of All Persons from Being Subjected to Torture (1975)); *LaFrance v. Bohlinger*, 499 F 2d 29, 34 (1st Cir. 1974) ("It is unthinkable that a statement obtained by torture or by other conduct belonging only in a police state should be admitted at the government's behest in order to bolster its case."). Nevertheless, certain United States courts have indicated some reticence concerning the admissibility of state practices to support an individual claim that evidence was, in fact, acquired by torture. *See Yousef*, 327 F.3d at 129 n. 59.

94. *Belmarsh II*, [2005] UKHL 71 at [18].

95. *R. v. Horseferry Road Magistrates' Court, ex parte Bennett*, [1994] 1 AC 42, 61–62, 74, 76, quoted in *Belmarsh II*, [2005] UKHL 71 at [19]. The House also observed that this principle exists in United States law, as well. *See id.* (citing *Toscanino*, 500 F.2d at 275-76). *See also R. v. Looseley*, [2001] UKHL 53, [1]; *R. v. Mullen*, [2000] QB 520, 535–36.

96. *See* Douglas E. Edlin, *Judges and Unjust Laws: Common Law Constitutionalism and the Foundations of Judicial Review* (University of Michigan Press, 2008), 144–49.

97. *Belmarsh II*, [2005] UKHL 71 at [22].

98. *See Belmarsh II*, [2005] UKHL 71 at [70] ("The executive and the judiciary have different functions and different responsibilities. It is one thing for tainted information to be used by the executive when making operational decisions or by the police when exercising their investigatory powers, including powers of arrest. These steps do not impinge upon the liberty of individuals or, when they do, they are of an essentially short-term interim character. Often there is an urgent need for action. It is an altogether different matter for the judicial arm of the state to admit such information as evidence when adjudicating definitively upon the guilt or innocence of a person charged with a criminal offence. In the latter case repugnance to torture demands that proof of facts should be found in more acceptable sources than information extracted by torture.") (Lord Nicholls), [94]–[95] ("[T]he 2001 Act makes the exercise by the Secretary of State of his extraordinary powers subject to judicial supervision. . . . It [the

SIAC] is to form its own opinion, after calm judicial process, as to whether it considers that there are reasonable grounds for such suspicion or belief. It is exercising a judicial, not an executive function. Indeed, the fact that the exercise of the draconian powers conferred by the Act was subject to review by the judiciary was obviously an important reason why Parliament was willing to confer such powers on the Secretary of State. . . . In my opinion Parliament, in setting up a court to review the question of whether reasonable grounds exist for suspicion or belief, was expecting the court to behave like a court. In the absence of clear express provision to the contrary, that would include the application of the standards of justice which have traditionally characterised the proceedings of English courts. It excludes the use of evidence obtained by torture, whatever might be its source.") (Lord Hoffmann), [161]–[162] (Lord Brown). There is an alternative that is not contained in the existing statutory scheme in which prosecutors, rather than the police or the courts, would make the determination regarding the quality and sufficiency of the evidence. *See* Clive Walker, *Keeping Control of Terrorists Without Losing Control of Constitutionalism*, 59 Stan. L. Rev. 1395, 1429–30 (2007).

99. *Belmarsh II*, [2005] UKHL 71 at [91]. *See also id.* at [137] (Lord Rodger), [150] (Lord Carswell), [164] (Lord Brown). The Supreme Court of the United States reached its own version of the same conclusion in *Brown v. Mississippi*, 297 U.S. 278, 285, 286, 287 (1936) ("[T]he trial equally is a mere pretense where the state authorities have contrived a conviction resting solely upon confessions obtained by violence. The due process clause requires 'that state action, whether through one agency or another, shall be consistent with the fundamental principles of liberty and justice which lie at the base of all our civil and political institutions.' . . . It would be difficult to conceive of methods more revolting to the sense of justice than those taken to procure the confessions of these petitioners, and the use of the confessions thus obtained as the basis for conviction and sentence was a clear denial of due process. . . . The duty of maintaining constitutional rights of a person on trial for his life rises above mere rules of procedure and wherever the court is clearly satisfied that such violations exist, it will refuse to sanction such violations and will apply the corrective.") (Hughes, C.J.) (citations and quotation marks omitted).

100. *See Belmarsh II*, [2005] UKHL 71 at [83]; *Belmarsh*, [2004] UKHL 56 at [36]. *See also* Jeremy Waldron, *Torture and Positive Law: Jurisprudence for the White House*, 105 Colum. L. Rev. 1681, 1741–42 (2005) ("A third point [regarding the use of torture by the state] addresses the issue of the rule of law—the enterprise of subjecting 'the engines of state' to legal regulation and restraint. We hold ourselves committed to a general and quite aggressive principle of legality, which means that law does not just have a little sphere of its own in which to operate, but expands to govern and regulate every aspect of official practice. . . . I think we should be concerned about the effect not just on American law but on the rule of law of a weakening or an undermining of the legal prohibition on torture. We have seen how the prohibition on torture operates as an archetype of various parts of American constitutional law and law enforcement culture generally. I believe it also operates as an archetype of the ideal we call the rule of law. That agents of the state are not permitted to torture those who fall into their hands seems an elementary incident of the rule of law as it is understood in the modern world. If this protection is not assured, then the prospects for the rule of law generally look bleak indeed.").

101. *See, e.g.*, Brian Z. Tamanaha, *On the Rule of Law: History, Politics, Theory* (Cambridge University Press, 2004), 52 ("The judiciary is the point of most direct confrontation between the government, law, and the individual, and it can therefore serve as the best barrier against lawless governmental actions."); Scott Gordon, *Controlling the State: Constitutionalism from Ancient Athens to Today* (Harvard University Press, 1999), 256 ("During the seventeenth century not only did Parliament become established as a powerful political institution; the foundation was also laid for the role of the judiciary as a protective buffer between the government and the citizenry, a role that it plays in all modern constitutional polities."); R. C. van Caenegem, *An Historical Introduction to Western Constitutional Law* (Cambridge University Press, 1995), 98 ("The parliamentary and constitutional monarchy which . . . took shape in England . . . provided a solid central government, which protected the national interest, but was nevertheless bound to operate within the parameters of the law, *inter alia*, because of the impact of an influential and independent judicature."); Paul O. Carrese, *The Cloaking of Power: Montesquieu, Blackstone, and the Rise of Judicial Activism* (University of Chicago Press, 2003), 182–83 ("The first cause of an independent judiciary and its subsequent rise to power in eighteenth- and nineteenth-century America seems to be the blending of Montesquieu's complicated liberal constitutionalism with the common-law tradition of mixed constitutionalism, something undertaken nowhere more extensively than in America. . . . Hamilton and Marshall argued for judicial independence, a common-law profession, and judicial review so as to establish judges as guardians of constitutional tradition and limited government.").

102. *R. (on the application of Evans) v. Attorney General*, [2015] UKSC 21, [51]–[52], [53] (Lord Neuberger). Lord Kerr and Lord Reed joined Lord Neuberger's opinion. Lord Mance and Baroness Hale concurred with Lords Neuberger, Kerr, and Reed regarding the outcome but resolved the case on administrative grounds.

103. *Evans*, [2015] UKSC 21 at [54] (citing *Anisminic, Ltd. v. Foreign Compensation Commission*, [1969] 2 AC 147). *See also id.* at [55]–[57] (discussing specific applications of the principle of legality in protecting fundamental rights) (citing *R. v. Cheltenham Commissioners*, (1841) 1 QB 467; *R. v. Secretary of State for the Home Department, ex parte Pierson*, [1998] AC 539; *R. v. Secretary of State for the Home Department, ex parte Simms*, [2000] 2 AC 115; *Jackson v. Attorney General*, [2005] UKHL 56; *AXA General Insurance, Ltd. v. HM Advocate*, [2011] UKSC 46). For further discussion of the principle of legality in UK constitutional and administrative law, *see* Edlin, *Judges and Unjust Laws*, 179–87.

104. *See* Johan Steyn, *Guantanamo Bay: The Legal Black Hole*, 53 Int'l and Comp. L. Q. 1 (2004). The phrase actually has a longer history in English judicial opinions, but I want to restrict its meaning to the context of the detainees in Guantanamo and Belmarsh. Even with that limitation, however, the phrase appears in *R. (on the application of Abbasi and another) v. Secretary of State for Foreign and Commonwealth Affairs*, [2002] EWCA Civ 1598, [22].

105. The use of the term "lawlessly" is intended to comprise both of its common usages, *i.e.*, the government cannot act contrary to, or in the absence of, legal standards. *Cf.* Waldron, *Torture and Positive Law*, 105 Colum. L. Rev. at 1726–27, 1734–39, 1741–43; H. W. R. Wade, *Constitutional and Administrative Aspects of the* Anisminic *Case*, 85 Law Q. Rev. 198, 200 (1969).

106. Steyn, *The Legal Black Hole*, 11.

Chapter 6

1. Judith S. Kaye, *The Human Dimension in Appellate Judging: A Brief Reflection on a Timeless Concern*, 73 Cornell L. Rev. 1004, 1015 (1988).

2. Nomination of John G. Roberts, Jr. to be Chief Justice of the United States: Confirmation Hearing Before the S. Comm. on the Judiciary, 109th Cong. (2005), 55. For further comments on the "judge-as-umpire" trope, *see, e.g.*, Erwin Chemerinsky, *Seeing the Emperor's Clothes: Recognizing the Reality of Constitutional Decision Making*, 86 B.U. L. Rev. 1069, 1069–70 (2006) ("At his confirmation hearings for the Chief Justice position, Judge John Roberts began the proceedings by analogizing his future role to that of a baseball umpire. Although both make decisions, it is hard to think of a less apt analogy. An umpire applies rules created by others; the Supreme Court, through its decisions, creates rules that others play by. An umpire's views should not make a difference in how plays are called; a Supreme Court Justice's views make an enormous difference. . . . Why did Chief Justice Roberts, who obviously knows better, use such a disingenuous analogy? Undoubtedly, he wanted to begin the confirmation hearings by delivering the message that his views would not matter and, accordingly, there was no reason for the Senators to be concerned about his views or his refusal to discuss them. . . . I have personally heard th[is view] echoed by scholars and commentators. But the statements are indeed nonsense. . . . [H]ow can a judge's own views and experience not matter?").

3. Nominations of William H. Rehnquist and Lewis F. Powell, Jr. to be Associate Justices of the Supreme Court of the United States: Confirmation Hearing Before the S. Comm. on the Judiciary, 92d Cong. (1971), 77 (statement of Justice Rehnquist).

4. Jeffrey A. Segal, Harold J. Spaeth, and Sara C. Benesh, *The Supreme Court in the American Legal System* (Cambridge University Press, 2005), 31–32.

5. *See* above at 58–59, 181–82n45 and accompanying text. *See also* Connie S. Rosati, *Some Puzzles about the Objectivity of Law*, 23 Law & Phil. 273, 286, 303 (2003) ("[W] hat is really of interest to us when we attempt to investigate the objectivity of law is not best understood in terms of a framework that appeals to various senses or kinds of objectivity applicable to different domains. . . . [L]aw is something we make, and the conventional origins of law seem terribly at odds with the idea that legal facts are utterly independent of our beliefs, judgments, attitudes, or reactions concerning what the law is.").

6. *See* above at 29, 156n54.

7. *See* above at 10.

8. I suggested functional effectiveness as a form of objectivism that might be used to explain the judicial process as distinct from the forms of objectivism that are used to explain law. *See* above at 17, 21, 29, 36–37, 79, 113, 137n23, 148n4, 157n56.

9. *See* Rosati, *Some Puzzles about the Objectivity of Law*, 306–7.

10. *See* Rosati, *Some Puzzles about the Objectivity of Law*, 308–9.

11. *See* Rosati, *Some Puzzles about the Objectivity of Law*, 290. *See also* above at 142n70.

12. *See Obergefell v. Hodges*, 192 L. Ed. 2d 609, 625 (2015) ("[T]he reasons marriage is fundamental under the Constitution apply with equal force to same-sex couples. A first premise of the Court's relevant precedents is that the right to personal choice regarding marriage is inherent in the concept of individual autonomy. This abiding connection between marriage and liberty is why *Loving* invalidated interracial marriage

bans under the Due Process Clause.") (citing *Loving v. Virginia*, 388 U.S. 1, 12 (1967)) (other citation omitted).

13. *Obergefell*, 192 L. Ed. 2d at 628–29.

14. *Obergefell*, 192 L. Ed. 2d at 621–22 (quoting *Lawrence v. Texas*, 539 U.S. 558, 575 (2003) and citing *United States v. Windsor*, 133 S. Ct. 2675 (2012)).

15. *See* above at 81–82, 84–85, 87–88.

16. *See Lawrence v. Texas*, 539 U.S. 558, 604–5 (2003) ("Today's opinion dismantles the structure of constitutional law that has permitted a distinction to be made between heterosexual and homosexual unions, insofar as formal recognition in marriage is concerned. If moral disapprobation of homosexual conduct is 'no legitimate state interest' for purposes of proscribing that conduct . . . what justification could there possibly be for denying the benefits of marriage to homosexual couples exercising 'the liberty protected by the Constitution'? . . . This case 'does not involve' the issue of homosexual marriage only if one entertains the belief that principle and logic have nothing to do with the decisions of this Court.") (Scalia, J., dissenting). Scalia also does not believe that *Loving* serves as precedent for striking bans on same-sex marriage. *See id.* at 599–601 (arguing that laws differentiating people on the basis of race should be analyzed under strict scrutiny but laws differentiating people on the basis of sexual orientation should be analyzed according to a rational basis test).

17. *Lawrence*, 539 U.S. at 602 (Scalia, J., dissenting).

18. In *Lawrence*, for example, Scalia indicated his belief that the majority's opinion was driven by a "law-profession culture, that has largely signed on to the so-called homosexual agenda" despite the reality (as he saw it) "that the attitudes of that culture are not obviously 'mainstream'"). 539 U.S. at 602–3.

19. *See* Guyora Binder and Robert Weisberg, *The Critical Use of History: Cultural Criticism of Law*, 49 Stan. L. Rev. 1149, 1151–52 (1997) ("[T]he legal representation of social will bears little resemblance to scientific observation. It is more like the literary representation of generic themes. . . . Like preferences, none of these entities exists independent of its representations. These representations are judged aesthetically rather than epistemologically: They are judged according to the experience they enable rather than their truth to experience. So too can we judge law aesthetically, according to the society it forms, the identities it defines, the preferences it encourages, and the subjective experience it enables. We can 'read' and criticize law as part of the making of a culture.").

20. *See* above at 22–24, 150–51n19.

21. The German term *weltanschauung* originated in Kant's first *Critique* and encompasses (in its modern usage) our understandings of history, art, culture, society, and the experiences of our interior world and the external world.

22. *See* Joan Gadol, *Leon Battista Alberti: Universal Man of the Early Renaissance* (University of Chicago Press, 1969), 107.

23. Clarence Thomas, *My Grandfather's Son* (Harper Collins, 2007), 75.

24. *See, e.g.*, Stephen L. Carter, *Reflections of an Affirmative Action Baby* (Basic Books, 1991), 12, 50–62. *Cf.* Linda Hamilton Krieger, *Civil Rights Perestroika: Intergroup Relations after Affirmative Action*, 86 Calif. L. Rev. 1251, 1263–64 (1998); Ellis Cose, *The Rage of a Privileged Class* (Harper Collins, 1993), 122–23.

25. *Grutter v. Bollinger*, 539 U.S. 306, 372 (2003) (Thomas, J., concurring in part and dissenting in part).

26. *Grutter*, 539 U.S. at 373 (citation omitted).

27. *See, e.g.*, *Adarand Constructors, Inc. v. Pena*, 515 U.S. 200, 241 (1995) ("[T]here can be no doubt that racial paternalism and its unintended consequences can be as poisonous and pernicious as any other form of discrimination. So-called 'benign' discrimination teaches many that because of chronic and apparently immutable handicaps, minorities cannot compete with them without their patronizing indulgence. Inevitably, such programs engender attitudes of superiority or, alternatively, provoke resentment among those who believe that they have been wronged by the government's use of race. These programs stamp minorities with a badge of inferiority.") (Thomas, J., concurring in part and concurring in the judgment).

28. *Fisher v. University of Texas at Austin*, 133 S.Ct. 2411, 2432 (2013) (Thomas, J., concurring) (citations omitted).

29. Thomas graduated in 1974 and Sotomayor graduated in 1979.

30. *See* Thomas, *My Grandfather's Son*, 74–75; Sonia Sotomayor, *My Beloved Life* (Knopf, 2013), 145–46, 189.

31. Sotomayor describes experiencing this primarily at Princeton, while Thomas experienced it primarily at Yale. *See* Sotomayor, *My Beloved Life*, 128, 143–45; Thomas, *My Grandfather's Son*, 74.

32. *See* Sotomayor, *My Beloved Life*, 129–30, 133–35; Thomas, *My Grandfather's Son*, 51.

33. Sotomayor, *My Beloved Life*, 145. *Cf.* Thomas, *My Grandfather's Son*, 71.

34. *Compare* Thomas, *My Grandfather's Son*, 86 ("One high-priced lawyer after another treated me dismissively. . . . Many asked pointed questions unsubtly suggesting that they doubted I was as smart as my grades indicated.") *with* Sotomayor, *My Beloved Life*, 188, 189 ("[T]he partner facing me asked whether I believed in affirmative action. . . . [']Do you think you would have been admitted to Yale Law School if you were not Puerto Rican?'").

35. Sotomayor, *My Beloved Life*, 191.

36. 134 S. Ct. 1623 (2014).

37. Mich. Const. art. I, § 26(1).

38. *Schuette* was a 6–2 decision. Justice Kagan did not participate. Justice Breyer, who joined the majority in *Grutter*, concurred in the *Schuette* judgment, because in his view "the Constitution permits, though it does not require, the use of the kind of race-conscious programs that are now barred by the Michigan Constitution," 134 S. Ct. at 1649, and because the case "does not involve a reordering of the *political* process; it does not in fact involve the movement of decisionmaking from one political level to another." 134 S. Ct. at 1650 (emphasis in original).

39. *Schuette*, 134 S. Ct. at 1630.

40. *Schuette*, 134 S. Ct. at 1638.

41. 393 U.S. 385 (1969).

42. 458 U.S. 457 (1982).

43. *Schuette*, 134 S. Ct. at 1659 (citation omitted).

44. *Schuette*, 134 S. Ct. at 1659.

45. *Schuette*, 134 S. Ct. at 1660.

46. *Schuette*, 134 S. Ct. at 1662.

47. *Schuette*, 134 S. Ct. at 1653 (quoting *Seattle*, 458 U.S. at 467).

48. *Schuette*, 134 S. Ct. at 1662.

49. *Schuette*, 134 S. Ct. at 1660.

50. *See Regents of the Univ. of Cal. v. Bakke*, 438 U.S. 265, 315–18 (1978).

51. *See Grutter*, 539 U.S. at 325 ("[W]e endorse Justice Powell's view [in *Bakke*] that student body diversity is a compelling state interest that can justify the use of race in university admissions.").

52. *See Grutter*, 539 U.S. at 328–33.

53. *Schuette*, 134 S. Ct. at 1660.

54. *Grutter*, 539 U.S. at 371, 372 (Thomas, J., concurring in part and dissenting in part). *See also Fisher*, 133 S. Ct. at 2431 ("Blacks and Hispanics admitted to the University as a result of racial discrimination are, on average, far less prepared than their white and Asian classmates. Tellingly, neither the University nor any of the 73 amici briefs in support of racial discrimination has presented a shred of evidence that black and Hispanic students are able to close this substantial gap during their time at the University. . . . But, as a result of the mismatching, many blacks and Hispanics who likely would have excelled at less elite schools are placed in a position where underperformance is all but inevitable because they are less academically prepared than the white and Asian students with whom they must compete. Setting aside the damage wreaked upon the self-confidence of these overmatched students, there is no evidence that they learn more at the University than they would have learned at other schools for which they were better prepared.") (Thomas, J., concurring). This is not the place to discuss the "mismatch" theory endorsed by Justice Thomas. Very briefly, however, I should note that this argument has gained purchase among opponents of affirmative action. *See, e.g.*, Stephan Thernstrom and Abigail Thernstrom, *America in Black and White: One Nation, Indivisible* (Simon & Schuster, 1997), 391–97, 405–11; Richard H. Sander and Stuart Taylor, Jr., *Mismatch: How Affirmative Action Hurts Students It's Intended to Help, and Why Universities Won't Admit It* (Basic Books, 2012); Richard H. Sander, *A Systemic Analysis of Affirmative Action in American Law Schools*, 57 Stan. L. Rev. 367, 371–72 (2004). The argument has also been challenged by proponents of affirmative action. *See, e.g.*, William G. Bowen and Derek Bok, *The Shape of the River: Long-Term Consequences of Considering Race in College and University Admissions* (Princeton University Press, 1998), 59–68, 114–15, 142–44, 258–65; Thomas J. Kane, "Misconceptions in the Debate Over Affirmative Action in College Admissions" in Gary Orfield and Edward Miller, eds., *Chilling Admissions: The Affirmative Action Crisis and the Search for Alternatives* (Harvard Education Publishing Group, 1998), 18–23; Ian Ayres and Richard Brooks, *Does Affirmative Action Reduce the Number of Black Lawyers?*, 57 Stan. L. Rev. 1807, 1811–40 (2005); David L. Chambers, *et al.*, *The Real Impact of Eliminating Affirmative Action in American Law Schools: An Empirical Critique of Richard Sander's Study*, 57 Stan. L. Rev. 1855, 1868–74 (2005); David B. Wilkins, *A Systematic Response to Systematic Disadvantage: A Response to Sander*, 57 Stan. L. Rev. 1915, 1919–41 (2005).

55. *See generally* Helen Norton, *The Supreme Court's Post-Racial Turn Towards a Zero-Sum Understanding of Equality*, 52 Wm. & Mary L. Rev. 197, 206–7 (2010)

("Courts, policymakers, and scholars have long struggled with a vigorous and perhaps intractable debate: whether antidiscrimination law should be understood as driven by antisubordination as opposed to anticlassification values. Antisubordination advocates urge that the Equal Protection Clause should be understood to bar those government actions that have the intent or the effect of perpetuating traditional patterns of hierarchy. Under this view, government actions that seek to undermine such hierarchies, including those expressly based on race, do not offend antidiscrimination values. This approach thus finds 'no moral or constitutional equivalence between a policy that is designed to perpetuate a caste system and one that seeks to eradicate racial subordination.' Those who urge an anticlassification understanding of the Equal Protection Clause, in contrast, take the view that the Constitution prohibits government from '[r]educ[ing] an individual to an assigned racial identity for differential treatment.' They thus consider differential race-based treatment as uniformly morally and legally repugnant regardless of motive.") (footnotes deleted).

56. *See* above at 71–72, 73–75.

57. *See* above at 169nn178–182.

58. 530 F.3d 87 (2d Cir. 2008), *reh'g denied en banc,* 530 F.3d 88 (2d Cir. 2008), *rev'd,* 557 U.S. 557 (2009).

59. *Ricci v. DeStefano,* 554 F. Supp. 2d 142, 153 (D. Conn. 2006).

60. Nomination of Sonia Sotomayor to be an Associate Justice of the Supreme Court of the United States: Confirmation Hearing Before the S. Comm. on the Judiciary, 111th Cong. (2009), 7–8 (italics in original).

61. Benjamin Vargas is his name. *See Ricci,* 557 U.S. at 607.

62. Judge Parker was nominated to the United States District Court for the Southern District of New York by Bill Clinton.

63. Sotomayor, *My Beloved Life,* 176.

64. *See* Angela Onwuachi-Willig, *Just Another Brother on the SCT?: What Justice Clarence Thomas Teaches Us About the Influence of Racial Identity,* 90 Iowa L. Rev. 931, 948–52, 954–59 (2005); Stephen F. Smith, *Clarence X?: The Black Nationalist Behind Justice Thomas's Constitutionalism,* 4 NYU J.L. & Liberty 583, 614–24 (2009).

65. *See* Rosati, *Some Puzzles about the Objectivity of Law,* 286, 301.

References

Adams, Charles Francis, ed. *Memoirs of John Quincy Adams, 1795–1848* (J. B. Lippincott & Co., 1874).

Adler, Matthew D. *Judicial Restraint in the Administrative State: Beyond the Countermajoritarian Difficulty*, 145 U. Pa. L. Rev. 759 (1997).

Alexy, Robert. *A Theory of Legal Argumentation: The Theory of Rational Discourse as Theory of Legal Justification* (Oxford University Press, 1989).

Allan, T. R. S. *Constitutional Justice: A Liberal Theory of the Rule of Law* (Oxford University Press, 2001).

Allison, Henry E. *Kant's Theory of Taste: A Reading of the* Critique of Aesthetic Judgment (Cambridge University Press, 2001).

Anastaplo, George. *The Amendments to the Constitution: A Commentary* (Johns Hopkins University Press, 1995).

Anastaplo, George. *The Constitution of 1787: A Commentary* (Johns Hopkins University Press, 1989).

Anderson, Benedict. *Imagined Communities: Reflections on the Origin and Spread of Nationalism* (rev. ed.) (Verso, 1991).

Aquinas, Thomas. *The Treatise on Law* (R. J. Henle, ed.) (University of Notre Dame Press, 1993).

Arendt, Hannah. *Between Past and Future: Eight Exercises in Political Thought* (Penguin Books, 2006).

Arendt, Hannah. *Lectures on Kant's Political Philosophy* (Ronald Beiner, ed.) (University of Chicago Press, 1982).

Arendt, Hannah. *The Life of the Mind: Thinking* (Harcourt Brace Jovanovich, 1978).

Ashworth, Andrew. *Principles of Criminal Law* (5th ed.) (Oxford University Press, 2006).

Atiyah, P. S. "Form and Substance in Legal Reasoning," in Neil MacCormick and Peter Birks, eds., *The Legal Mind: Essays for Tony Honoré* (Oxford University Press, 1986).

Atiyah, P. S., and R. S. Summers. *Form and Substance in Anglo-American Law: A Comparative Study of Legal Reasoning, Legal Theory, and Legal Institutions* (Oxford University Press, 1987).

Ayres, Ian, and Richard Brooks. *Does Affirmative Action Reduce the Number of Black Lawyers?*, 57 Stan. L. Rev. 1807 (2005).

Azmy, Baher. *Constitutional Implications of the War on Terror:* Rasul v. Bush *and the Intra-Territorial Constitution*, 62 N.Y.U. Ann. Surv. Am. L. 369 (2007).

Bair, Robert R., and Robin D. Coblentz. *The Trials of Mr. Justice Samuel Chase*, 27 Md. L. Rev. 365 (1967).

Baker, J. H. *An Introduction to English Legal History* (4th ed.) (Oxford University Press, 2007).

Baker, Thomas E. *Rationing Justice on Appeal: The Problems of the U.S. Courts of Appeals* (West Publishing Co., 1994).

Barak, Aharon. *The Judge in a Democracy* (Princeton University Press, 2006).

Barak, Aharon. *The Role of a Supreme Court in a Democracy*, 53 Hastings L.J. 1205 (2002).

Barber, N. W. *Sovereignty Re-examined: The Courts, Parliament, and Statutes*, 20 Oxford J. Leg. Stud. 131 (2000).

Barnett, Vincent M., Jr. *Constitutional Interpretation and Judicial Self-Restraint*, 39 Mich. L. Rev. 213 (1940).

Barton, J. L. *The Story of Marital Rape*, 108 Law Q. Rev. 260 (1992).

Baum, Lawrence. *Judges and Their Audiences: A Perspective on Judicial Behavior* (Princeton University Press, 2006).

Beck, Lewis White. *Essays on Kant and Hume* (Yale University Press, 1978).

Beiner, Ronald. *Philosophy in a Time of Lost Spirit: Essays on Contemporary Theory* (University of Toronto Press, 1997).

Bell, David. *The Art of Judgement*, 96 Mind 221 (1987).

Bell, John. "The Acceptability of Legal Arguments," in Neil MacCormick and Peter Birks, eds., *The Legal Mind: Essays for Tony Honoré* (Oxford University Press, 1986).

Beltran, Jordi Ferrer, and Giovanni Battista Ratti, eds. *The Logic of Legal Requirements: Essays on Defeasibility* (Oxford University Press, 2012).

Berkowitz, Roger. *The Gift of Science: Leibniz and the Modern Legal Tradition* (Harvard University Press, 2005).

Berman, Harold J. *Law and Language: Effective Symbols of Community* (Cambridge University Press, 2013).

Bickel, Alexander M. *The Least Dangerous Branch: The Supreme Court at the Bar of Politics* (2nd ed.) (Yale University Press, 1986).

Binder, Guyora, and Robert Weisberg. *The Critical Use of History: Cultural Criticism of Law*, 49 Stan. L. Rev. 1149 (1997).

Bix, Brian. *Law, Language, and Legal Determinacy* (Oxford University Press, 1993).

Bix, Brian. *On the Dividing Line Between Natural Law Theory and Legal Positivism*, 75 Notre Dame L. Rev. 1613 (2000).

Black, Charles L., Jr. *The People and the Court: Judicial Review in a Democracy* (Macmillan, 1960).

Blackburn, Simon. "Rule-Following and Moral Realism," in Steven Holtzman and Christopher Leich, eds., *Wittgenstein: To Follow a Rule* (Routledge & Kegan Paul, 1981).

Blackstone, William. *Commentaries on the Laws of England* (Oxford University Press, 1769).

Bobbitt, Philip. *Constitutional Fate: Theory of the Constitution* (Oxford University Press, 1982).

Bogdanor, Vernon. *The New British Constitution* (Hart Publishing, 2009).

Bowen, William G., and Derek Bok. *The Shape of the River: Long-Term Consequences of Considering Race in College and University Admissions* (Princeton University Press, 1998).

Bowie, Andrew. *Aesthetics and Subjectivity: From Kant to Nietzsche* (2nd ed.) (Manchester University Press, 2003).

Braden, George D. *The Search for Objectivity in Constitutional Law*, 57 Yale L.J. 571 (1948).

Brennan, William J., Jr. *In Defense of Dissents*, 37 Hastings L.J. 427 (1986).

Brennan, William J., Jr. *Reason, Passion, And "The Progress Of The Law"*, 42 Record of the Ass'n of the Bar of the City of New York 948 (1987).

Breslin, Beau. *From Words to Worlds: Exploring Constitutional Functionality* (Johns Hopkins University Press, 2009).

Brink, David O. "Legal Interpretation, Objectivity, and Morality," in Brian Leiter, ed., *Objectivity in Law and Morals* (Cambridge University Press, 2001).

Brownell, Roy E. II. *Vice Presidential Secrecy: A Study in Comparative Constitutional Privilege and Historical Development*, 84 St. John's L. Rev. 423 (2010).

Brudner, Alan. *Constitutional Goods* (Oxford University Press, 2004).

Buchanan, James M., and Gordon Tullock. *The Calculus of Consent: Logical Foundations of Constitutional Democracy* (University of Michigan Press, 1962).

Burbank, Stephen B. *The Architecture of Judicial Independence*, 72 S. Cal. L. Rev. 315 (1999).

Burbank, Stephen B. *The Courtroom as Classroom: Independence, Imagination and Ideology in the Work of Jack Weinstein*, 97 Colum. L. Rev. 1971 (1997).

Burgess, Craig. *Kant's Key to the Critique of Taste*, 39 Phil. Q. 484 (1989).

Burke, Edmund. *The Works of the Right Honorable Edmund Burke* (Oxford University Press, 1906).

Burns, Robert P. *A Theory of the Trial* (Princeton University Press, 1999).

Butler, Lynda L. *The Politics of Takings: Choosing the Appropriate Decisionmaker*, 38 Wm. & Mary L. Rev. 749 (1997).

Calabresi, Steven G., and Stephanie Dotson Zimdahl. *The Supreme Court and Foreign Sources of Law: Two Hundred Years of Practice and the Juvenile Death Penalty Decision*, 47 Wm. & Mary L. Rev. 743 (2005).

Campos, Paul. *Three Mistakes About Interpretation*, 92 Mich. L. Rev. 388 (1993).

Cardozo, Benjamin N. *Law and Literature and Other Essays and Addresses* (Harcourt, Brace and Co., 1931).

Cardozo, Benjamin N. *The Nature of the Judicial Process* (Yale University Press, 1921).

Carpenter, William S. *Judicial Tenure in the United States with Especial Reference to the Tenure of Federal Judges* (Yale University Press, 1918).

Carrese, Paul O. *The Cloaking of Power: Montesquieu, Blackstone, and the Rise of Judicial Activism* (University of Chicago Press, 2003).

Carter, Stephen L. *Constitutional Improprieties: Reflections on* Mistretta, Morrison, *and Administrative Government*, 57 U. Chi. L. Rev. 357 (1990).

Carter, Stephen L. *Reflections of an Affirmative Action Baby* (Basic Books, 1991).

Chambers, David L., *et al. The Real Impact of Eliminating Affirmative Action in American Law Schools: An Empirical Critique of Richard Sander's Study*, 57 Stan. L. Rev. 1855 (2005).

Chemerinsky, Erwin. *Seeing the Emperor's Clothes: Recognizing the Reality of Constitutional Decision Making*, 86 B.U. L. Rev. 1069 (2006).

Chukwumerije, Okezie. *Rhetoric Versus Reality: The Link Between the Rule of Law and Economic Development*, 23 Emory Int'l L. Rev. 383 (2009).

Clancy, Kevin, John Bartolomeo, David Richardson, and Charles Wellford. *Sentence Decisionmaking: The Logic of Sentence Decisions and the Extent and Sources of Sentence Disparity*, 72 J. Crim. L. & Criminology 524 (1981).

Cleveland, Sarah H. *Our International Constitution*, 31 Yale J. Int'l Law 1 (2006).

Cohen, Joel. *Blindfolds Off: Judges on How They Decide* (American Bar Association, 2014).

Cohen, Joshua. *Philosophy, Politics, Democracy: Selected Essays* (Harvard University Press, 2009).

Cohen, Ted and Paul Guyer. "Introduction," in Ted Cohen and Paul Guyer, eds., *Essays in Kant's Aesthetics* (University of Chicago Press, 1982).

Coke, Edward. *Institutes of the Laws of England* (Flesher, Lee & Pakeman, 1644).

Coke, Edward. *The Selected Writings of Sir Edward Coke* (Steve Sheppard, ed.) (Liberty Fund, 2003).

Coleman, Jules. "Authority and Reason," in Robert P. George, ed., *The Autonomy of Law: Essays on Legal Positivism* (Oxford University Press, 1996).

Coleman, Jules L., and Brian Leiter. *Determinacy, Objectivity, and Authority*, 142 U. Pa. L. Rev. 549 (1993).

Constable, Marianne. *Our Word Is Our Bond: How Legal Speech Acts* (Stanford University Press, 2014).

Cook, Beverly B. *Public Opinion and Federal Judicial Policy*, 21 Am. J. Pol. Sci. 567 (1977).

Cooper, George R., and Clare D. McGillem. *Probabilistic Methods of Signal and System Analysis* (3rd ed.) (Oxford University Press, 1998).

Corbin, Arthur Linton. *Corbin on Contracts: A Comprehensive Treatise on the Rules of Contract Law* (West Publishing Co., 1960).

Corso, Lucia. *Should Empathy Play Any Role in the Interpretation of Constitutional Rights?*, 27 Ratio Juris 94 (2014).

Corwin, Edward S. *The Supreme Court and Unconstitutional Acts of Congress*, 4 Mich. L. Rev. 616 (1906).

Cose, Ellis. *The Rage of a Privileged Class* (Harper Collins, 1993).

Crawford, Donald W. *Kant's Aesthetic Theory* (University of Wisconsin Press, 1974).

Crawford, Donald W. *Reason-Giving in Kant's Aesthetics*, 28 J. of Aesthetics and Art Criticism 505 (1970).

Dannenbaum, Tom. *Nationality and the International Judge: The Nationalist Presumption Governing the International Judiciary and Why It Must Be Reversed*, 45 Cornell Int'l L. J. 77 (2012).

Davidson, Donald. *Subjective, Intersubjective, Objective* (Oxford University Press, 2001).

Davidson, Kenneth M., Ruth Bader Ginsburg, and Herma Hill Kay. *Sex-Based Discrimination* (West Publishing Co., 1974).

Davidson, Paul. *The Keynes Solution: The Path to Global Economic Prosperity* (Palgrave Macmillan, 2009).

Denneny, Michael. "The Privilege of Ourselves: Hannah Arendt on Judgment," in Melvyn A. Hill, ed., *Hannah Arendt: The Recovery of the Public World* (St. Martin's Press, 1979).

Diamond, Shari Seidman, and Hans Zeisel. *Sentencing Councils: A Study of Sentence Disparity and Its Reduction*, 43 U. Chi. L. Rev. 109 (1975).

Dicey, A. V. *Introduction to the Study of the Law of the Constitution* (8th ed.) (Liberty Fund, 1982).

Dicey, A. V. *Lectures on the Relation between Law and Public Opinion in England during the Nineteenth Century* (Macmillan, 1905).

Dickson, Julie. *Evaluation and Legal Theory* (Hart Publishing, 2001).

Dorf, Michael C. *Legal Indeterminacy and Institutional Design*, 78 N.Y.U. L. Rev. 875 (2003).

Dragich, Martha J. *Will the Federal Courts of Appeals Perish If They Publish? Or Does the Declining Use of Opinions to Explain and Justify Judicial Decisions Pose a Greater Threat?*, 44 Am. U. L. Rev. 757 (1995).

Drobak, John N., and Douglass C. North. *Understanding Judicial Decision-Making: The Importance of Constraints on Non-Rational Deliberations*, 26 Wash. U. J. L. & Pol'y 131 (2008).

Duarte d'Almeida, Luis. *Allowing for Exceptions: A Theory of Defences and Defeasibility in Law* (Oxford University Press, 2015).

Duberstein, John. *Excluding Torture: A Comparison of the British and American Approaches to Evidence Obtained by Third Party Torture*, 32 N.C. J. Int'l L. & Com. Reg. 159 (2006).

Duff, Peter. *The Scottish Criminal Jury: A Very Peculiar Institution*, 62 Law & Contemp. Prob. 173 (1999).

Dworkin, Ronald. *Justice in Robes* (Harvard University Press, 2006).

Dworkin, Ronald. *Law's Empire* (Harvard University Press, 1986).

Eagleton, Terry. *The Ideology of the Aesthetic* (Blackwell, 1990).

Edlin, Douglas E. *A Constitutional Right to Judicial Review: Access to Courts and Ouster Clauses in England and the United States*, 57 Am. J. Comp. L. 67 (2009).

Edlin, Douglas E. *Judges and Unjust Laws: Common Law Constitutionalism and the Foundations of Judicial Review* (University of Michigan Press, 2008).

Eisenberg, Melvin A. *Disclosure in Contract Law*, 91 Calif. L. Rev. 1645 (2003).

Eisenberg, Melvin Aron. *The Nature of the Common Law* (Harvard University Press, 1988).

Eisgruber, Christopher L. *The Next Justice: Repairing the Supreme Court Appointments Process* (Princeton University Press, 2007).

Eskridge, William N., Jr. *The New Textualism*, 37 UCLA L. Rev. 621 (1990).

Fabre, Cécile. *A Philosophical Argument for a Bill of Rights*, 30 Brit. J. Pol. Sci. 77 (2000).

Farber, Daniel A. *The Supreme Court, the Law of Nations, and Citations of Foreign Law: The Lessons of History*, 95 Calif. L. Rev. 1335 (2007).

Feldman, Heidi Li. *Objectivity in Legal Judgment*, 92 Mich. L. Rev. 1187 (1994).

Ferejohn, John. *Independent Judges, Dependent Judiciary: Explaining Judicial Independence*, 72 S. Cal. L. Rev. 353 (1999).

Filvaroff, David B. and Raymond E. Wolfinger. "The Origin and Enactment of the Civil Rights Act of 1964," in Bernard Grofman, ed., *Legacies of the 1964 Civil Rights Act* (University Press of Virginia, 2000).

Finnis, John. "Natural Law and Legal Reasoning," in Robert P. George, ed., *Natural Law Theory: Contemporary Essays* (Oxford University Press, 1992).

Finnis, John. *Natural Law and Natural Rights* (2nd ed.) (Oxford University Press, 2011).

Finnis, John. *Philosophy of Law: Collected Essays* (Oxford University Press, 2011).
Fish, Stanley. *Doing What Comes Naturally: Change, Rhetoric, and the Practice of Theory in Literary and Legal Studies* (Duke University Press, 1989).
Fiss, Owen M. *The Forms of Justice*, 93 Harv. L. Rev. 1 (1979).
Fiss, Owen. *The Law as It Could Be* (New York University Press, 2003).
Fortescue, John. *De Laudibus Legum Angliae* (S. B. Chrimes, ed.) (Cambridge University Press, 1942).
Frank, Jerome. *Courts on Trial: Myth and Reality in American Justice* (Princeton University Press, 1949).
Franke, Katherine. *Introduction: Symposium Honoring the Advocacy, Scholarship, and Jurisprudence of Justice Ruth Ginsburg*, 25 Colum. J. Gender & L. 1 (2013).
Frankel, Marvin E. *The Sentencing Morass and a Suggestion for Reform*, 3 Crim. L. Bull. 365 (1967).
Freckmann, Anke, and Thomas Wegerich. *The German Legal System* (Sweet & Maxwell, 1999).
Freed, Daniel J. *Federal Sentencing in the Wake of Guidelines: Unacceptable Limits on the Discretion of Sentencers*, 101 Yale L.J. 1681 (1992).
Fried, Charles. *Saying What the Law Is: The Constitution in the Supreme Court* (Harvard University Press, 2004).
Friedman, Barry and Andrew D. Martin. "Looking for Law in All the Wrong Places: Some Suggestions for Modeling Legal Decision-making," in Charles Gardner Geyh, ed., *What's Law Got To Do With It?: What Judges Do, Why They Do It, and What's at Stake* (Stanford University Press, 2011).
Gadol, Joan. *Leon Battista Alberti: Universal Man of the Early Renaissance* (University of Chicago Press, 1969).
Gardner, John. *Law as a Leap of Faith: Essays on Law in General* (Oxford University Press, 2012).
George, Robert P. *Natural Law*, 52 Am. J. Juris. 55 (2007).
Gerhardt, Michael J. *Constitutional Humility*, 76 U. Cin. L. Rev. 23 (2007).
Gerhardt, Michael J. *The Power of Precedent* (Oxford University Press, 2008).
Gerhardt, Michael J. *The Role of the Judge in the Twenty-First Century: What's Old Is New Again*, 86 B.U. L. Rev. 1267 (2006).
Gewirtz, Paul. *On "I Know It When I See It,"* 105 Yale L.J. 1023 (1996).
Geyh, Charles Gardner. *Judicial Independence, Judicial Accountability, and the Role of Constitutional Norms in Congressional Regulation of the Courts*, 78 Ind. L. J. 153 (2003).
Geyh, Charles Gardner. *Straddling the Fence Between Truth and Pretense: The Role of Law and Preference in Judicial Decision Making and the Future of Judicial Independence*, 22 Notre Dame J. L. Ethics & Pub. Pol'y 435 (2008).
Geyh, Charles Gardner. *When Courts and Congress Collide: The Struggle for Control of America's Judicial System* (University of Michigan Press, 2006).
Geyh, Charles Gardner, and Emily Field Van Tassel. *The Independence of the Judicial Branch in the New Republic*, 74 Chi.-Kent L. Rev. 31 (1998).
Giles, Marianne. *Judicial Law-Making in the Criminal Courts: The Case of Marital Rape*, [1992] Crim. L. Rev. 407.

Gillman, Howard. *The Votes That Counted: How the Court Decided the 2000 Presidential Election* (University of Chicago Press, 2001).

Ginsburg, Martin D. *Some Reflections on Imperfection*, 39 Ariz. St. L.J. 949 (2007).

Ginsburg, Ruth Bader. *The Changing Complexion of Harvard Law School*, 27 Harv. Women's L.J. 303 (2004).

Ginsburg, Ruth Bader. *"A Decent Respect to the Opinions of Humankind": The Value of a Comparative Perspective in Constitutional Adjudication*, 1 F.I.U. L. Rev. 27 (2006).

Ginsburg, Ruth Bader. *A Tribute to Justice Sandra Day O'Connor*, 119 Harv. L. Rev. 1239 (2006).

Glenn, H. Patrick. *Legal Traditions of the World: Sustainable Diversity in Law* (5th ed.) (Oxford University Press, 2014).

Goldman, Ari L. "Gerald Gunther, Legal Scholar, Dies at 75," N.Y. Times, Aug. 1, 2002.

Goodhart, A. L. *English Law and the Moral Law* (Stevens & Sons, 1953).

Goodpaster, Gary. *On the Theory of American Adversary Criminal Trial*, 78 J. Crim. L. & Criminology 118 (1987).

Goodson, Timothy J. *Duck, Duck, Goose: Hunting for Better Recusal Practices in the United States Supreme Court in Light of* Cheney v. United States District Court, 84 N.C. L. Rev. 181 (2005).

Gordon, Scott. *Controlling the State: Constitutionalism from Ancient Athens to Today* (Harvard University Press, 1999).

Graber, Mark A. *Resolving Political Questions Into Judicial Questions: Tocqueville's Thesis Revisited*, 21 Const. Comment. 485 (2004).

Gray, John Chipman. *The Nature and Sources of the Law* (Ashgate, 1997).

Green, Leslie. *Positivism and the Inseparability of Law and Morals*, 83 N.Y.U. L. Rev. 1035 (2008).

Green, Michael Steven. *Dworkin's Fallacy, or What the Philosophy of Language Can't Teach Us about the Law*, 89 Va. L. Rev. 1897 (2003).

Greenawalt, Kent. *Conflicts of Law and Morality* (Oxford University Press, 1987).

Greenawalt, Kent. *Discretion and Judicial Decision: The Elusive Quest for the Fetters that Bind Judges*, 75 Colum. L. Rev. 359 (1975).

Greenawalt, Kent. *Law and Objectivity* (Oxford University Press, 1992).

Greenawalt, Kent. *Policy, Rights, and Judicial Decision*, 11 Ga. L. Rev. 991 (1977).

Greenhouse, Linda. "An Intense Attack by Justice Thomas on Cross-Burning," N.Y. Times, Dec. 12, 2002.

Grossman, Joel B. *Lawyers and Judges: The ABA and the Politics of Judicial Selection* (John Wiley & Sons, 1965).

Gugliotta, Guy, and Eleanor Randolph. "A Mentor, Role Model and Heroine of Feminist Lawyers," Wash. Post, June 15, 1993.

Guyer, Paul. *Disinterestedness and Desire in Kant's Aesthetics*, 36 J. Aesthetics & Art Criticism 449 (1978).

Guyer, Paul. "Introduction," in Paul Guyer, ed., *The Cambridge Companion to Kant and Modern Philosophy* (Cambridge University Press, 2006).

Guyer, Paul. *Kant and the Claims of Taste* (2nd ed.) (Cambridge University Press, 1997).

Guyer, Paul. *Kant and the Experience of Freedom: Essays on Aesthetics and Morality* (Cambridge University Press, 1993).

Guyer, Paul. "Pleasure and Society in Kant's Theory of Taste," in Ted Cohen and Paul Guyer, eds., *Essays in Kant's Aesthetics* (University of Chicago Press, 1982).

Guyer, Paul. *Values of Beauty: Historical Essays in Aesthetics* (Cambridge University Press, 2005).

Guyer, Paul, and Henry Allison. "Dialogue: Paul Guyer and Henry Allison on Allison's *Kant's Theory of Taste*," in Rebecca Kukla, *Aesthetics and Cognition in Kant's Critical Philosophy* (Cambridge University Press, 2006).

Haines, Charles Grove. *The American Doctrine of Judicial Supremacy* (2nd ed.) (University of California Press, 1932).

Halberstam, Malvina. *Ruth Bader Ginsburg: The First Jewish Woman on the United States Supreme Court*, 19 Cardozo L. Rev. 1441 (1998).

Hale, Matthew. *The History of the Pleas of the Crown* (Nutt & Gosling, 1736).

Hall, Melinda Gann. *Introduction to "An Analysis of the Rehnquist Court's Establishment Clause Jurisprudence: A New Marriage of Legal and Social Science Approaches,"* 1999 L. Rev. M.S.U.-D.C.L. 865 (1999).

Halpin, Andrew. *Reasoning with Law* (Hart Publishing, 2001).

Hamilton, Alexander, John Jay, and James Madison. *The Federalist* (Liberty Fund, 2001).

Hammond, Grant. *Judicial Recusal: Principles, Process and Problems* (Hart Publishing, 2009).

Hart, Henry M., Jr. and Albert M. Sacks. *The Legal Process: Basic Problems in the Making and Application of Law* (Foundation Press, 1994).

Hart, H. L. A. *The Ascription of Responsibility and Rights*, 49 Proc. Aristotelian Soc'y 171 (1949).

Hart, H. L. A. *The Concept of Law* (3rd ed.) (Oxford University Press, 2012).

Hart, H. L. A. *Essays in Jurisprudence and Philosophy* (Oxford University Press, 1983).

Hart, H. L. A. *Positivism and the Separation of Law and Morals*, 71 Harv. L. Rev. 593 (1958).

Hart, H. L. A. *Punishment and Responsibility: Essays in the Philosophy of Law* (2nd ed.) (Oxford University Press, 2008).

Hatch, Orrin G. *The Constitution as the Playbook for Judicial Selection*, 32 Harv. J. L. & Pub. Pol'y 1035 (2009).

Holmes, Oliver Wendell. *The Path of the Law*, 10 Harv. L. Rev. 457 (1897).

Hurley, S. L. *Natural Reasons: Personality and Polity* (Oxford University Press, 1989).

Ingber, Stanley. *Judging without Judgment: Constitutional Irrelevancies and the Demise of Dialogue*, 46 Rutgers L. Rev. 1473 (1994).

Isenbergh, Joseph. *Activists Vote Twice*, 70 U. Chi. L. Rev. 159 (2003).

Jaffe, Louis L. *English and American Judges as Lawmakers* (Oxford University Press, 1969).

Jardine, David. *A Reading on the Use of Torture in the Criminal Law of England Previously to the Commonwealth* (Baldwin & Cradock, 1837).

Johnson, Timothy R. *Oral Arguments and Decision Making on the United States Supreme Court* (State University of New York Press, 2004).

Kahn, Ronald. *The Commerce Clause and Executive Power: Exploring Nascent Individual Rights in* National Federation of Independent Business v. Sebelius, 73 Md. L. Rev. 133 (2013).

Kalman, Laura. *The Strange Career of Legal Liberalism* (Yale University Press, 1996).

Kane, Thomas J. "Misconceptions in the Debate Over Affirmative Action in College Admissions," in Gary Orfield and Edward Miller, eds., *Chilling Admissions: The Affirmative Action Crisis and the Search for Alternatives* (Harvard Education Publishing Group, 1998).

Kant, Immanuel. *The Critique of Judgement* (James Creed Meredith, trans.) (Oxford University Press, 1928).

Kant, Immanuel. *Groundwork of the Metaphysics of Morals* (Mary Gregor, trans.) (Cambridge University Press, 1998).

Kaufman, Irving R. *The Anatomy of Decisionmaking*, 53 Fordham L. Rev. 1 (1984).

Kaufman, Irving R. *Chilling Judicial Independence*, 88 Yale L.J. 681 (1979).

Kay, Herma Hill. *Symposium: Celebration of the Tenth Anniversary of Justice Ruth Bader Ginsburg's Appointment to the Supreme Court of the United States*, 104 Colum. L. Rev. 1 (2004).

Kaye, Judith S. *The Human Dimension in Appellate Judging: A Brief Reflection on a Timeless Concern*, 73 Cornell L. Rev. 1004 (1988).

Kemal, Salim. *Kant and Fine Art: An Essay on Kant and the Philosophy of Fine Art and Culture* (Oxford University Press, 1986).

Kerber, Linda K. *No Constitutional Right to Be Ladies: Women and the Obligations of Citizenship* (Hill & Wang, 1998).

Klebanow, Diana, and Franklin L. Jonas. *People's Lawyers: Crusaders for Justice in American History* (Routledge, 2002).

Kommers, Donald P., and Russell A. Miller. *The Constitutional Jurisprudence of the Federal Republic of Germany* (3rd ed.) (Duke University Press, 2012).

Körner, Stephan. *Kant* (Yale University Press, 1955).

Kramer, Matthew H. *Objectivity and the Rule of Law* (Cambridge University Press, 2007).

Krieger, Linda Hamilton. *Civil Rights Perestroika: Intergroup Relations after Affirmative Action*, 86 Calif. L. Rev. 1251 (1998).

Kronman, Anthony T. *Mistake, Disclosure, Information, and the Law of Contracts*, 7 J. Legal Stud. 1 (1978).

Lane, Charles. "Scalia Tells Congress To Mind Its Own Business," Wash. Post, May 19, 2006.

Lay, Donald P. *Rethinking the Guidelines: A Call for Cooperation*, 101 Yale L.J. 1755 (1992).

Leiter, Brian. *Objectivity and the Problems of Jurisprudence*, 72 Tex. L. Rev. 187 (1993).

Lepore, Ernie, and Kirk Ludwig. *Donald Davidson: Meaning, Truth, Language, and Reality* (Oxford University Press, 2005).

Lewis, Neil A. "Rejected as a Clerk, Chosen as a Justice: Ruth Joan Bader Ginsburg," N.Y. Times, June 15, 1993.

Lithwick, Dahlia. "Personal Truths and Legal Fictions," N.Y. Times, Dec. 17, 2002.

Llewellyn, Karl. *The Common Law Tradition: Deciding Appeals* (Little, Brown & Co., 1960).

Longuenesse, Béatrice. *Kant and the Capacity to Judge: Sensibility and Discursivity in the Transcendental Analytic of the* Critique of Pure Reason (Princeton University Press, 1998).

Longuenesse, Béatrice. "Kant's Leading Thread in the Analytic of the Beautiful," in Rebecca Kukla, ed., *Aesthetics and Cognition in Kant's Critical Philosophy* (Cambridge University Press, 2006).

Lucas, J. R. "On Processes for Resolving Disputes," in Robert S. Summers, *Essays in Legal Philosophy* (Blackwell, 1970).

Lyons, David. *Moral Aspects of Legal Theory: Essays on Law, Justice, and Political Responsibility* (Cambridge University Press, 1993).

Lyons, David. *Open Texture and the Possibility of Legal Interpretation*, 18 Law and Phil. 297 (1999).

MacCormick, Neil. "*The Concept of Law* and The Concept of Law," in Robert P. George, ed., *The Autonomy of Law: Essays on Legal Positivism* (Oxford University Press, 1996).

MacCormick, Neil. *Institutions of Law: An Essay in Legal Theory* (Oxford University Press, 2007).

MacCormick, Neil. *Legal Reasoning and Legal Theory* (Oxford University Press, 1978).

MacCormick, Neil. *Practical Reason in Law and Morality* (Oxford University Press, 2008).

MacCormick, Neil. *Rhetoric and the Rule of Law: A Theory of Legal Reasoning* (Oxford University Press, 2005).

Macedo, Stephen. *Morality and the Constitution: Toward a Synthesis for "Earthbound" Interpreters*, 61 U. Cin. L. Rev. 29 (1992).

Macey, Jonathan R. *Promoting Public-Regarding Legislation Through Statutory Interpretation: An Interest Group Model*, 86 Colum. L. Rev. 223 (1986).

Margolick, David, Evgenia Peretz, and Michael Shnayerson. *The Path to Florida*, Vanity Fair (Oct. 2004).

Marino, Patricia. *What Should A Correspondence Theory Be and Do?*, 127 Phil. Stud. 415 (2006).

Martindale, Charles. *Latin Poetry and the Judgement of Taste: An Essay in Aesthetics* (Oxford University Press, 2005).

Mayeda, Graham. *Uncommonly Common: The Nature of Common Law Judgment*, 19 Can. J.L. & Juris. 107 (2006).

Mayeri, Serena. *The Strange Career of Jane Crow: Sex Segregation and the Transformation of Anti-Discrimination Discourse*, 18 Yale J.L. & Human. 187 (2006).

McCloskey, Robert G. *The American Supreme Court* (5th ed.) (University of Chicago Press, 2010).

McConnell, Michael W. *Moderation and Coherence in American Democracy*, 99 Calif. L. Rev. 373 (2011).

McDonald, Forrest. *Novus Ordo Seclorum: The Intellectual Origins of the Constitution* (University Press of Kansas, 1985).

McDowell, John. *Mind, Value, and Reality* (Harvard University Press, 1998).

McGinnis, John O. *Foreign To Our Constitution*, 100 Nw. U. L. Rev. 303 (2006).

Meerbote, Ralf. "Reflection on Beauty," in Ted Cohen and Paul Guyer, eds., *Essays in Kant's Aesthetics* (University of Chicago Press, 1982).

Merryman, John Henry, and Rogelio Pérez-Perdomo. *The Civil Law Tradition: An Introduction to the Legal Systems of Europe and Latin America* (3rd ed.) (Stanford University Press, 2007).

Meyer, Linda. *Between Reason and Power: Experiencing Legal Truth*, 67 U. Cin. L. Rev. 727 (1999).

Meyer, Linda Ross. *The Justice of Mercy* (University of Michigan Press, 2010).

Meyer, Linda. *"Nothing We Say Matters": Teague and New Rules*, 61 U. Chi. L. Rev. 423 (1994).
Miller, Arthur S., and Ronald F. Howell. *The Myth of Neutrality in Constitutional Adjudication*, 27 U. Chi. L. Rev. 661 (1960).
Minow, Martha. *Stripped Down Like a Runner or Enriched by Experience: Bias and Impartiality of Judges and Jurors*, 33 Wm. & Mary L. Rev. 1201 (1992).
Montefiore, Alan. "Objectivity, Impartiality and Open-Mindedness," in Alan Montefiore, ed., *Neutrality and Impartiality: The University and Political Commitment* (Cambridge University Press, 1975).
Moore, Michael. *The Interpretive Turn in Modern Theory: A Turn for the Worse?*, 41 Stan. L. Rev. 871 (1989).
Moore, Michael. "Law as a Functional Kind," in Robert P. George, ed., *Natural Law Theory: Contemporary Essays* (Oxford University Press, 1992).
Moore, Michael. *Moral Reality*, 1982 Wis. L. Rev. 1061 (1982).
Moore, Michael. *Moral Reality Revisited*, 90 Mich. L. Rev. 2424, 2492 (1992).
Moore, Michael. *A Natural Law Theory of Interpretation*, 58 S. Cal. L. Rev. 277 (1985).
Murdoch, Iris. *Metaphysics as a Guide to Morals* (Penguin Books, 1993).
Murphy, Walter F. *Civil Law, Common Law, and Constitutional Democracy*, 52 La. L. Rev. 91 (1991).
Nelson, William E. Marbury v. Madison: *The Origins and Legacy of Judicial Review* (University Press of Kansas, 2000).
Neuborne, Burt. *A Symposium on the Legacy of Justice William J. Brennan, Jr.: Introduction of Justice Ruth Bader Ginsburg*, 95 Calif. L. Rev. 2213 (2007).
Newman, Jon O. *The New Commission's Opportunity*, 8 Fed. Sent. Rep. 8 (1995).
Newmyer, R. Kent. *The Supreme Court under Marshall and Taney* (Crowell, 1968).
Nielsen, Mark. Mistretta v. United States *and the Eroding Separation of Powers*, 12 Harv. J. L. & Pub. Pol'y 1049 (1989).
North, Douglass C. *Dealing with a Non-Ergodic World: Institutional Economics, Property Rights, and the Global Environment*, 10 Duke Envtl. L. & Pol'y F. 1 (1999).
North, Douglass C. *Understanding the Process of Economic Change* (rev. ed.) (Princeton University Press, 2005).
Norton, Helen. *The Supreme Court's Post-Racial Turn Towards a Zero-Sum Understanding of Equality*, 52 Wm. & Mary L. Rev. 197 (2010).
Nussbaum, Martha C. *Emotion in the Language of Judging*, 70 St. John's L. Rev. 23 (1996).
Nussbaum, Martha C. *Poets as Judges: Judicial Rhetoric and the Literary Imagination*, 62 U. Chi. L. Rev. 1477 (1995).
O'Connor, Sandra Day. *Justice O'Connor Reflects on Arizona's Judiciary*, 43 Ariz. L. Rev. 1 (2001).
Onwuachi-Willig, Angela. *Just Another Brother on the SCT?: What Justice Clarence Thomas Teaches Us About the Influence of Racial Identity*, 90 Iowa L. Rev. 931 (2005).
Orrego, Cristóbal. "Hart's Last Legal Positivism: Morality Might Be Objective, Legality Certainly Is Not," in Kenneth Einar Himma, ed., *Law, Morality, and Legal Positivism* (Franz Steiner Verlag, 2004).
Patterson, Dennis. *Law and Truth* (Oxford University Press, 1996).
Patterson, Dennis. *Normativity and Objectivity in Law*, 43 Wm. & Mary L. Rev. 325 (2001).

Peratis, Kathleen. *Rhetoric of Justice Ruth Bader Ginsburg: Brief Comparison of the Language of the Advocate with the Language of the Justice*, 25 Colum. J. Gender & L. 35 (2013).
Perry, Stephen R. *Judicial Obligation, Precedent and the Common Law*, 7 Oxford J. Leg. Stud. 215 (1987).
Perry, Stephen R. *The Varieties of Legal Positivism*, 9 Can. J.L. & Juris. 361 (1996).
Pettys, Todd E. *Judicial Discretion in Constitutional Cases*, 26 J.L. & Politics 123 (2011).
Pillow, Kirk. "Understanding Aestheticized," in Rebecca Kukla, ed., *Aesthetics and Cognition in Kant's Critical Philosophy* (Cambridge University Press, 2006).
Pollock, Frederick. *The Law of Torts* (11th ed.) (Stevens & Sons, 1920).
Posner, Richard A. *The Federal Courts: Challenge and Reform* (2nd ed.) (Harvard University Press, 1996).
Posner, Richard A. *How Judges Think* (Harvard University Press, 2008).
Posner, Richard A. *Legal Reasoning From the Top Down and From the Bottom Up: The Question of Unenumerated Constitutional Rights*, 59 U. Chi. L. Rev. 433 (1992).
Posner, Richard A. *The Problematics of Moral and Legal Theory* (Harvard University Press, 1999).
Posner, Richard A. *The Problems of Jurisprudence* (Harvard University Press, 1990).
Posner, Richard A. *Reflections on Judging* (Harvard University Press, 2013).
Posner, Richard A. "What Am I, a Potted Plant? The Case Against Strict Constructionism," in David M. O'Brien, ed., *Judges on Judging: Views from the Bench* (4th ed.) (CQ Press, 2013).
Postema, Gerald J. "*A Similibus ad Similia*: Analogical Thinking in Law," in Douglas E. Edlin, ed., *Common Law Theory* (Cambridge University Press, 2007).
Postema, Gerald J. "Law's Autonomy and Public Practical Reason," in Robert P. George, ed., *The Autonomy of Law: Essays on Legal Positivism* (Oxford University Press, 1996).
Postema, Gerald J. "Objectivity Fit for Law," in Brian Leiter, ed., *Objectivity in Law and Morals* (Cambridge University Press, 2001).
Pound, Roscoe. *The Theory of Judicial Decision*, 36 Harv. L. Rev. 940 (1923).
Pound, Roscoe. "What Is the Common Law?," in Roscoe Pound, ed., *The Future of the Common Law* (Peter Smith, 1965).
Powell, H. Jefferson. *Constitutional Conscience: The Moral Dimension of Judicial Decision* (University of Chicago Press, 2008).
Powell, H. Jefferson. *The Three Independences*, 38 U. Rich. L. Rev. 603 (2004).
Powell, Lewis F., Jr. "What Really Goes On at the Supreme Court," in David M. O'Brien, ed., *Judges on Judging: Views from the Bench* (4th ed.) (CQ Press, 2013).
Prosser, William L. *Law of Torts* (4th ed.) (West Publishing Co., 1971).
Provine, Doris Marie. "Courts in the Political Process in France," in Herbert Jacob, *et al.*, *Courts, Law, and Politics in Comparative Perspective* (Yale University Press, 1996).
Pryor, William H., Jr. *Not-So-Serious Threats to Judicial Independence*, 93 Va. L. Rev. 1759 (2007).
Radin, Max. *The Requirement of Written Opinions*, 18 Calif. L. Rev. 486 (1930).
Rädler, Peter. "Independence and Impartiality of Judges," in David S. Weissbrodt and Rüdiger Wolfrum, eds., *The Right to a Fair Trial* (Springer, 1998).
Rakove, Jack N. *Original Meanings: Politics and Ideas in the Making of the Constitution* (Knopf, 1996).

Rawls, John. *Political Liberalism* (Columbia University Press, 1993).

Raz, Joseph. *The Authority of Law: Essays on Law and Morality* (2nd ed.) (Oxford University Press, 2009).

Raz, Joseph. *Dworkin: A New Link in the Chain*, 74 Calif. L. Rev. 1103 (1986).

Raz, Joseph. *Ethics in the Public Domain: Essays in the Morality of Law and Politics* (Oxford University Press, 1994).

Raz, Joseph. "Legal Principles and the Limits of Law," in Marshall Cohen, ed., *Ronald Dworkin and Contemporary Jurisprudence* (Rowman & Allanheld, 1983).

Raz, Joseph. "On the Authority and Interpretation of Constitutions," in Larry Alexander, ed., *Constitutionalism: Philosophical Foundations* (Cambridge University Press, 1998).

Reid, John. *Doe Did Not Sit—The Creation of Opinions by an Artist*, 63 Colum. L. Rev. 59 (1963).

Roberts, Florrie Young. *Disclosure Duties in Real Estate Sales and Attempts to Reallocate the Risk*, 34 Conn. L. Rev. 1 (2001).

Rosati, Connie S. *Some Puzzles about the Objectivity of Law*, 23 Law & Phil. 273 (2003).

Ruger, Theodore W. *Justice Harry Blackmun and the Phenomenon of Judicial Preference Change*, 70 Mo. L. Rev. 1209 (2005).

Russell, Peter H. "Toward a General Theory of Judicial Independence," in Peter H. Russell and David M. O'Brien, eds., *Judicial Independence in the Age of Democracy: Critical Perspectives from around the World* (University Press of Virginia, 2001).

Salmond, John W., ed. *The Science of Legal Method* (Macmillan, 1921).

Salomone, Rosemary C. *Same, Different, Equal: Rethinking Single-Sex Schooling* (Yale University Press, 2003).

Samuelson, Paul. "Classical and Neoclassical Monetary Theory," in Robert W. Clower, ed., *Monetary Theory: Selected Readings* (Penguin, 1969).

Sander, Richard H. *A Systemic Analysis of Affirmative Action in American Law Schools*, 57 Stan. L. Rev. 367 (2004).

Sander, Richard H., and Stuart Taylor, Jr. *Mismatch: How Affirmative Action Hurts Students It's Intended to Help, and Why Universities Won't Admit It* (Basic Books, 2012).

Savile, Anthony. *Aesthetic Reconstructions: The Seminal Writings of Lessing, Kant, and Schiller* (Blackwell, 1987).

Scalia, Antonin. *A Matter of Interpretation: Federal Courts and the Law* (Princeton University Press, 1997).

Scalia, Antonin. *Originalism: The Lesser Evil*, 57 U. Cin. L. Rev. 849 (1989).

Scalia, Antonin. *The Rule of Law as a Law of Rules*, 56 U. Chi. L. Rev. 1175 (1989).

Schaper, Eva. "Taste, Sublimity, and Genius: The Aesthetics of Nature and Art," in Paul Guyer, ed., *The Cambridge Companion to Kant and Modern Philosophy* (Cambridge University Press, 2006).

Schauer, Frederick. *Giving Reasons*, 47 Stan. L. Rev. 633 (1995).

Schauer, Frederick, and Virginia Wise. *Legal Positivism as Legal Information*, 82 Cornell L. Rev. 1080 (1997).

Schauer, Frederick. "Positivism Before Hart," in Michael Freeman and Patricia Mindus, eds., *The Legacy of John Austin's Jurisprudence* (Springer, 2013).

Schiller, F. C. S. *Solipsism*, 18 Mind 169 (1909).

Schlag, Pierre. *Normativity and the Politics of Form*, 139 U. Pa. L. Rev. 801 (1991).

Schlesinger, Arthur M., Jr. *The Age of Roosevelt: The Politics of Upheaval, 1935–1936* (Houghton Mifflin, 1960).

Segal, Jeffrey A., and Harold J. Spaeth. *The Supreme Court and the Attitudinal Model* (Cambridge University Press, 1993).
Segal, Jeffrey A., Harold J. Spaeth, and Sara C. Benesh. *The Supreme Court in the American Legal System* (Cambridge University Press, 2005).
Shaffer, Gregory, and Tom Ginsburg. *The Empirical Turn in International Legal Scholarship*, 106 Am. J. Int'l L. 1 (2012).
Shapiro, Martin. *Judges as Liars*, 17 Harv. J. L. & Pub. Pol'y 155 (1994).
Shell, Susan Meld. *Kant and the Limits of Autonomy* (Harvard University Press, 2009).
Shetreet, Shimon, and Sophie Turenne. *Judges on Trial: The Independence and Accountability of the English Judiciary* (2nd ed.) (Cambridge University Press, 2013).
Shklar, Judith N. *Legalism: Law, Morals, and Political Trials* (Harvard University Press, 1964).
Smith, Barbara Herrnstein. *Belief and Resistance: Dynamics of Contemporary Intellectual Controversy* (Harvard University Press, 1997).
Smith, Dale. *Can Anti-Objectivists Support Judicial Review?*, 31 Austl. J. Leg. Phil. 50 (2006).
Smith, Stephen F. *Clarence X?: The Black Nationalist Behind Justice Thomas's Constitutionalism*, 4 NYU J.L. & Liberty 583 (2009).
Smith, Tara. *Judicial Review in an Objective Legal System* (Cambridge University Press, 2015).
Smith, Tara. *Originalism's Misplaced Fidelity: "Original" Meaning Is Not Objective*, 26 Const. Comment. 1 (2009).
Smith, Tara. *Originalism, Vintage or Nouveau: "He Said, She Said" Law*, 82 Fordham L. Rev. 619 (2013).
Smith, Thomas. *De Republica Anglorum: A Discourse on the Commonwealth of England* (L. Alston, ed.) (Cambridge University Press, 1906).
Soames, Scott. *Philosophy of Language* (Princeton University Press, 2010).
Soper, Philip. "Law's Normative Claims," in Robert P. George, ed., *The Autonomy of Law: Essays on Legal Positivism* (Oxford University Press, 1996).
Soper, Philip. *A Theory of Law* (Harvard University Press, 1984).
Sotomayor, Sonia. *A Latina Judge's Voice*, 13 Berkeley La Raza L.J. 87 (2002).
Sotomayor, Sonia. *My Beloved Life* (Knopf, 2013).
Spencer, J. R. "Criminal Law," in Louis Blom-Cooper, Brice Dickson, and Gavin Drewry, *The Judicial House of Lords, 1876–2009* (Oxford University Press, 2009).
Stavropoulos, Nicos. *Objectivity in Law* (Oxford University Press, 1996).
Stearns, Maxwell L. *Constitutional Process: A Social Choice Analysis of Supreme Court Decision Making* (University of Michigan Press, 2000).
Stearns, Maxwell L. *Standing Back From the Forest: Justiciability and Social Choice*, 83 Calif. L. Rev. 1309 (1995).
Steiner, George. *Real Presences* (University of Chicago Press, 1989).
Stephen, James Fitzjames. *A History of the Criminal Law of England* (Macmillan, 1883).
Stevens, Robert. *The Act of Settlement and the Questionable History of Judicial Independence*, 1 Oxford U. Commonw. L. J. 253 (2001).
Steyn, Johan. *Guantanamo Bay: The Legal Black Hole*, 53 Int'l and Comp. L. Q. 1 (2004).
Stick, John. *Can Nihilism Be Pragmatic?*, 100 Harv. L. Rev. 332 (1986).

Stith, Kate, and José A. Cabranes. *Fear of Judging: Sentencing Guidelines in the Federal Courts* (University of Chicago Press, 1998).

Stroud, Barry. *The Quest for Reality: Subjectivism and the Metaphysics of Colour* (Oxford University Press, 1999).

Sunstein, Cass R. "Incommensurability and Kinds of Valuation: Some Applications in Law," in Ruth Chang, ed., *Incommensurability, Incomparability, and Practical Reason* (Harvard University Press, 1997).

Tamanaha, Brian Z. *Beyond the Formalist-Realist Divide: The Role of Politics in Judging* (Princeton University Press, 2010).

Tamanaha, Brian Z. *Law as a Means to an End: Threat to the Rule of Law* (Cambridge University Press, 2006).

Tamanaha, Brian Z. *On the Rule of Law: History, Politics, Theory* (Cambridge University Press, 2004).

Tasioulas, John. *The Legal Relevance of Ethical Objectivity*, 47 Am. J. Juris. 211 (2002).

Thernstrom, Stephan, and Abigail Thernstrom. *America in Black and White: One Nation, Indivisible* (Simon & Schuster, 1997).

Thomas, Clarence. *My Grandfather's Son* (Harper Collins, 2007).

Tur, Richard H. S. *Defeasibilism*, 21 Oxford J. Leg. Stud. 355 (2001).

Tushnet, Mark. *A Court Divided: The Rehnquist Court and the Future of Constitutional Law* (W. W. Norton, 2005).

Vanaskie, Thomas I. *The Independence and Responsibility of the Federal Judiciary*, 46 Vill. L. Rev. 745 (2001).

van Caenegem, R. C. *The Birth of the English Common Law* (2nd ed.) (Cambridge University Press, 1988).

van Caenegem, R. C. *European Law in the Past and the Future: Unity and Diversity over Two Millennia* (Cambridge University Press, 2002).

van Caenegem, R. C. *An Historical Introduction to Western Constitutional Law* (Cambridge University Press, 1995).

Wade, H. W. R. *Constitutional and Administrative Aspects of the* Anisminic *Case*, 85 Law Q. Rev. 198 (1969).

Wade, Paula. *White's Defeat Poses Legal Dilemma: How Is a Replacement Justice Picked?*, Com. Appeal (Memphis, Tenn.), Aug. 3, 1996.

Waldron, Jeremy. "The Irrelevance of Moral Objectivity," in Robert P. George, ed., *Natural Law Theory: Contemporary Essays* (Oxford University Press, 1992).

Waldron, Jeremy. *Kant's Legal Positivism*, 109 Harv. L. Rev. 1535 (1996).

Waldron, Jeremy. "Legal Judgment and Moral Reservation," in Agustín José Menéndez and John Erik Fossum, eds., *Law and Democracy in Neil MacCormick's Legal and Political Theory: The Post-Sovereign Constellation* (Springer, 2011).

Waldron, Jeremy. *Torture and Positive Law: Jurisprudence for the White House*, 105 Colum. L. Rev. 1681 (2005).

Walker, Clive. *Keeping Control of Terrorists Without Losing Control of Constitutionalism*, 59 Stan. L. Rev. 1395 (2007).

Warren, W. Preston. *Modes of Objectivity*, 39 Phil. & Phenomenological Res. 74 (1978).

Wathen, Daniel, and Barbara Riegelhaupt. *The Speeches of Frank M. Coffin: A Sideline to Judging*, 63 Me. L. Rev. 467 (2011).

Wechsler, Herbert. *Toward Neutral Principles of Constitutional Law*, 73 Harv. L. Rev. 1 (1959).

Weinstein, Jack B. *A Trial Judge's Reflections on Departures from the Federal Sentencing Guidelines*, 5 Fed. Sent. Rep. 6 (1992).

Wellington, Harry H. *Common Law Rules and Constitutional Double Standards: Some Notes on Adjudication*, 83 Yale L. J. 221 (1973).

Wenzel, Christian Helmut. *An Introduction to Kant's Aesthetics: Core Concepts and Problems* (Blackwell, 2005).

West, Robin L. *Are There Nothing But Texts in This Class? Interpreting the Interpretive Turns in Legal Thought*, 76 Chi.-Kent L. Rev. 1125 (2000).

White, Penny J. *An America without Judicial Independence*, 80 Judicature 174 (1997).

Wilkins, David B. *A Systematic Response to Systematic Disadvantage: A Response to Sander*, 57 Stan. L. Rev. 1915 (2005).

Winter, Steven L. *A Clearing in the Forest: Law, Life, and Mind* (University of Chicago Press, 2001).

Wittgenstein, Ludwig. *Philosophical Investigations* (P. M. S. Hacker and Joachim Schulte, eds.) (4th ed.) (Wiley-Blackwell, 2009).

Wright, Ronald F. *Sentencers, Bureaucrats, and the Administrative Law Perspective on the Federal Sentencing Commission*, 79 Calif. L. Rev. 3 (1991).

Wyzanski, Charles E., Jr. *A Trial Judge's Freedom and Responsibility*, 65 Harv. L. Rev. 1281 (1952).

Young, Ernest A. *Foreign Law and the Denominator Problem*, 119 Harv. L. Rev. 148 (2005).

Zamulinski, Brian. *Rehabilitating the Declaratory Theory of the Common Law*, 2 J. L. & Cts. 171 (2014).

Zinkin, Melissa. "Intensive Magnitudes and the Normativity of Taste," in Rebecca Kukla, ed., *Aesthetics and Cognition in Kant's Critical Philosophy* (Cambridge University Press, 2006).

Zipursky, Benjamin C. *Legal Coherentism*, 50 SMU L. Rev. 1679 (1997).

Zipursky, Benjamin C. "The Model of Social Facts," in Jules Coleman, ed., *Hart's Postscript: Essays on the Postscript to* The Concept of Law (Oxford University Press, 2001).

Zweigert, Konrad, and Hein Kötz. *Introduction to Comparative Law* (3rd ed.) (Oxford University Press, 1998).

Index of Subjects

Judicial decisions that appear in the text are indexed. All judicial decisions cited in this book are listed in the table of authorities.

Index of Names

Printed and bound by CPI Group (UK) Ltd, Croydon, CR0 4YY

16/09/2026

14963487-0005